Green City Rising

T0367075

GEOGRAPHIES OF JUSTICE AND SOCIAL TRANSFORMATION

SERIES EDITORS

Mathew Coleman, *Ohio State University*
Sapana Doshi, *University of California, Merced*

FOUNDING EDITOR

Nik Heynen, *University of Georgia*

ADVISORY BOARD

Deborah Cowen, *University of Toronto*
Zeynep Gambetti, *Boğaziçi University*
Geoff Mann, *Simon Fraser University*
James McCarthy, *Clark University*
Beverley Mullings, *Queen's University*
Harvey Neo, *Singapore University of Technology and Design*
Geraldine Pratt, *University of British Columbia*
Ananya Roy, *University of California, Los Angeles*
Michael Watts, *University of California, Berkeley*
Ruth Wilson Gilmore, *CUNY Graduate Center*
Jamie Winders, *Syracuse University*
Melissa W. Wright, *Pennsylvania State University*
Brenda S. A. Yeoh, *National University of Singapore*

Green City Rising

CONTAMINATION, CLEANUP,
AND COLLECTIVE ACTION

BY ERIN GOODLING
ILLUSTRATIONS BY ALI CAT LEEDS

The University of Georgia Press
Athens

© 2024 by the University of Georgia Press
Athens, Georgia 30602
www.ugapress.org
All rights reserved
Set in Minion 10.25 / 13.5 by Rebecca A. Norton

Most University of Georgia Press titles are
available from popular e-book vendors.

Printed digitally

Library of Congress Cataloging-in-Publication Data
Names: Goodling, Erin Katherine, 1981– author. | Leeds, Ali Cat, illustrator.
Title: Green city rising : contamination, cleanup, and collective action /
    by Erin Goodling ; illustrations by Ali Cat Leeds.
Identifiers: LCCN 2023048976 (print) | LCCN 2023048977 (ebook) |
    ISBN 9780820363851 (hardback) | ISBN 9780820363844 (paperback) |
    ISBN 9780820363868 (ebook) | ISBN 9780820363875 (pdf)
Subjects: LCSH: Green movement—Oregon—North Portland Harbor. |
    Community development—Oregon—North Portland Harbor. |
    Environmentalism—Oregon—North Portland Harbor—Citizen participation. |
    Environmental justice.
Classification: LCC GE198.O74 G66 2024 (print) | LCC GE198.O74 (ebook) |
    DDC 304.2/80979549—dc23/eng/20231221
LC record available at https://lccn.loc.gov/2023048976
LC ebook record available at https://lccn.loc.gov/2023048977

In memory of Art McConville, Roy Pascoe, and Mike Summers, who all loved the river.

CONTENTS

PREFACE

Over the last decade, I have splashed and fished in the Willamette River with Portland Harbor Community Coalition (PHCC) members. Joined water ceremonies under the St. John's Bridge organized by the American Indian Movement. Attended birthday parties in church basements, funerals on sidewalks. Listened to hip-hop music at festivals in parking lots and symphonies on the Willamette's banks. I have heard stories about nocturnal life from unhoused people living in makeshift shelters along the river: massive oceangoing ships that slip in and out under the cover of darkness, small critters scurrying to and fro. One day on a walk along the river, a person living in a blue tent described in great detail his relationship with riverine animals. The previous night he had awoken to rustling in the nearby saplings. The moonlight illuminated a nutria attempting to drag a thick branch down to the water. But the four-inch diameter log was too bulky for the little beaver-like creature to grasp. "So I got up and helped him," he explained. He said he had a decade worth of such interspecies stories of life on the river.

I have also heard stories of damaged and stolen ancestral fishing grounds. Asthma and other health problems caused by exposure to industrial emissions. Children subsisting on fish with PCB levels one hundred times what is deemed safe. I have gotten to know Black families who were segregated to the nearby Albina area, only to have entire blocks of their neighborhoods bulldozed for the Memorial Coliseum, Emanuel Hospital, the interstate freeway, and, more recently, hipster bars and yoga studios. I have watched cleanup crews tear down life-saving makeshift riverfront shelters, with police looking on, leaving trash and traumatized people in their wake.

And I have witnessed the commitments made by PHCC members and supporters to fighting for a more just future of the Portland Harbor and beyond. This work is driven not only by a quest for redress for violence of years present and past, but also by visions of more beautiful times to come. In framing PHCC's work in this dialectic way in *Green City Rising*—that is, in exposing oppression while simultaneously uplifting the joy, life, and agency of ordinary people and communities—I am attempting to heed Black geographies scholar Katherine McKittrick's (2011:959) insistence that researchers avoid reifying narratives that obscure the "human relationality" of ordinary people collectively engaged in struggle, taking a "desire-based" as opposed to a "damage-centred" analytical frame (Tuck et al., 2014).

My own knowledge of the Portland Harbor is rooted in familial ties to the river and nearby land. Growing up in the Parkrose neighborhood of East Portland in the 1980s, nearly every weekend my younger siblings and I shared seatbelts in my dad's 1940s buttercup yellow Dodge pickup truck as we drove five miles west along the Columbia River, downstream toward the wetlands and fields abutting the watershed's slough system behind Portland International Airport. The slough is part of the Columbia River's floodplain, adjacent to its confluence with the Willamette River. Levees constructed beginning in 1917 now mostly separate the massive Columbia from its slough and lake system. Dotted with blackberry brambles and lined with tall, swaying cottonwood trees, an eighty-acre plot of land within this slough system was home to a dozen horses and mules cared for by my grandpa, dad, and uncles for half a century. Each fall beginning around 1965, my family took these animals hunting for deer and elk in the Wallowa Mountains of eastern Oregon. Broadmoor Golf Course, where my grandpa worked in the maintenance department, owned the land where the horses and mules lived. Until the golf course owners sold the land in 2010, they allowed my family to use it as a home for the animals, as well as for growing hay, fruit trees, and a vegetable garden.

While the adults got to work trimming the mules' hooves and repairing fences on our weekly excursions to "the field" in my dad's little truck, my siblings and cousins and I explored the urban wilderness. We built forts with scrap wood, collected sweet-smelling hoof trimmings for show-and-tell, and clambered back and forth on logs crossing the slough. We loved summer best of all, when our garden overflowed with corn, tomatoes, cucumbers, and squash, with cicadas buzzing in the hot still air. We all shared in the work of tending the vegetables, learning from my Hungarian great-grandma, Oma. Most of the year, the Pacific Northwest rains provided ample water for our garden. But in late summer, after the old plum trees sagged heavy with fruit the color of sunsets and drought set in, we dropped one end of a hose into the slough and pumped water through a sprinkler to keep the vegetables from withering. As an adult, I now know that the slough likely contained toxic discharge acquired on its journey to the Willamette River. Nevertheless, we loved that garden, and along with venison from the Wallowas and whatever was on sale at WinCo Foods, it fed my whole extended family well. Many years before I understood the hydrology of the area, our garden and the field also connected me from a young age to the Willamette and Columbia Rivers via the upstream slough system.

Stretching back further, ancestors on my mom's side also indirectly connected me to the rivers. My Irish Catholic great-grandpa was born in 1900, right off of Mississippi Avenue and adjacent to the present-day Swan Island industrial area of the Portland Harbor. As a child, I spent hours sitting cross-legged on his scratchy green living room carpet, knee-to-knee with my cousins, listening to wild tales of his youth. These included stories about walking through "hobo jungles" on the way to catfish fries with friends on the Willamette's bank. Several decades later in the 1980s, his grandson—my uncle—took a job in the shipyards. Though never excluded from unions on the basis of his skin color, as Black shipyard workers were until the 1960s, my uncle and his coworkers continue to deal with health issues likely caused and complicated by years of sandblasting lead paint off old ships.

These personal ties to Portland's waterways primed my initial engagement with PHCC. In 2013, a friend introduced me to the alliance of Black, Indigenous, immigrant and refugee, and houseless-led groups. After attending meetings and helping with community organizing efforts for several months, PHCC leaders asked if I would consider documenting the coalition's work, so that other grassroots organizations could learn from their experiences. I was a student at the time, working on a graduate degree in urban studies at Portland State University, and had been thinking about potential action research projects, with implications for real-world community organizing and not just academia. In PHCC's early days, a lack of documentation of comparable cases made it difficult to glean insights from groups facing similar environmental justice challenges, namely fighting for environmental justice in the context of a city that purported to be "green for all." Organizers relied on piecemeal anecdotes and occasional phone calls with groups in Seattle and other cities to inform Portland-based strategies. These were helpful, but ultimately it remained difficult to strategize a path forward toward environmental remediation that would actually benefit frontline communities, rather than contribute to gentrification and displacement. PHCC leaders hoped that my inside experience with the coalition might result in an amplification of the perspectives of those most affected by contamination and least likely to benefit from status quo sustainability initiatives and environmental cleanups. This narrative might then in some modest way, we hoped, serve as a record, bearing witness to struggles for a cleaned-up river and inform the efforts of other groups working in similar circumstances elsewhere and in the years to come in Portland.

The particular life experiences, identities, and locations—the positionalities—of PHCC members and supporters, including my own as a white, cisgender activist-researcher born and raised in Portland, are fundamental to the coalition's narrative and work, and in turn the contents of this book. As feminist geographer Gillian Rose (1997:308) notes, "siting is intimately involved in sighting." That is, what one sees has everything to do with one's vantage point, with regard to a host of mediating factors including race, ethnicity, gender, social and economic status, and so on. Instead of pursing an unattainable objectivity or, on the flipside, falsely assuming that researcher and research subject occupy similar positions, Rose implores researchers to position different kinds of knowledges in conversation with one another. PHCC members and supporters have strived to produce, as Rose suggests, "knowledges that learn from other kinds of knowledges," and this book is a humble attempt at extending that conversation.

To research and write this book, I have put my own stories of growing up near the harbor into dialogue with others' stories from near and far. Doing so has required my own acute awareness of my positionality, as someone whose whiteness has allowed me to benefit from ongoing settler colonial and anti-Black, white supremacist systems. Many of my ancestors made their way to the Portland area from Ireland, Germany, and elsewhere in western and eastern Europe, first on steam liners crossing the Atlantic Ocean in the late 1700s and later in covered wagons traversing the Oregon Trail in the mid-1800s. More recently, during World War II, my paternal grandma and great-grandma—Oma, who taught me so much about gardening—lost their farm in rural Hungary to Axis powers. My grandma then married my grandpa, a U.S. Army mess hall cook stationed in Europe during the Korean War. Together they journeyed to the U.S. West Coast to raise their children near my grandpa's family, in East Portland. Thanks to the G.I. Bill, they qualified for a publicly subsidized home mortgage—available to them in the postwar years on the basis of their white skin. My parents, and now my own family, have also benefited from other similar publicly funded programs. In other words, I am a full benefactor of the U.S. government's policies of granting acreage and homes to white settlers in the Portland area who did little more than show up to already-occupied land. Given this unearned privilege, I have strived to develop research questions in collaboration with people on the front lines of fighting for a more just city and world; to follow the leads of those coordinating day-to-day organizing activities; and to operate in a transparent, ethical way in my interactions, research activities, and editing decisions. No doubt this is a work in progress, and I have made mistakes; I continue to learn and am grateful for those patient enough to teach me.

In what follows, I present the story of PHCC's origins and first five years, from 2012 through 2016, as a narrative that has emerged from many different knowledges. While bridges of understanding may not ever entirely traverse the deep chasms of life experience that exist between each of PHCC's member groups and supporters, this is a coalition that has nevertheless endeavored to build productive linkages between diverse peoples in service to a better future. Indeed, for the past to serve a purpose in the present for cross-race, cross-class coalitions such as PHCC, it must be excavated, remembered, communicated, negotiated—hence, collectively produced. My role has been to help stitch various threads together and to put PHCC's story into conversation with other times and places. To do so, I have consulted archives and secondary histories, synthesized insights drawn from informal conversations and formal interviews with coalition members, and consulted my own notes from participation in hundreds of coalition meetings and events from 2013 through 2016. PHCC representatives and supporters have read and commented on various versions of this account. In dialogue with coalition members and while writing drafts of this book, I have also recalled my own memories. The version offered here is therefore partly—though very far from solely—my own. May it serve as one enduring record of the Portland Harbor and its people.

ACKNOWLEDGMENTS

I owe a long list of people an enormous debt of gratitude for their support throughout this project. First and foremost, I want to thank members and supporters of the Portland Harbor Community Coalition (PHCC) past and present, named and unnamed in this book, as well as so many others who have been instrumental in Portland's social and environmental justice movements over the years whom I have gotten to know and learn from, including Abudulhadi "Hadi" Mohammed, Aileen McPherson, Alejandra Ruíz, Alex Gillow-Wiles, Alex Lopez, Amber Dunks, Ana Mendoza, Art McConville, Benjamin Donlon, Bob Sallinger, Callie Riley, Cassie Cohen, Cherrell Edwards, Coya Crespin, D Pei Wu, Danielle Klock, Donovan Smith, Edward Hill, Faduma Ali, Hannah Buehler, Ibrahim Mubarak, Irina Phillips, Jackie Calder, Jade Arellano, Jeff Liddicoat, Jeri Jimenez, Jim Robison, Jonathan Guzmán-Lopez, Joy Alise Davis, JR Lilly, Julia McKenna, Kaia Sand, Kaitlyn Dey, Kas Guillozet, Katrina Holland, Laquida Landford, Laura Stevens, Linda Senn, Leo Rhodes, Lisa Fay, Loretta Hankel, Lucia Llanos, Manuela Interián, María Jiménez, Mary Ann Warner, Mike Summers, Monica Beemer, Pam Phan, Paul Boden, Pepe Espinoza, Perla Medina Alvarez, Rahsaan Muhammad, Ranfis Giannettino Villatoro, Rose Highbear, Roy Pascoe, Scout Zabel, Shadow, Steve Goldstein, Sydney Eckhardt, Trish Summers, Vadim Riskin, Velia, Vince Masiello, Violeta Alvarez, Wilma Alcock, and so many others. I can only hope that the words on these pages help amplify in some small way the knowledge and experiences of such dedicated humans.

Second, I cannot thank the members of my dissertation committee at Portland State University (PSU) enough for their belief in this project and their help making it come to fruition. Nathan McClintock, the chair of my committee, took me under his wing soon after we both arrived at PSU. When I first contacted Nathan, I had never read, let alone researched and written, an academic article. He patiently helped me channel the critical perspective and skills I had developed over the previous decade as a youth worker, high school teacher, and organizer, and not only learn to navigate the world of academia but also to make research useful to movement groups. Sy Adler also offered invaluable support. More than anyone, Sy pushed me to think historically, connecting the past to the present in service of the future. Lisa K. Bates served as a model phronetic scholar. Equally at ease doing complicated statistical analyses and talking story with teenagers, Lisa is a role model for the kind of activist-researcher that I aspire to be. Throughout this project, she reminded me that my first commitment was always to PHCC members and their work. The first day I met Veronica Dujon, in a graduate seminar, she asserted how critical it is to continually ask three questions: Who wins? Who loses? Who decides? I have sought to make these questions central to my own work ever since.

Sincere appreciation is also due to colleagues and mentors at PSU and elsewhere. Classmates—now friends—who have helped shape my thinking in valuable ways include Amy Coplen, Anandi van Diepen-Hedayat, Betsy Breyer, Cameron Herrington, Claire Bach, Fiona Gladstone, Ingrid Behrsen, Jamaal Green, Jen Turner, Khanh Pham, Kenya Dubois, Lauren Brown, Marissa Matsler, Mary Ann Rozance, Max Ritts, Melanie Malone, Mike Simpson, Pam Phan, Paul Manson, Tara Goddard, Sam Stritzl, and Samantha Hamlin. Three classmates/colleagues—Anthony Levenda, Ellie Harmon, and Dillon Mahmoudi—deserve extra special thanks as fellow members of the DZ writing group; I am confident I would not have finished this book without their friendship and support. And I have benefited enormously from the formal and informal guidance, collegiality, and friendship of faculty members at PSU and other institutions, some of whom so helpfully commented on various pieces of this project: Alan Yeakley, Amy Lubitow, Ananya Roy, Carl Abbott, Charlene Mollett, Chris Hawn, Chris Herring, Dilara Yarborough, Ellen Kohl, Greg Schrock, Henrik Ernstson, Isabelle Anguelovski, Jason Jurjevich, Jennifer Allen, Jennifer Dill, Jessie Speer, Jill Harrison, Juan De Lara, Karen Gibson, Levi Van Sant, Malini Ranganathan, Marisa Zapata, Moriah McSharry McGrath, Monica Farías, Naomi Adiv, Natchee Barnd, Nik Heynen, Paroj Banerjee, Paula Carder, Richard Milligan, Richard White, Sanjeev Routray, Thad Miller, and others. Additionally, I am so grateful to PSU's National Science Foundation Integrative Graduate Education and Research Traineeship (NSF-IGERT) program staff and faculty for their deep commitments to interdisciplinary research and student-centered approach to learning, especially Darrell Brown, Dave Ervin, Elise Granek, and Kim Heavener. I also so appreciate the good people at the University of Georgia Press, especially Mick Gusinde-Duffy, Lea Johnson, Sapana Doshi, and Mat Coleman; anonymous reviewers who offered incisive feedback on this manuscript; and Jane Curran and Erin Clancy for their careful editing and indexing support. Additionally, I am enormously grateful to Andy Kent and everyone at the Antipode Foundation, for their support of this project and emerging (activist) scholars in general.

Members of the Critical Race Lab at the University of Oregon (UO)—Carla Macal Montenegro, Cristina Faiver-Serna, Fiona de los Rios, Sophia Ford, Tianna Bruno, Zoë Gammell Brown—welcomed me with open arms and provided so much wise counsel for three years while I worked on this manuscript and other projects. I will be forever thankful to you all, and I commit to attempting to pass along the kind of care you showed me to other comrades wherever I find myself in life. I am especially grateful to Laura Pulido, who took me under her wing at UO through exceptionally difficult times, always offering honest critique, generous compliments, and steady camaraderie. I am also so incredibly lucky to have connected with Lisa Fink at UO, who has contributed to my own growth as a scholar and human. And I am indebted to Simon Richards, whose wisdom and intuitive sense as a reader helped shape this manuscript in critical ways.

Ali Cat Leeds: your ability to visually depict together the human and biophysical world blows me away, and I so, so appreciate you for creating the illustrations included in this book despite many trials and tribulations. You responded to PHCC members' feedback with grace, and the result is a stunning series of drawings to open each chapter.

Finally, I have so much gratitude for past teachers, mentors, and friends Art Leo, Susan Brookhart, Dave Corkran, Ann Staley, Laura Conklin, and Jordia Blumenstein, for helping me learn to love to write. And I owe my family giant hugs of appreciation. My in-laws, Alan and Sharon Horton, gave me the gift of many hours to write, and Kai the gift of much love and time to adventure with grandparents. Veronica, Jared, Julian, and Valentina are like extended family members, loving us like their own. Thanks to our amazing neighbors, Drew, Martina, Marcela, Dodge, and little Lupe, we weathered the worst of the Covid-19 pandemic; we know we will remain friends for years to come, wherever life takes us. Lifelong *ohana* Crissy Marti and Kim Donohue, Auntie Aggie and Uncle Sal, and friends Alison Schneider, Beth Cohen, Diana Denham, Erin West, Katie Brennan, Lara Scanlon, Lindsey Kneuven, Jay Leary, Jude Lieberman, Marc Antinoro, Rachel Copeland, Scott Warner, Taylor Rezvani, Ty Hall, and Veronica Ledeaux have helped me experience so much joy and stay grounded; I appreciate you all more than you know. My siblings, Peter and Emilie and their families; cousins and aunts and uncles; and grandparents and great-grandparents and ancestors continue to offer the same unconditional love as they have since I can remember. I cannot begin to imagine life without you. My parents, Jesse and Cecilia Goodling, demonstrate every day what it truly means to live in reciprocity with those around us; the only way I have to thank you is to attempt to keep the reverberations going in all my own relationships. Last but definitely not least, Joe and Kai: you guys make sure I feel loved, every single day. Thank you.

This research was made possible through generous financial and in-kind support of PSU's Institute for Sustainable Solutions; an Ernie Bonner Equity Planning Scholarship; a PSU Laurel's Fellowship; the PSU Library Special Collections Dissertation Fellowship; and two Maurie Clark Dissertation Fellowships. Additionally, this material is based upon work supported by National Science Foundation (NSF) NSF Grant #0966376: "Sustaining Ecosystem Services to Support Rapidly Urbanizing Areas." An NSF Postdoctoral Research Fellowship (Grant #1808869), an Antipode Scholar-Activist Award, and an Antipode Right to the Discipline Award also supported parts of the research and writing included here. Any opinions, findings, and conclusions or recommendations expressed in this material are those of the author and do not necessarily reflect the views of the NSF or other funders.

Parts of this book are based on ideas developed in earlier work, including my own articles appearing in *Antipode* and *Environment and Planning E*; a comic book co-developed with Stephen Christian, Cassie Cohen, Donovan Smith, and PHCC members; an op-ed coauthored with Donovan Smith in *Street Roots*; and a chapter in *Urban Cascadia and the Pursuit of Environmental Justice*, edited by Nik Janos and Corina McKendry.

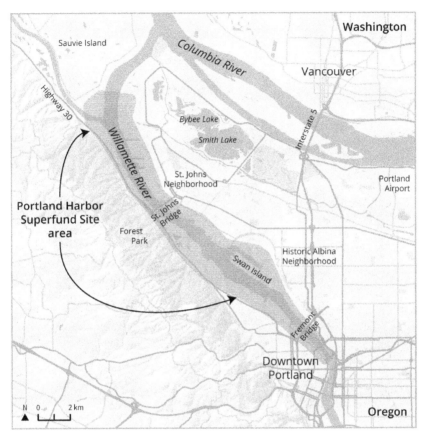

Map of the Portland Harbour by Dillon Mahmoudi

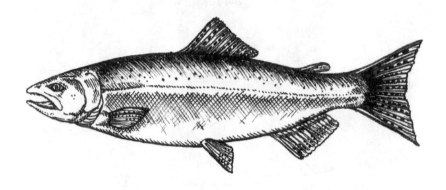

Chinook Salmon
Oncorhynchus tshawytscha
Threatened

INTRODUCTION

One gray morning in June 2016, Rahsaan Muhammad stood tall behind a portable podium, addressing fifty people gathered on the sidewalk:

> We are here today representing over a dozen organizations that are saying NO! We want a comprehensive cleanup . . . What they are proposing is truly insufficient. We are talking about a site that is ten miles long, over 22,000 acres. We're talking about dredging that needs to be done, shorelines that need to be cleaned up.

Reporters cocked digital recorders toward Rahsaan, scribbling on little notepads. He continued:

> There are billions of dollars that have already been pocketed by corporations like Bayer CropScience, Chevron, Gunderson, Exxon, BP, Shell, Schnitzer Steel, Toyota, the U.S. Navy, just to name a few—and we all can look at their records and what they make yearly and see that that 750 [million dollars] that you all are playin' with, tryin' to clean up the harbor, is really an insult and a joke.

> We are here, men, women, and children, ALL different nations—make no mistake about this—this coalition is representative of ALL the communities of color, ALL the Native tribes. . . . We are ALL on board with *cleaning up* our harbor *at the expense of those* who are responsible for *polluting* the harbor.

The crowd clapped and cheered, raising fists into the misty air. Huddled with fellow activists in support of Rahsaan, I shivered in the uncharacteristically chilly early summer morning air as I shifted my nine-month-old child, Kai, from one hip to the other.

Given Rahsaan's emphasis on the need to remediate industrial pollutants emitted into a river by multinational corporations, this might at first appear to be a story of an environmental justice (EJ) fight in a place known for manufacturing, such as Pittsburgh or Detroit. Or, given Rahsaan's mention of diverse communities leading efforts to push for change, a report coming from Chicago or Los Angeles, two cities with deep histories of coalition-based organizing.

Instead, this story is set in the Pacific Northwest city of Portland, Oregon, on unceded land of the Chinook, Multnomah, Tualatin Kalapuya, and many other bands and tribes. With miles of bike lanes, a vibrant farm-to-table movement, and myriad outdoor recreation opportunities, Portland regularly tops "most sustainable" lists. And with a population of nearly 650,000—76 percent non-Hispanic white—Portland is the whitest major city in the United States. Why, and how, in one of the most ostensibly environmentally friendly (and whitest) places in the country, are diverse Portlanders fighting for the kinds of EJ issues that affect Latinx communities in California's Central Valley, where pesticides and other chemicals poison the air and water? Or Indigenous communities in the Dakotas, where oil companies are attempting to lay a vast network of pipelines? Or low-income Black and white communities in Louisiana, where a stretch of the Mississippi River has been designated a "Cancer Alley" due to the plethora of nearby industrial plants emitting lethal substances? What kinds of challenges are Rahsaan and his comrades facing, and what strategies have helped people involved develop new relationships with each other and the land?

Contradictions of a Paradigmatic Sustainable City

I contend that examining grassroots collective action in Portland has the potential to lend key insights into the struggle for a more just world during the "sustainability era"—a time of growing mainstream consciousness about the promises and perils of human (in)action with regard to pollution, climate change, and other forms of environmental degradation. *Green City Rising* addresses the contradictions of fighting for EJ in so-called green cities, such as Portland, where sustainability initiatives too often reify existing racialized, gendered disparities. My goal in writing this book is to highlight struggles for EJ in a place where urban sustainability has become mainstream, underscoring the perspectives of those who have carried the burdens of toxic industry for generations, and who are now leading the way toward what urban planning scholar Julian Agyeman (2013) calls a more *just* sustainability. I argue that at the same time as the mainstream sustainability paradigm forecloses opportunities for frontline groups to meaningfully shape urbanization processes, sustainability's contradictions simultaneously present possibilities for progress toward a more just, green future. At the heart of this argument is an assertion that we—planners, policymakers, researchers, natural resource managers, environmentalists, green city boosters, activists, and ordinary residents—must be willing to tell and hear a different story about urban sustainability. This narrative must center the perspectives of historically and presently uprooted communities and their bold visions for an antiracist, decolonial world.

The paradoxes of green development are particularly stark in Portland. Rahsaan and fellow members of the Portland Harbor Community Coalition (PHCC), an alliance of Indigenous, Black, immigrant, refugee, and houseless-led groups with a mission to raise the voices of those most impacted by pollution in the Portland Harbor, had assembled that gray summer morning to condemn the Environmental Protection Agency's (EPA's) *Portland Harbor Superfund Site: Superfund Proposed Plan*. The EPA listed the harbor as a Superfund site in 2000. This designation ensured that cleanup of a ten-mile stretch of the Willamette River, flowing north out of downtown Portland nearly to the confluence with the Columbia River, would receive federal oversight.[1] But Rahsaan and PHCC asserted that the strategy outlined in the EPA's *Proposed Plan* would actually do little to repair damage from over a century of industrial activity. According to PHCC, the estimated cost of the proposed cleanup—$750 million dollars—was far from enough to remediate the harsh contaminants left behind by decades of wartime shipbuilding and ship-breaking, fertilizer manufacturing, lumber processing, and other highly toxic activities. And it was far, far from enough to even begin conversations about reconciliation and reparations, let alone to rectify harm done to Indigenous and Black communities. At stake in the *Proposed Plan*, PHCC affirmed, was the health of a beloved urban river and its watershed, and in turn the wellbeing of the fish, birds, plants, and peoples who have depended on the river for generations.

Notwithstanding its sullied harbor, Portland is at the forefront of today's green urbanism movement. The city has been heralded as "a model city for living the good life" (Stephenson, 2021) for its climate protection and land use system, the "bike capital of the US" (Duffy, 2014) for its network of dedicated bike lanes, and a "mighty gastropolis" (Brooks et al., 2012) for its renowned farm fresh food scene. Portlanders can head east for world-class skiing and hiking in the Cascade Mountains or west for surfing in the Pacific Ocean; both are within a two-hour drive, and Lonely Planet listed the city as one of its top twenty global destinations of 2017, on account of such "eco-friendly activities" (Sullivan, 2016). Scholars recognize Portland's role in promoting green urbanism in cities across North America and beyond (McCann, 2017). Indeed, Portland is a paradigmatic "sustainable city" in nearly every sense, with considerable influence on urban greening trends worldwide.

The opportunity to pursue urban swimming and kayaking in the Willamette River—despite the harbor's Superfund listing—is a key part of the city's sustainability success story. Self-identified "riverlution" boosters deem the city's main urban waterway a perfect place to cool off on hot summer afternoons, when crowds of millennials and Gen Zers line downtown docks from happy hour onward into the night, sipping beer and blasting music with the cityscape in the background. For a decade, until 2022, thousands of people participated in an annual "Big Float" festival, filling the water with fluorescent pink and yellow inner-tubes every July. In spring 2016, mayor-elect Ted Wheeler even delivered his ballot via "tiny triathlon," ceremonially swimming across the Willamette, biking along the waterfront, walking a few blocks to Pioneer Courthouse Square, and dropping his voting card in the box (Acker, 2016a). A few months later, Mayor Wheeler took another public dip, starting what would become an annual tradition throughout his tenure. He remarked, "Today we're going to swim in the water, the water quality is very good. We're not going to stop and eat mud on the bottom of the river" (quoted in Acker, 2016b).[2]

Contrasting the messaging of a handful of environmental and EJ groups, Wheeler's statement sums up conventional narratives of the Portland Harbor, asserting that the river is perfectly fine . . . for leisure pursuits. The media, EPA officials, and many planners and policymakers by and large offer a simple storyline that minimizes ongoing harm: *For much of the twentieth century, the Portland Harbor was a cesspool of refuse from the pulp and paper industry, municipal sewage and stormwater runoff. Following completion of massive public infrastructure investments, including construction of the $1.4 billion "Big Pipe" in 2011, toxic runoff into the Willamette River has dramatically declined. The river is now clean!*

For the majority of Portland residents, toxins in the mud pose relatively little danger, as Mayor Wheeler suggests. The river is indeed likely clean enough to safely kayak and swim, most of the time, for most people. But as Indigenous scholar Roxanne Dunbar-Ortiz explains, such mainstream narratives of North America are lacking not in their "facts, dates, or details," but rather in their "*essence*" (2014:5; emphasis added). Toxins buried in the soil and sediment, such as polychlorinated biphenyls (PCBs), sometimes called "forever chemicals" for their inability to break down, prevent thousands of people from safely engaging in cultural traditions and life-sustaining activities, including fishing. Moreover, the largely white-led riverlution is part and parcel of the city's green development boom, which has fueled the most recent round of displacement and exclusion of PHCC members' communities. Make no mistake: PHCC recognizes that past river remediation has laid an important foundation for continued decontamination. And many PHCC members enjoy canoeing, fishing, swimming, and other riverfront pastimes. But conventional histories of the Portland Harbor largely obscure who has carried the burdens of harbor pollution—and who has benefited and suffered as a result of Portland's greening thus far.

People from a dozen or so organizations that constituted PHCC's core member groups stood with Rahsaan that morning on the sidewalk. Supporters from key environmental, labor, and neighborhood groups also joined in solidarity. I was there as an organizer and activist-researcher, supporting and documenting PHCC's fight at the request of coalition members. Issues at stake for PHCC's constituents included fish, human, and habitat health; public access to the river; community control over land; living-wage cleanup jobs; affordable housing; treatment of houseless people living in the harbor; and much more. This list of issues points to disparities resulting from the harbor's contamination—and its cleanup. White-washed histories, such as those that celebrate the harbor's improvements without critically examining differential impacts of pollution and remediation, Dunbar-Ortiz (2014:5) asserts, allow people to sidestep important questions around "reparations, restitution, and reordering society." Counternarratives, like those produced by groups such as PHCC, do the opposite, serving to affirm the existence and experience of entire communities often erased in mainstream storylines.

Purpose and Interventions

Green City Rising addresses fights for EJ in paradigmatic green cities, such as Portland, where sustainability initiatives often reinforce existing racialized patterns of exclusion, oppression, and violence—and where ordinary people are leading efforts toward a more just world. The case of PHCC enables me to make three interrelated arguments. First, I contend that the mainstream sustainable city-building paradigm forecloses opportunities for grassroots groups to meaningfully shape urban greening processes, at the same time as it presents new possibilities for progress toward a more just, green future. Such opportunities arise in part because of the ways in which diverse groups such as PHCC, whose members have varied relationships to land and access to public participation processes, are striving to push fresh narratives of years past, to interact across lines of difference in humanity-affirming ways, and to advance bold visions of worlds yet to come. I further contend that the sustainable city-building paradigm more broadly influences the approach to social change that grassroots groups like PHCC take, especially with regard to the ways in which advocates strategically engage and disengage with public agencies at different times and scales. In the case of PHCC, this has meant sometimes following established participation channels put forth by local and federal government agencies, while other times acknowledging there may be little to gain by going through mainstream channels and pursuing more direct action and mutual aid avenues instead. And finally, I argue that while many of today's EJ struggles may be located in so-called green cities, they are nevertheless tied to temporally and geographically distant circumstances. For instance, while the Portland Harbor is the *place* that ties PHCC members together today, few actually live near the harbor due to a host of displacing forces. Moreover, people often invoke their connections to other times and places when talking about their motivations to fight for a more just, green harbor. In this way, *Green City Rising* speaks to scalar politics and "place attachment," including what it means when those fighting for improvements to a place have deep ties to the land and water but are culturally or economically excluded from living there.

In advancing these arguments, this book addresses a variety of questions. How does the sustainability paradigm influence social and climate/EJ struggles, and vice versa? How are diverse frontline groups attempting to reconcile the racist, colonial past and present while also redefining what an environmental and EJ movement can be, and who it can serve? What cracks exist in the "green growth machine" that might be exploited for more humane processes and outcomes? How do ordinary people come to understand the disjuncture between what *is* and what *is possible* in the sustainable city? What impels them to act on this understanding? What strategies do they use, and with what challenges and successes?

Such questions have their roots in conversations about urban sustainability and the environmental and climate justice movements. A wide variety of actors, including urban planners, policymakers, natural resource practitioners, real estate professionals, industrial corporations, nonprofit organizations, grassroots activist groups, and many others shape and are shaped by sustainability and EJ initiatives. Moreover, many academic disciplines' core questions encompass environmental politics and EJ struggles, including urban studies, urban planning, geography, sociology, anthropology, Black studies, Indigenous studies, environmental studies, and public policy. I draw on all of these, especially urban studies and planning, as well as urban political ecology, a subfield of geography that is concerned with the racialized, classed, and gendered power differentials inherent in socio-ecological relations. These traditions maintain that while sustainability and EJ movements have converged at various moments, they have their own distinct lineages, goals, and politics. Advocates of sustainability and EJ are often at odds with one another, even as both purportedly seek more healthful environments. The distinction is rooted in who is at the helm, their tellings of the past, and the extent to which their goals and strategies articulate a truly transformative future for all.

In the remainder of this introduction, I first critically trace the historical roots of the sustainability and EJ movements, providing a lineage for PHCC's present-day work. I then outline debates about the efficacy of various EJ movement approaches, with an emphasis on the ways in which agents of change engage and disengage with the state; PHCC has experienced the pros and cons of varying tactics. I end with a detailed look at "radical incrementalism," a hybrid approach to systemic change that helps describe the way in which PHCC has gone about its work. Together, these sections provide important historical, geographic, and social and EJ movement context for the story of PHCC that unfolds in the chapters to come.

Rise of the Urban Sustainability Fix

The urban sustainability paradigm that groups such as PHCC are attempting to challenge today emerged in the early 1970s, when three research areas—conservation, overpopulation, and model-based ecosystem ecology—converged. This merging happened around the same time as the early oil shocks and economic crises of the 1970s. Such global-scale events provided fresh political opportunities for a popular critique of modernism, ushering in more widespread support for a new socio-environmental paradigm. Throughout the 1980s, the concept of sustainability began to appear in more and more consulting, government, and nonprofit contexts, used to appeal to a multiplicity of concerns ranging from environmental to economic to social. Ultimately, it was the organizing framework for the United Nations' World Commission on Environment and Development (WCED), commonly known as the Brundtland Commission, that solidified the salience of sustainability throughout the Global North. In 1987, the Brundtland Commission issued a groundbreaking report, *Our Common Future*, which emphasized poverty reduction coupled with ecological concerns and intergenerational equity. The report set the stage for discussions at the 1992 Earth Summit in Rio de Janeiro. There, national leaders from around the world passed Agenda 21, which enumerated several environmental principles intended to guide nations in pursuit of economic development. Ecology's subfield of climate science also adopted sustainability rhetoric, and businesses began to recognize the potential of its popular appeal (Gottlieb, 2001; Redclift, 2005).

Prior to Agenda 21, throughout the 1960s and 1970s, U.S.-based environmentalists had sought governmental support for more progressive policies at the federal level. Popular backing for environmental initiatives had not been robust enough at the local level to amount to a critical mass, and municipal governments tended to cater foremost to business rather than environmental interests (Molotch, 1976; Portney, 2005). Agenda 21, however, promoted new ideas, with heavy emphasis on the role of the local level in combating emerging socio-ecological challenges. In tandem with growing popular concern for environmental issues, Agenda 21 pushed municipalities to materialize as hubs of the sustainability paradigm. The decline of manufacturing in U.S. urban areas following World War II also opened the political space necessary for increased attention to environmental issues at the city level, as stricter environmental regulations would no longer threaten employment bases as intensively as they once did. By 2005, forty-two U.S. cities had initiated sustainable cities programs to "improve their livability" (Portney, 2005:579), and dozens have since established climate action plans (Schrock et al., 2015). Many of these invoke the Brundtland Commission definition of sustainable development: "development that meets the needs of the present without compromising the ability of future generations to meet their own needs" (WCED, 1987).

Why did business, and cities, suddenly appear to become pro-environment? Answering this question is key to understanding how sustainability ultimately came to prominence—and how sustainability's original equity and environmental aspirations became so watered down. One key reason that the sustainability framework gained so much traction at the local level was that it provided ample rhetorical space to attend to city-scale economic growth initiatives, at the same time as it spoke to growing social and environmental concerns. Whereas traditional environmentalism had been subject to critiques of elitism, class indifference, and economic damage to communities, sustainability rhetoric held a more populist tone and therefore had coalition-building potential; the very slipperiness of the concept likely contributed to its growing popularity (Gunder, 2006; Vos, 2007). But in its conceptual openness, sustainability also appealed to growth machine-minded actors: the market, with proper incentives, they presumed, would be capable of "delivering human prosperity and ecological integrity" for all (Krueger and Gibbs, 2007:2).

A critical reading of sustainability's genealogy, coupled with a Marxian analysis of uneven development situated within larger processes of settler colonialism and racial capitalism, clarifies sustainability's linkages to neoliberal urbanization. Since World War II, the United States has seen a handful of periods marked by overaccumulation and devaluation in certain sectors, themselves part of larger circuits of production. Profit-making in the primary circuit occurs through the production and consumption of goods and services. Secondary circuit profits accrue through the built environment, or "fixed capital." Tertiary circuit surplus value is generated through research and development, technology, education, and social services. When any one circuit becomes saturated, with overaccumulation of capital or labor-threatening profits, the state and private interests "switch" the flow of capital into other circuits and spaces (Harvey, 1989; Hackworth, 2007).[3]

Particularly relevant for the rise of sustainability, the built environment is central to the capital-switching process. Following World War II, with the slowdown of wartime manufacturing and veterans returning in search of housing and work, the United States faced a predicament: postwar U.S. cities offered little room for expansion of housing, and unemployment rates threatened to balloon. Seeking to engineer a "spatial fix," government, corporate, financial, and real estate sectors colluded to prompt a state-led expansion of physical infrastructure, making possible newly built suburban neighborhoods. Suburbanization fostered immense growth in the housing sector, making up for the loss of revenue in manufacturing. At the same time, however, suburban growth—and racist fears—facilitated a "hollowing out" of central cities by white, middle-class households (Beauregard, 2006; Harvey, 1989; Jonas and While, 2007; Logan and Molotch, 2007; Massey and Denton, 1993; R. Walker, 1981).

Suburban expansion may well have "solved" the postwar economic crisis. But growth on the outskirts of urban areas was only a temporary fix. Starved by a shrinking tax base and saddled with debt following the exodus of both manufacturing and wealthier residents, cities were in financial trouble. At the same time, corporate, private, and national debt ballooned, and inflation loomed large. In 1973, postwar, debt-fueled suburban growth and inner-core disinvestment ultimately culminated in a worldwide property and financial market collapse. With secondary circuit growth slowing way down, and stagflation devaluing the credit-based "fictitious" capital markets that had powered suburbanization, a fresh fix was necessary. This time market actors turned to a conservative, anti-Keynesian approach that prioritized privatization, deregulation, the lifting of tariffs and embargoes, and a decentralization of power and responsibility to the local level (Brenner and Theodore, 2002; Hackworth, 2007; Peck and Tickell, 2002).

As with the post–World War II exodus of people and capital from central cities, the fix accompanying this "neoliberal turn" would once again possess a substantial spatial component. Seeking municipal-scale revenue generation, cities partnered with growth machine actors to remake devalued inner-city neighborhoods as sites of accumulation. Instead of through industry, growth this time occurred through real estate and amenity-based development. Public subsidies "lubricated" private profits in the secondary circuit (N. Smith, 2002). Crucially, city boosters began to capitalize on growing popular environmental concerns, and sustainability discourse became part and parcel of the urban core reinvestment process in many cities. Urban greening projects unfolding over the next few decades, such as brownfield redevelopment, public transit installation, green space development, urban agriculture provisioning, and bike infrastructure expansion, came to constitute what While et al., (2004) dub an "urban sustainability fix."

Despite any original redistributive leanings, those who have benefited from urban greening are largely white and middle class or wealthy. Comprising "the same old growth machine but with a decorative skin" (Logan and Molotch, 2007:xx), sustainability framings simultaneously address the environmental concerns of a growing number of people; attract investors, tourists, and highly educated residents; and satisfy the demands of investors and developers. In a spatial "seesawing" of capital, private and public investment has flowed out of many suburban spaces and back into central cities. But as inner-core housing prices have risen, working-class residents have been forced outward in a process coined as "eco-gentrification" (Dooling, 2009; Quastel, 2009), "environmental gentrification" (Checker, 2011), and "accumulation by green dispossession" (Safransky, 2014). Though many celebrate this so-called (green) revitalization of urban cores, others characterize it as a "revanchist" process (N. Smith, 1996), highlighting how this "consummate expression of neoliberal urbanism" (N. Smith, 2002:446) has resulted in the forced removal of lower-income, racialized communities while catering to the aesthetic tastes of a wealthier, whiter "creative class" (Hanlon, 2009; Katz et al., 2010; Kneebone and Garr 2010; Peck, 2005)—what sociologists Kenneth Gould and Tammy Lewis (2019) refer to as the "sustainability class."

While the neoliberal green urbanism paradigm may well have solved a crisis at the municipal level, in so doing it shifted a dire emergency to the household and community scale (Checker, 2011). Those who are displaced and excluded from newly greened neighborhoods are often the same residents who have suffered and continue to suffer from legacies of slavery, ongoing settler colonialism, and other forms of dispossession, displacement, and exploitation. And these same communities have been disproportionately exposed to pollution for decades (Anguelovski, 2016; Banzhaf and McCormick, 2012; Dillon, 2014; Reese, 2018). Moreover, as anthropologist Melissa Checker's (2020) recent research on communities fighting for EJ in New York City reveals, several years of sustainable urban development—a so-called win-win-win approach for the environment, the economy, and social equity—have added up to a "double bind" for EJ communities. By double bind, Checker means that attempts to resolve one conflict result in new challenges. When New York needed a place to site a facility to treat sludge dredged from gentrifying Brooklyn's Gowanus Canal Superfund Site, for instance, officials turned to Staten Island, home to a highly diverse population that already suffers from numerous environmental injustices.

Perhaps nowhere is the tendency of the mainstream urban sustainability movement to reproduce racialized disparities clearer in the United States than along urban waterfronts. Such spaces where land meets water have long been sites of violence, from riverine influxes of white colonists to the theft of Indigenous lands and genocide of Indigenous peoples, to the sale of enslaved Black people, to the construction of wartime ships at the center of the military industrial complex and empire-building practices (Bunce and Desfor, 2007). When manufacturing and production vacated many U.S. cities throughout the mid-twentieth century, industry left behind ports and their infrastructure, including docks, warehouses, ship repair yards, ship terminals, cargo handling facilities, and salvage yards. Since the 1970s, as throughout hollowed-out cities, *green* growth machine coalitions made up of developers, real estate investors, entertainment and tech industry actors, outdoor recreation enthusiasts, and government officials have recognized the profit-making possibilities in such "underutilized" waterfronts, putting urban harbors at the forefront of conflicts around economic restructuring and who has a right to control cities' destinies.

Urban sustainability, along riverfronts and throughout U.S. cities and beyond, has thus become fully subsumed into racial capitalism.[4] The mainstreaming of top-down urban greening initiatives has reproduced and further entrenched, as opposed to remedied, racialized health disparities and housing instability, particularly near urban harbors and within inner-core neighborhoods. Conventional narratives about sustainability gloss over such disparate impacts, suggesting that a rising green tide will lift all boats. Sustainability boosters render green development an apolitical—what critical geographers call a "postpolitical"—project, advancing a storyline that all will benefit and omitting the meaningful input of frontline communities that might contend otherwise. Notably, mainstream sustainability discourse is, by and large, also ahistorical, its gaze set resolutely on a utopic green future with little analysis of how to remedy past (and present-day) inequities (Davidson and Iveson, 2014; Swyngedouw, 2007, 2009). Groups such as PHCC are asserting a new narrative, one that brings this underside to light—and in so doing attempts to chart a new path forward.

Movements for Environmental Justice

The neoliberal urban sustainability era is not only the *context* in which today's environmental justice movement leaders work. EJ-focused agents of change, including PHCC members, are directly responding to the mainstream sustainability paradigm at the same time as they are attempting to fashion urban greening into something more attuned to categories of difference, to historical context, and to a more radical shift in socio-ecological relations. Current EJ struggles are grounded in decades and centuries of organizing. With direct roots in the civil rights, anti-toxics, Indigenous, labor, and traditional environmental movements, the EJ movement has mobilized people to advocate for improved living conditions around transportation, land use, public health, toxins, housing, occupational safety, and more. EJ scholar David Pellow (2016:222) defines EJ communities as those facing a "disproportionate burden of environmental harm."[5] Poor communities of all races and ethnicities experience environmental and climate injustice, and Black, Indigenous, Latinx, and other communities of color experience the highest burdens of environmental pollutants, with persistent racial differences occurring across levels of socioeconomic status (Agyeman, 2013; Brulle and Pellow, 2006; Bullard, 2000; Bullard et al., 2008; Corburn, 2005; Morello-Frosch et al., 2001; Pellow, 2018; Pellow and Brulle, 2005; D. Taylor, 2000).

The U.S.-based EJ movement dates to the early 1980s, when protesters responded to the dumping of toxic PCBs in Warren County, North Carolina. In 1987, the United Church of Christ published "Toxic Wastes and Race in the United States," bringing attention to the disproportionate risk of commercial toxic waste exposure for BIPOC (Black, Indigenous, and people of color) communities. Less than a decade later, in 1991, the First People of Color Environmental Leadership Summit laid out the EJ movement's core principles. Key tenets include the precautionary principle, which shifts the legal burden of proof onto the perpetrator, rather than forcing communities to prove that they are being harmed. Other important principles emphasize democratizing problem definition and making scientific research more transparent and participatory. The EJ movement is also concerned with *limiting* environmental risk in order to promote well-being for all, rather than merely spreading environmental risk around more equitably. Notably, EJ activists brought environmentalism to "the city" by conceptualizing "the environment" as the places where people live, work, play, pray, and learn, as opposed to some wild place outside of an urbanized landscape.

In the first two decades of the twenty-first century, movements for urban sustainability and EJ have collided, often in conflict-oriented ways, though sometimes productively. A growing number of groups fighting for the right to live in toxin-free places—such as PHCC—are also fighting for benefits of and the ability to shape the green urbanism movement, including gaining access to green space, improving public transportation options, reducing congestion and unhealthy air, developing more pedestrian-friendly neighborhoods, accessing housing that is truly affordable and close to the places people spend time, and fighting climate injustice. Agyeman (2013) refers to such efforts that bridge traditional EJ with more recent explicitly equity-focused sustainability efforts as a "just sustainability" paradigm.

Others have described communities taking a more expansive approach to EJ work as utilizing a tactic that is "just green enough" (JGE) (e.g., Anguelovski, 2016; Curran and Hamilton, 2012, 2018; Wolch et al., 2014). A JGE strategy implies an effort to maintain industrial jobs at the same time as communities seek to curb emissions and benefit from environmental improvements. The JGE model, Winifred Curran and Trina Hamilton (2018:6) argue, "is a call to rethink what we mean by 'green' and to offer an alternative vision of what a remediated neighborhood can look like." Some challenge the JGE conceptualization, however, arguing that some grassroots groups may well be working to preserve industry in the midst of more equitable urban greening schemas—but that some are also actively fighting for anti-displacement strategies as part of a "just transition" that moves society away from today's industry-induced climate crisis (i.e., Sze and Yeampierre, 2018). Black, Indigenous, and other communities of color are on the front lines of this work, and many view it as a racial justice project (Kim, 2017). Such groups indeed challenge what Miriam Greenberg (2015) calls "the sustainability edge" that characterizes mainstream, market-oriented sustainability discourse.

The vast majority of research on just sustainability movements focuses on particular neighborhoods, often in New York City, featuring David and Goliath-type stories of a lower-income, Black, Indigenous, and people of color-led groups facing corporate polluters backed by public agencies with no pretense to being green. Grassroots groups, particularly those working in cross-class, cross-race coalitions that do not map neatly to a particular neighborhood, such as PHCC, have received less attention—especially those working in purportedly green cities outside of New York. Yet, a growing number of people are attempting to come together across lines of difference, in and from disparate geographies, to address what geography and urban planning scholar Sarah Safransky (2018) refers to as an urban land question that is deeply entangled with interconnecting issues of capital and class, racism and colonialism. Agents of change in North American green cities are working under conditions of what critical pedagogy scholar La Paperson (2014) calls "settler environmentalism." Such conditions entail discourse characterizing the land in dualistic terms: as simultaneously "desecrated, in pain, in need of rescue," at the same time as it is "sacred, wild, and preserve-able." Continuing a trend over three centuries, a triad of key actors is imbricated in today's land use conflicts: white settlers "whose power lies in shaping the land into his wealth," Indigenous people, "whose claim to land must be extinguished," and descendants of enslaved people, who "must be kept landless" (116–117).

In coalitions such as PHCC, members of these three groups, as well as immigrants, refugees, and other newcomers of various racial, ethnic, and class backgrounds, are coming together. They are attempting to hold industry, public agencies, and "re-invading" (i.e., upper-middle-class, white) environmentalists and sustainability advocates accountable. Such groups are grappling with questions of how to establish some sort of community control in a way that does not merely redistribute land stolen from Indigenous peoples to other oppressed groups. And they are focused on a particular place, even if that place is no longer (or in some cases has never been) "home" to those on the front lines, due to complex histories of displacement, dispossession, and forced migration. PHCC's struggle, in other words, is one of spatial alienation and forced removal, at the same time as it is one of togetherness and claim staking.

Critical Environmental Justice and (Dis)engagements with the Sustainability State

"Critical EJ" scholars offer a firm foundation for thinking about this most recent wave of green city changemaking in all its historical nuances, and open space to consider the complexities of cross-race, cross-class organizing such as that of PHCC. Pellow (2018) explains that while "first generation" EJ practice and scholarship focused primarily on disproportionate exposure to toxins for communities of color, sometimes referred to as *distributional justice*, today, grassroots groups are also explicitly fighting for other forms of justice, including *procedural* and *representational justice*. In other words, EJ groups today are concerned with more than solely reducing disproportionate impacts of environmental burdens; meaningful recognition and input, and self-determination, are often fundamental pieces of their demands.[6]

According to Pellow (2018), a new generation of EJ research and practice—*Critical EJ*—builds on this expanded perspective of justice and develops EJ thinking in four key ways. First, in addition to enlarging notions of justice beyond distributive and juridical frames to encompass procedural and other forms of justice, researchers and activists are also giving greater attention to the complex ways in which social categories of difference, such as race, class, gender, sexuality, and disability, intersect to magnify the ways in which people experience systemic violence. In doing so, Critical EJ takes cues from the Black feminist tradition's intersectional lens. *Intersectionality* refers not simply to an additive list of identities, but rather to the ways in which different forms of systemic violence become multiplied when combined. The ways in which Black women experience oppression, for instance, are distinct from the experiences of both white women and Black men; the survival strategies and resistance efforts that Black women pursue likewise differ (Cho et al., 2013; Crenshaw, 1991; Ducre, 2018).

Intersecting hazards are also a core part of Critical EJ analysis. Environmental racism becomes embodied for low-income Black communities in intersecting ways via not only exposure to air pollution, a traditional EJ issue, but also through anti-Black police violence, which also literally "constricts breath," as exemplified in the death of Eric Garner at the hands of the New York Police Department (Dillon and Sze, 2016). This example highlights what Pellow refers to as the "intersecting axes of domination and control" that have differential impacts along lines of race and class. Elsewhere, I have extended Pellow's critical EJ framework to argue that a conjoined lens of intersectionality and intersecting hazards is particularly crucial for understanding how people living unhoused experience environmental injustice (Goodling, 2019). Police sweeps in downtown and residential areas push people into toxic spaces, and when houseless communities express concerns, they risk further forced removal; such systemic violence vis-à-vis environmental hazards is further multiplied and magnified for unhoused people along lines of race, gender, age, disability, and so on.

Pellow's other three pillars address the role of the state in perpetuating environmental racism, bring attention to complex spatial and temporal dimensions of environmental injustice, and grapple with the ways in which entire populations are deemed expendable—and are fighting back. Expendability implies that there is no escape, no possibility of moving to safety. The state perpetuates the expendability of particular groups through its track record of refusing to intervene in meaningful ways in the interests of EJ communities. At the federal level, Executive Order (EO) 12898 sits at the heart of this analysis. In 1994, President Bill Clinton instituted EO 12898, mandating that all federally funded projects overtly address EJ issues. But as of January 2014, out of 298 Title VI complaints filed against the EPA—grievances registered "in response to perceived discrimination by a public agency using federal funds"— all but *two* had been dismissed. In other words, EO 12898 has done little to actually improve the environments of vulnerable communities (Pulido et al., 2016; see also Engelman Lado, 2017; Harrison, 2019, 2022).

Yet, the EPA and state-level environmental agencies, interdisciplinary scholar Jill Harrison (2019) asserts, nevertheless maintain unique capacity to reduce harms caused by industrial activity in ways that individuals, environmental organizations, and other actors cannot. These agencies have the power to regulate polluters and to force industrial corporations to make changes, even if they have yet to actually carry out comprehensive initiatives in a way that benefits those who are most impacted by toxic industries. Harrison attributes inaction at the federal level to organizational inertia over the last forty years, even under Obama, whose administration vocally supported EJ. Such inaction is notwithstanding the herculean efforts by EJ activists and EJ staff and supporters within the EPA and state-level regulatory agencies. Factors contributing to inertia are diverse and include funding restrictions, anemic regulatory authority, neoliberal weakening of government more broadly, court decisions that "underspecify" agencies' authority, and technical limitations (17). Severely exacerbating impacts of these "standard narrative" explanations, Harrison argues, is a regulatory workplace culture that slows progress on EJ initiatives. Day-to-day cultural elements that undermine EJ efforts within agencies such as the EPA include disagreement among agency staff about the appropriateness of various EJ reforms and outright rejection of EJ initiatives brought forth by EJ staff—notwithstanding explicit commitments to EJ, such as EO 12898. Until agency staff and leadership "treat EJ as *central* to what these organizations do," and until they "define EJ in ways that align with longstanding EJ movement principles," Harrison contends, it is unlikely that environmental regulatory agencies will make much progress on EJ reforms.

The primary state-sponsored levers meant to help marginalized groups thus do remarkably little on their behalf. This analysis echoes Luke Cole and Sheila Foster, who, in *From the Ground Up*, argue that pursuing legal strategies has amounted to little success for the EJ movement. Likewise, geographers Tyler McCreary and Richard Milligan (2018:x) argue that pursuit of state recognition by Indigenous and Black groups in North America, in a context of ongoing settler colonialism and racial capitalism, "functions more to elide historic drivers and geographic processes of marginalization than to disrupt white supremacy and settler colonialism." Moreover, the process of invoking regulatory agencies' tools requires enormous amounts of time and energy for grassroots groups, often to little avail (Pulido et al., 2016).

Geography and ethnic studies scholars Laura Pulido and her colleagues (2016) therefore argue that EJ activists ought to disengage from public agencies and instead pursue a more militant path; EJ groups will have a higher likelihood of success, they contend, by pursuing change *outside* the state's participatory channels such as through direct action and more self-reliant strategies, rather than from within government participation processes. Pellow (2018), likewise, argues that EJ movement agents of change ought to work to deepen direct democracy in all its manifestations regardless of whether such actions engage the state, as doing so promises a greater likelihood of more just process and outcomes. In an interview with Pulido (2017:52), Pellow asserts that the EPA's track record on EO 12898 communicates its priorities loud and clear: "The government has informed communities of color that poisoning them is in the national interest! Do we really want to place our faith in the idea that the state can give us environmental justice?" Harrison (2015, 2019, 2022), however, cautions against discounting the crucial role that strong environmental regulations can play in protecting communities, and urges EJ groups to put full-court pressure on regulatory agencies to carry out EO 12898. Her analysis emerges in large part from conversations with EJ leaders around the country (Harrison 2015, 2016, 2019). In Harrison's interviews, some dismissed campaigns aimed at government regulatory agencies. Much of the concern she heard was based in a logic not of pursuing alternative strategies toward stricter protective regulations, but rather focused on "hands-on" projects such as building community gardens that had little to do with compelling government regulation—in essence, neoliberalizing activism.[7]

PHCC is neither wholly disengaging from the state's participatory channels nor pursuing the neoliberal avenue against which Harrison cautions. As *Green City Rising* illustrates, PHCC has simultaneously engaged with the state *selectively* and at times *confrontationally* as opposed to unequivocally and submissively—at the same time as the coalition, and especially PHCC member organization Right 2 Survive, a houseless-led group, has pursued bottom-up initiatives aimed at creating a new system within the shell of the old. As the old International Workers of the World maxim goes, this is a mode of prefigurative politics, one that seeks to transform structures from the inside out. PHCC's hybrid approach neither entirely embraces engagement with state agencies nor entails full-scale disengagement. PHCC acknowledges the limits of engaging with regulatory agencies, while simultaneously holding strong to a belief that public agencies must be impelled to act—all the while pursuing access to the kinds of environmental amenities that are promised, though rarely delivered, to all in so-called green cities. PHCC is far from unique in this regard. In *Evolution of a Movement: Four Decades of California Environmental Justice Activism*, for instance, Tracey E. Perkins (2022) analyzes the trade-offs inherent in taking more reformist versus revolutionary tactics within the EJ movement in California. Ultimately, she argues that institutional (reformist) tactics have resulted in incremental progress for EJ movements—albeit at the risk of watering down demands. The case of PHCC provides an opportunity to examine how to build upon and integrate calls for simultaneously attempting to hold the state accountable, engaging in confrontations with the state, and drawing on more radical avenues to social change that may sometimes entail complete disengagement, making space for a primarily mutual aid and direct action approach.

Radical Incrementalism in the U.S. Context

South African critical urban scholar Edgar Pieterse (2008) offers a framework to begin thinking through the hybrid approaches pursued by PHCC and other grassroots groups. Drawing on twenty years as an activist, teacher, policy manager, researcher, and in other roles, Pieterse argues that neither the pole of "Marxist revolution" nor that of managerial mainstream "good governance" is sufficient to enact and understand transformative politics in fast-growing African cities—and as I contend here, nor in so-called sustainable cities in the United States. He suggests that two concepts, "radical incrementalism" and "recursive political empowerment," open space for a more generous reading of how change happens, and indeed how grassroots groups might intentionally pursue change in some contexts. By radical incrementalism, Pieterse means "bringing change into the world through discrete avenues: surreptitious, sometimes overt, and multiple small revolutions that at unanticipated and unexpected moments galvanize into deeper ruptures that accelerate tectonic shifts of the underlying logics of domination and what is considered possible." By "recursive empowerment," Pieterse brings attention to the *agents* of change: the galvanization process, he asserts, depends upon grassroots groups that themselves operate in democratic, reflexive ways, enabling people to build their own capacity as they develop collective power that is more than the sum of its parts. Empowerment of the urban "poor" and "abandoned," Pieterse explains, "is fundamentally an individual process that deepens with time if individual efforts are consciously embedded in more collective forms of solidarity and mutual empowerment" (8). It is through engagement in bottom-up analysis, political education, and collective action that new circuits of knowledge come into being, enacting transformative change that does not rely on a "benign state" nor "good policy plus political will" (7).[8]

Radical incrementalism was the focus of a workshop I attended in 2014, with Pieterse and two dozen organizers, artists, and researchers at the African Centre for Cities at the University of Cape Town, South Africa. Most participants were local to Cape Town, while a handful of us had traveled from around the world to attend. One of the main aims was, following urban scholar Ananya Roy (2009), to decenter urban theory making from the "great cities" of Western Europe and North America. "It is time to blast open theoretical geographies," Roy contends, "to produce a new set of concepts in the crucible of a new repertoire of cities" (820). The workshop's framing document elaborates on radical incrementalism in this way:

> Radical incrementalism [entails] citizens, sometimes in collaboration with researchers and civil servants, engaging the State on a project-by-project basis to achieve incremental institutional changes. This field of antagonism and collaboration goes beyond re-distribution of material resources, but requires a shift in "who is in the know"—a shift in competencies and a re-coding of the city's administration. . . . [It is] the mechanism by which residents of the city slowly re-wire and re-structure their city administration to better suit the actual city it is set up to govern. It [might] provoke new imaginaries of what is possible . . . and make possible the articulation of new identities, groups and demands.[9]

In attending to systemic shifts that occur in incremental fashion as opposed to via sudden revolution, this framework is attuned to the process and agents of change alike. It also assumes the state as complicit in injustice *at the same time as* it holds potential for agonistic yet progressive politics. In so doing, this lens opens space to account for the sometimes seemingly contradictory ways in which groups such as PHCC strategically engage and disengage with government agencies, incorporate political education into their work, and pursue hands-on projects that improve the day-to-day lives of constituents incrementally—while serving as models and catalysts for more radical systemic change that might transpire on a larger scale, in relationship to many other agents of change using a variety of tactics.

PHCC's radically incremental approach may stem partially from a propensity toward neoliberal subjectivity, but perhaps more fundamentally from the *contradictions* of the neoliberal sustainability context in which the group is working. As in Cape Town, where public agencies promise that economic development will benefit all residents, Black and white, poor and middle class alike, the sustainability paradigm promises improved environmental conditions for all, including fresh air and clean water. Sustainable city boosters also promise equitable access to green benefits of the built environment, including public transit, decent housing, walkable and bikeable neighborhoods, expanded parks, living-wage green jobs, and more. Yet, these are the same amenities that are part and parcel of eco-gentrification and displacement, and that have largely accrued for white, wealthier residents.

Such built environment improvements come under the control of local agencies, while environmental cleanup is largely under the purview of regulatory agencies such as the EPA or state bureaus. Given this multi-scalar governance structure, it is an incredibly complex task for frontline communities to bring about an improved urban environment in the sustainability era—and to actually have access to environmental improvements rather than be displaced by rising housing costs tied to urban greening. But it is precisely on this contradiction, between the promises of the sustainable city and unjust outcomes, that groups such as PHCC focus in articulating new narratives of what can and should be, by and for whom, and why.

Certainly, the granting structures of the EPA and other funders hold sway over EJ groups such as PHCC. In recent years, government and philanthropic foundations have moved away from funding organizations pursuing regulatory and policy change and litigation, in favor of those seeking to build gardens, trails, and alternative energy infrastructure. As a result, fewer groups are engaging in regulatory and policy reforms in order to reduce hazards, and more are pursuing nonregulatory means to bring about access to environmental amenities (Harrison, 2019; see also Harrison 2015, 2016, 2022). Nevertheless, there remain many exceptions to this trend, as Harrison acknowledges, including PHCC. At the same time as PHCC seeks to bolster environmental regulations and fully remediate the harbor, the coalition also seeks access to the environmental amenities and fundamental provisions, such as housing and decent-paying jobs, that are promised to all sustainable city residents. The case of PHCC therefore offers an opportunity to understand how grassroots groups navigate the murky waters of green city environmental injustice, paying particular attention to complex scalar questions, to the role of the state in socio-ecological change processes, and to the imaginaries put forth and negotiated by diverse frontline groups.

The contradictions that PHCC has encountered in attempting to push the harbor toward a more liberatory future informs a theory of change that helps explain what is happening in cities across the United States in this era of mainstream environmental concern. Like so many groups, PHCC simultaneously seeks to bring urban ecosystems into a more healthful state and ensure that marginalized communities have what they need to survive and thrive. PHCC has attempted to push for change by implicitly taking a radical incrementalist approach, adapted to the U.S. sustainable city context. This path has entailed selectively engaging *and* disengaging with the EPA and local public agencies, sometimes cautiously and cooperatively and other times confrontationally, and it has meant pursuing regulatory as well as nonregulatory mechanisms of change. In so doing, PHCC members have simultaneously prioritized short-term survival *and* long-term structural shifts, focusing on exterminating hazards as part of building access to a healthy, sustainable world. While far from perfect, the process by which the coalition has pursued change has endeavored to be democratic, centering the voices of those most affected while embracing the humble support of some who have benefited from the harbor's contamination and cleanup. PHCC's particular radically incremental approach stems from the scalar contradictions of the sustainability context in which many EJ groups are now working; the case of PHCC therefore offers an opportunity to understand the logic and utility of a hybrid approach to change, one that groups in cities across the country have similarly embraced.

Indeed, EJ activists are advancing visions of *indispensability* (to echo Pellow, 2018), that is, of the fundamental necessity to view communities as interconnected, interdependent, and capable of operating in solidarity. It remains to be seen what will unfold, but in the meantime the case of PHCC offers a window into the intricacies of pursuing environmental justice in an era characterized by growing environmental consciousness, at the same time as it is marked by neoliberal deregulation and apolitical sustainability discourse. The range of issues on PHCC's radar begins to illustrate some of the complexities involved in the Portland Harbor's *contamination*, the harbor's *cleanup*, and PHCC-led *collective action* for a more just, green future.

My role with PHCC has been to help stitch together various narratives of the harbor's contamination and cleanup. I have also incorporated facts, figures, and stories from archives and secondary histories, from informal conversations and formal interviews with coalition members, and from my own experiences in hundreds of PHCC-related functions that took place from 2013 through 2016. Unless otherwise noted, all quotes from coalition members and others involved in the harbor cleanup are from conversations and interviews I conducted and are used with permission. For a more extended description of my positionality and role within PHCC, see the preface to this book.

At its heart, *Green City Rising* is a story of ordinary people, inspired by a beloved river, who are attempting to come together across lines of race and class to undo our society's commitment to the interconnected domination of land and people.[10] It is a story of a bottom-up effort to reclaim "the city" for fish, birds, and ordinary people, beginning with one urban watershed. And it is a story of the contradictions of so-called green cities and the challenges and successes that grassroots groups encounter in their endeavors to exploit those contradictions for more just ends.

Chapter Outline

Following this introduction is part 1, "Producing and Counter-Producing a Green City's Harbor." One main premise of this book is that the sustainable city-building paradigm simultaneously forecloses and opens opportunities for frontline groups such as PHCC to sway urban greening processes toward a more just, green future. Yet, neither this closing nor this opening happens on its own; *people* are behind the struggle for particular social and landscape configurations, whether resulting in theft and displacement, liberation and a more holistic way of life, or something in between. Such outcomes are centuries in the making, and they remain contested. The four chapters in part 1 examine some of the people and processes involved in contestations over the past, present, and future of the Portland Harbor. They focus on the conflicted ways in which the harbor has come to be, and come to be known, and addresses how and why one cross-class, cross-race alliance came together to fight for a more just green city. Even as they encounter age-old challenges to changing uneven power structures, groups such as PHCC are (re)defining what the EJ and environmental movements can be in the sustainability era.

Chapter 1, "'Little Bugs in the Mud': PHCC's Origins," situates the coalition in Portland's local EJ movement lineage and recounts how diverse groups initially joined up, shedding light on the relationship between today's fight for a more just sustainability and the EJ movement of years past. With roots in a classic EJ predicament, with polluters attempting to evade responsibility for cleanup and public agencies doing the bare minimum to engage the broader public and even less to tap frontline communities, PHCC ultimately emerged as an organization concerned with both remediating hazards *and* fighting for the benefits of and ability to shape the city's urban greening initiatives. This chapter describes Portland activists' early engagements with local and federal agencies around the harbor cleanup, setting the stage to dig into the long history of oppression and resistance in the harbor, inner workings of the coalition, and engagements between grassroots groups and public agencies in the chapters to come.

Understanding the contradictions confronting groups such as PHCC today also requires an examination of the historical relationship between activists—and their ancestors—and the places that are the focus of grassroots resistance. Chapter 2, "A Peoples' History of the Portland Harbor," addresses the deeper origins of the coalition, articulating a "peoples' view" of the harbor and how it differs from more mainstream accounts. Conventional narratives celebrate the harbor as an urban greening success story, highlighting how the Willamette River would be even more toxic than it is today without the efforts of public health experts, sanitary engineers, conservationists, and white, well-to-do anglers who expressed great concern about point-source pollution starting in the 1920s. Early remediation efforts indeed helped land Portland on the map as a leader in the nascent environmental movement. Yet, they also contributed to the city's present-day racialized disparities, giving rise to today's grassroots groups that are pursuing a more just sustainability. A *peoples'* history of the harbor, in contrast to more mainstream narratives, accounts for those who have been burdened by contamination and cleanup alike and emphasizes organizing around the interconnected issues of housing, labor, food sovereignty, racial justice, and many other topics that form a foundation for today's interlinked social and EJ movements. Drawing on archival materials, secondary histories, media reports, oral histories, interviews, planning documents, and participant observation, this chapter brings together the deep histories of the groups that make up PHCC in relation to the Portland Harbor, with particular focus on the endurance of Indigenous and Black communities in the face of ongoing settler colonialism and white supremacy.

The violence and resistance that have shaped the harbor possess not only a temporal element but also a subjective-spatial one. Chapter 3, "Our River, Our Future: More-than-Local Grassroots Activism," explores why people have gotten involved in cross-class, cross-race grassroots organizing for a more just sustainability in Portland. It centers on the role of landscape features—particularly urban rivers—in such organizing, examining complex "place attachments" involved in this work. People engage in social movements for a variety of reasons, and some are motivated by a combination of factors, such as a tangible survival need (e.g., food, shelter, safety), deep concern about a broader social or EJ issue, or a desire for connection and community. What is notable about the case of PHCC is that the river itself is a unifying motivator for nearly all coalition members, serving to stitch together seemingly disparate motivations. Yet it is not only the Willamette River generally nor the Portland Harbor specifically that has drawn people in, but also rivers in other parts of the world. Moreover, many PHCC members sense a strong connection to the harbor *even if they have never lived in its vicinity*. Such complex spatial attachments are particularly noteworthy given histories of dispossession and displacement. The Willamette River is therefore a central actor in this story, mediating PHCC members' relationships to the coalition and Superfund planning process.

Chapter 4, "*Producing* a Peoples' History of the Portland Harbor," charts the process by which coalition members have drawn on their riverine connections to put their own histories and relationships with the harbor into conversation to produce the new, shared history outlined in chapter 2. PHCC's peoples' history of the harbor emerged over a multiyear *process of becoming political*, which entailed interrelated collective identity formation and participation in coalition activities. These activities often involved elements of individual and shared remembering, teaching, and learning. A series of vignettes in this chapter helps illustrate how PHCC's collective historical narrative emerged. "Icebreaker" exercises at monthly member meetings, culturally specific events, the production of a short film, and collective testimony writing have all contributed to the development of PHCC's shared history, one that challenges white-washed versions of the harbor's history. As part 2 of this book goes on to illustrate, this collective narrative, in turn, has served to re-historicize and repoliticize the harbor, laying a foundation for ordinary people to collectively shape the harbor's future.

Whereas part 1 emphasizes the people engaged in PHCC's work, mediated by complex relationships to the landscape, part 2, "Challenging the (Green) Growth Machine," shifts to focus on some of the contradictions inherent in green city planning and in turn PHCC's approach to socio-environmental change. Collectively, the three chapters in part 2 address how grassroots groups sometimes simultaneously engage with *and* circumvent the state, at various scales. In so doing, PHCC has taken a "radically incremental" approach, implicitly following a blueprint for change articulated by Edgar Pieterse (2008) in the context of South African cities. For PHCC, a radically incremental approach in a U.S. green city setting has entailed engagements with state agencies that occur cooperatively and collaboratively, as well as interactions that are confrontational and antagonistic. The mechanisms of social change pursued by PHCC likewise have involved both regulatory and policy shifts, as well as nonregulatory means (i.e., direct action, mutual aid). The temporal scale of remedy has emphasized immediate survival, at the same time as longer-term, systemic shifts remain clear goals. Substantive areas of focus have involved not only hazard remediation but also access to green amenities. And the locus of expertise has been squarely democratic, while recognizing that there may be some role for technocratic experts to play—but only if their priorities align with those living and working on the front lines. In other words, PHCC has operated in a dialectic, tension-filled space in response to the promises and perils of the sustainable city paradigm.

Chapter 5, "Greenwashed Greenwashing: Challenging the Sustainable City's Classic Growth Machine," opens part 2 by recounting PHCC's shift to taking a more antagonistic approach in engagements with the City of Portland and analyzing what PHCC's encounters with the city reveal about the politics of so-called green cities. The coalition spent years prodding officials to engage frontline communities, to no avail. The City of Portland, in fact, actively foreclosed spaces for people to influence the harbor cleanup for several years, all the while publicly asserting how all would benefit from a cleaned-up harbor. Tired of waiting, PHCC took a more direct approach in spring 2015, showing up at the Portland City Hall *en masse* to highlight the lack of attention to social and EJ implications of the harbor cleanup. Later, it came to light that a legal battle between the city and water and sewer "ratepayers," and officials' related reticence to being saddled with undue liability for the cleanup, had had a chilling effect on the city's willingness to conduct a public involvement process around the harbor cleanup. Rather than green growth-oriented actors influencing the city to take a watered-down stance on EJ, as we might expect, it was *classic growth machine actors*, who made no pretense to being green, who implicitly pushed the city to depoliticize the planning process. The pervasiveness of a classic growth machine, in many ways, demystifies and de-fetishizes the idea of a "paradigmatic green city." EJ groups must be wary of greenwashing, therefore, and also of municipal leaders deploying sustainability discourse that in essence portrays classic polluters as greenwashers. What has transpired in Portland contradicts much thinking around how "green growth" works. The case of PHCC can serve as a cautionary tale for similar groups working in other cities, helping grassroots organizations understand the behind-the-scenes actors attempting to undermine social and EJ advances.

Chapter 6, "Remaking the City, Remaking Ourselves: Houseless-Led Community Organizing," delves deeply into the work of one of PHCC's core mem-

ber groups, Right 2 Survive (R2S), examining the origins of the organization
and the role of a community run by and for unhoused people within the coalition's efforts. By 2011, thousands of people were living unsheltered in the city
of Portland. As with the millions more living on the streets of cities across the
United States at the time, unhoused Portlanders were subjected to constant
dehumanization and criminalization, incurring fines and citations, enduring
"sweeps" that resulted in confiscation of life-saving possessions, surviving police and vigilante violence, and suffering trauma after trauma. People were also
banding together and rising up. Around the same time as PHCC was getting
started and attempting to engage public agencies about the harbor cleanup,
R2S was establishing an unsanctioned, self-organized "rest area" for houseless people with nowhere else to go. R2S's rest area provided a safe place for
people to sleep, at the same time as it became a hub for community organizing around a host of intersecting issues—including the harbor cleanup. A half-
dozen R2S members attended nearly every PHCC function for several years,
playing a central part in the coalition's work and pushing PHCC to consider
the needs of the city's most vulnerable residents. Key moments included the
collective production of a pamphlet highlighting ways to mitigate river-related
hazards for unhoused people, including toxic soil and police sweeps, and the
mobilization of over one hundred people living unhoused to testify on the
EPA's *Proposed Plan*. R2S played a key role in generating people power, analysis, and popular education materials for PHCC. The group also influenced
PHCC's overarching approach, in that the rest area implicitly utilized a radically incremental strategy. By demonstrating how to attend to immediate survival needs as a means of simultaneously building consciousness and forcing systemic change, R2S influenced other PHCC members to adopt a similar
mindset and prompted the coalition as a whole to indirectly embrace tenets of
radical incrementalism.

Finally, chapter 7, "(Dis)engagements With the Sustainability State," moves
beyond the local scale to examine PHCC's interactions with the EPA. For decades now, the EJ movement has largely called on the state, in particular the
EPA, to regulate the kinds of polluters who have contaminated the Portland
Harbor. But this strategy has proven less effective than hoped for, especially
at the federal level. Some EJ scholars and activists therefore urge EJ groups to
disentangle themselves from the state-led participatory programs and pursue
other, more autonomous and direct action channels toward change. Others
call for a renewed commitment to holding the state accountable and lament
that some EJ activists are pursuing a neoliberal path toward improvements
that prioritize small-scale projects such as community gardens without push-

ing for stricter state regulations and larger systemic change. This chapter articulates PHCC's experiences attempting to work with the EPA, highlighting the frustrations endured and rationale for ultimately disengaging from some EPA-led participatory channels in select moments. While pursuing access to the kinds of environmental amenities that are promised—though rarely delivered—to all in so-called green cities, PHCC has also acknowledged the limits of engaging with regulatory agencies *and* has held strong to a belief that public agencies must be impelled to act.

PART I

Producing and Counter-Producing a Green City's Harbor

Willamette Daisy
Erigeron decumbens
Endangered

CHAPTER 1

"Little Bugs in the Mud"
PHCC's Origins

A growing number of grassroots EJ groups that are working for improved environments today, such as PHCC, are fighting for the benefits of and ability to shape the green urbanism movement. Objectives include gaining access to green space, improving public transportation options, building pedestrian-friendly neighborhoods, ensuring housing that is truly affordable and close to the places people spend time, securing living-wage jobs in green industries, and pushing for a just transition to a healthier climate. Adversaries often include white-led environmental groups taking a color-blind approach and so-called green developers gunning for profits. But even in ostensibly sustainable cities, there is still plenty of classic growth coalition activity, with polluters attempting to mask contamination, block stricter regulations, and shield themselves from any financial responsibility for addressing harm. While it is crucial that organizers, researchers, students, policymakers, and others are attuned to the ways in which mainstream urban greening often perpetuates disparities, it is equally critical to pay attention to the ways in which old-fashioned environmental injustice simultaneously endures in these same green cities. The confluence of dynamics—polluters attempting to evade responsibility and sustainability boosters overlooking the equity implications of their work—makes for a highly complex world for EJ-focused groups to navigate.

This chapter outlines PHCC's origin story and includes protagonists we might expect to take center stage in fights over environmental contamination: corporations dealing in the oil, steel, and fertilizer industries; local and state government agencies, alongside the federal Environmental Protection Agency (EPA); conservation organizations; and grassroots groups representing Black and Indigenous people, immigrants and refugees, and poor people of various backgrounds. I also begin to illustrate public agencies' lack of meaningful engagement of frontline communities in the Portland Harbor. Much of the public involvement process that did occur earlier on in the cleanup process, it turns out, was led by representatives of polluters and entailed facilitators telling participants that highly toxic substances were akin to "little bugs in the mud." While PHCC evolved to also fight for the benefits of a cleaned-up harbor, the coalition first emerged in an attempt to hold polluters accountable. "'Little Bugs in the Mud': PHCC's Origins" unfolds in three parts. I first describe the work of some of PHCC's predecessors, which helps illustrate the coalition's linkages to the traditional EJ movement. Next, I recount events that unfolded in 2011–2012, when polluters took the helm of public engagement, raising red flags for local EJ leaders. Finally, I illustrate early meetings that led to the coalition's convergence, with attention to the kinds of groups that ended up joining together. This chapter sets the stage to examine the inner workings of the coalition and its later engagements with government agencies and polluters during the height of the cleanup planning process, in subsequent chapters.

Polluters at the Table, "Running Everything"

Leaders of the groups that would become PHCC's core membership base first convened in early 2012. To understand why they came together, however, it is necessary to first look back to 2000, when the EPA initially designated the Portland Harbor as a Superfund site and assembled the Portland Harbor Community Advisory Group (PHCAG). This early history foreshadows the tokenizing treatment that impacted communities would experience time and again over the next decade and a half as they engaged with public agencies.

Prior to joining the City of Portland's Office of Neighborhood Involvement as a program coordinator in 2006, Klamath tribal member Jeri Jimenez had become familiar with the complexity of the harbor cleanup planning process from her earlier work with the Workers' Organizing Committee and then as director of the Environmental Justice Action Group (EJAG). Jeri understood the EJ implications of the cleanup and worried that those who were affected by pollution were not being given adequate attention. In a 2016 interview with me reflecting on PHCC's origins, Jeri explains:

> [In the late 1990s], I was approached by the state and the county at times going, "Can you help us get this word out to these people who don't speak English? Because we're putting fish advisories out." . . . The state paid to have fish advisories put out, but none of them are saying anything about the effects. They're not saying, "Oh, as a pregnant woman you should only have one ounce a month." They're not saying any of this. They're just saying, "We're

saying it in Spanish, in English, in Russian, and Chinese; help us put those out." And we're saying, "Well, what is the effect?" [We saw] a report that showed . . . [one in] a thousand recreational fishers would contract cancer, but [one in] a hundred Native fishers—because they were subsistence fishers—would contract cancer from the fish.

For Jeri and other local environmental justice leaders, it was clear that Indigenous people and others relying on fish in the Portland Harbor for subsistence were at much greater risk of getting sick from pollution than the general population. This was an overt EJ issue. They agreed to help public agencies get the word out about the fish advisories.

Jeri and her EJAG comrades, however, remained concerned about health impacts. Drawing comparisons to the air pollution campaign they were also running against Oregon Steel Mill (now Evraz) at the time, EJAG leaders asked what good advisories did if people still breathed contaminated air because of where they lived or worked?[1] Similarly, what good were warning signs if people continued to eat contaminated fish for subsistence and cultural reasons? Damage would be—and had already been—done, regardless of fish advisories posted in multiple languages along the riverbanks. Jeri and others felt strongly that something more needed to be done about the environmental risks associated with pollution in the Portland Harbor.

State and county staff were not the only public agency representatives contacting Jeri and EJAG in the first decade of the 2000s. Familiar with the grassroots group's work on community-led brownfield cleanups with the City of Portland, the EPA also came knocking. Jeri recalls federal officials' request for assistance: "We [know you] already know how to build great community advisory groups, so help us." Specifically, the EPA asked EJAG to help build the Portland Harbor Community Advisory Group. According to the EPA, Superfund Community Advisory Groups (CAGs) entail community members coming together "to serve as the focal point for the exchange of information among the local community," as well as "the EPA, state regulatory agencies, and other relevant agencies involved in cleanup of the Superfund site" (EPA, 2016). Such groups, in the EPA's eyes, deliver a crucial public service: they provide "a public forum for community members to present and discuss their needs and concerns related to the Superfund decision-making process. A CAG can assist EPA in making better decisions on how to clean up a site. It offers EPA a unique opportunity to hear—and seriously consider—community preferences for site cleanup and remediation" (EPA, 2016).

At first, EJAG leaders appreciated the opportunity to weigh in on the cleanup. They quickly realized, however, that the reality of the CAG did not align with the EPA's stated intentions for the group. "We went to help them— but they didn't really listen," Jeri remembers, recollecting how the CAG's convening felt more like an official checkmark on a public participation worksheet than a process that would truly allow for community members to inform the Superfund decision-making process. She continues:

> We sat on the advisory group, maybe two years, and our member—who was an African-American man named Billy Washington—he used to play for the Oakland Raiders, and he had played [music] with Parliament for a while. He had also cleaned up messes in Kuwait, environmental messes in Kuwait. He knew, he had the expertise. And after about two years he was saying, "They've [the CAG] gone in a different direction, this is not good for the community . . . This isn't going to benefit us, so [let's] get out of it."

One of the chief issues for EJAG leaders was that representatives from potentially responsible parties—"PRPs" in EPA terminology, and simply "polluters" in EJAG parlance—were also members of the CAG. "Business was at the table," Jeri flatly stated. "The polluters were at the table, and they were running everything." Based on EJAG's experience fighting Oregon Steel/Evraz, community leaders found it unreasonable to expect that impacted communities would be able to participate in the CAG alongside PRPs and meaningfully influence the cleanup of contaminated soil and sediment.

Frustrated by the EPA's presumption that industry and impacted communities could productively work together under the CAG model, and realizing that EJAG's energy would be better spent engaging its base rather than sitting through hours and hours of CAG meetings, EJAG leaders withdrew from participating in the EPA's officially recognized advisory body. Instead, through the first decade of the 2000s, EJAG continued its focus on air pollution. At that time, there was discussion of adding four lanes to the Interstate 5 freeway, which cut through Portland's historically Black Albina neighborhood. Although Albina had by this point already lost many of its Black residents to gentrification (Gibson, 2007), Jeri recognized the immediate connection between expansion of the interstate freeway, EJAG's constituents' lives, and the work the group was already doing on air toxins: "*This* is our campaign, the I-5 freeway, and not expanding it, for all of these different reasons," she said. EJAG clearly had its hands full as it was, without jumping through CAG hoops.

In the years between EJAG's exit from the CAG and the nascent days of PHCC, EJAG wrapped up its air pollution campaign, and leaders scattered to begin new organizations and take on other projects. Jo Ann Hardesty, for one, went on to become the president of the Portland branch of the National Association for the Advancement of Colored People and then in 2018 was elected to the Portland City Council on an anti-police violence platform. Several people initiated a local chapter of Protocol for Assessing Community Excellence in Environmental Health, a coalition of government agencies, nonprofit groups, and community organizations focused on building a campaign around various environmental issues with human health impacts. Eventually, Jon Ostar, who had worked with EJAG as an intern attorney under Jeri Jimenez, started Organizing People / Activating Leaders—Environmental Justice Oregon (OPAL), an organization focused on transit justice and other EJ issues. Kevin Odell also left EJAG to help start OPAL and eventually founded a Portland branch of Groundwork USA. Groundwork Portland (GWPDX) came to focus on environmental workforce development and leadership development for Black, Indigenous, and other youth of color experiencing poverty, as well as advocacy around EJ issues more broadly. Much of GWPDX's early work revolved around community-led redevelopment of neighborhood brownfield sites, such as defunct gas stations and other pieces of contaminated land.

Although EJAG had disbanded, Jeri remained deeply committed to grassroots organizing around EJ issues. In 2009, when GWPDX's program director position opened, she encouraged someone she knew from the City of Portland, Cassie Cohen, to apply, unknowingly laying the first concrete steps for PHCC to take shape. Jeri recalls urging Cassie to submit her résumé for the position that would eventually transition into GWPDX's executive director: "I knew Cassie from the city, and then I knew [her] from the Center for Intercultural Organizing board, and she was looking for work, and I sent her the Groundwork job announcement." At first, Cassie was reluctant to apply, arguing that her background was in social work rather than EJ-oriented community organizing, and that as a white woman she might not be the best person to lead an organization fundamentally set up to serve diverse youth. But Jeri was adamant: "'You know how to organize because you organized all these people,' I told her." Jeri was referencing Cassie's work with the city as an intern from 2005 to 2007 and then as an employee from 2007 to 2009. Cassie worked on the visionPDX and Vision Into Action campaigns, both part of the City of Portland's landmark pre-Comprehensive Plan community visioning process. The "Portland Plan," as it came to be colloquially called, created a mandate for city planners to analyze all land use planning decisions through a lens of equity and racial justice. Jeri told Cassie, "If you apply, I'll support you." Cassie submitted her application and got the job, and she and Jeri met periodically throughout her time at GWPDX, from 2009 through early 2015.

In the Interim: "They Are Trying to Bamboozle Us"

While Portland's EJ leaders worked on improving air quality, building accessible transit, and remediating small-scale contaminated properties in low-income neighborhoods, Superfund cleanup planning moved forward with little to no input from members of frontline communities. Starting in late 2011, however, PRPs began doing their own direct outreach to those most likely to suffer the ill effects of harbor pollution. At this point, Jeri became less concerned that members of vulnerable groups were being excluded from the cleanup planning process, as she had been in the early days of the CAG, and more concerned with cooptation. A phone call in winter 2012 from a representative of a local Latinx-serving nonprofit left her troubled that impacted communities were being included "in order to be paid off," in Jeri's words, to adopt the perspectives of the polluters. The caller described outreach that the Portland Harbor Partnership (PHP) was conducting. Jeri recalls the conversation: "He said, 'Can you come watch this presentation, because I think they are trying to bamboozle us.'"

The PHP consisted of nine core PRPs: the Port of Portland, the Oregon Department of State Lands, Calbag Metals, Evraz Portland, Gunderson LLC, NW Natural, Schnitzer Steel, Vigor Industrial, and Portland General Electric. These PRPs worked with the Metropolitan Group, a "full-service strategic and creative agency" that "directly impact[s] social change" and "build[s] the power of voice and capacity of the people, organizations, and communities that drive social change," according to an earlier version of its website (Metropolitan Group, 2016). These nine PRPs also worked with the National Policy Consensus Center, a program of Portland State University's (PSU's) Hatfield School of Government. Together, these entities designed and carried out a public engagement campaign around the Superfund site cleanup from August 2011 to March 2012 (Rome and Bell, 2012), reported to have cost a half-million dollars (Mesh, 2012). The PHP aimed to raise awareness about the importance of the EPA-led process and to encourage involvement by all parts of the community in the upcoming decisions via public events, meetings, and other outreach avenues; and according to the Metropolitan Group, the PHP implemented a "groundbreaking new public education and engagement effort" around the Portland Harbor Superfund Site cleanup.

A final report prepared by graduate students attending PSU's Hatfield School described the PHP's outreach campaign as multifaceted and extensive. PHP's activities included a survey and focus groups, public events and community meetings, and development of social media and web-based tools.

The survey garnered 1,870 responses, and focus groups included 72 participants. Over 1,500 people attended meetings from 54 community, business, and other groups, including 14 neighborhood associations, and over 25,000 "direct impressions" were collected from tabling and other signage at various events. The campaign also included an "On the Waterfront" educational series, featuring lectures by local historians and other experts, developed with the support of the Oregon Historical Society, PSU, Oregon State University, the PHCAG, Freshwater Trust, and Willamette Partnership. More than 650 people attended the lectures. Notably, the survey campaign included a component called a "Charity Challenge." Upon completion of the PHP's survey, survey takers were invited to vote for one of four organizations—Oregon Food Bank, Friends of Trees, Oregon Historical Society, or Freshwater Trust—that would receive a $10,000 donation from the PHP (Rome and Bell, 2012).

The earlier Metropolitan Group website highlights outreach to communities of color and immigrant and refugee groups as a core part of the PHP's campaign: "A special emphasis has been placed on engaging a wide array of ethnic and cultural community groups through established community organizations." By working with three local, well-established community-based organizations, Immigrant Refugee and Community Organization, Latino Network, and Urban League, to "tailor culturally appropriate engagement plans to the specific constituencies" (Rome and Bell, 2012:5), the PHP aimed to demonstrate a commitment to impacted communities' priorities. Activities with these groups included focus groups, presentations, information booths at cultural events, surveys, and translation of feedback into English. Outreach resulted in input from over five hundred community members connected to these three groups.

According to a final report produced by PSU, four overarching themes emerged from the surveys and focus groups conducted with communities of color and the general population: "1) Concern over river contamination coupled with an appeal to clean the Willamette River quickly; 2) A request for more community parks and other forms of public access (e.g., fishing and boating docks, trails for hiking and biking, and community centers); 3) Restoration and preservation of wildlife and the natural environment; and 4) Responsible economic development" (Rome and Bell, 2012:1). The report summarizes one key takeaway from the nine-month outreach campaign: "It is clear from the data that residents of the Portland Metro Region would like a more publicly engaged, responsive, and effective cleanup process to begin" (1). But what followed was, from community leaders' perspectives, anything but that.

As soon as Jeri Jimenez got wind of the nature of the PHP's presentations, she decided to attend a presentation to see for herself what was going on. She describes her first impression:

> Oh my gosh, yes this is so bad. . . . For more than thirty years, the governments—meaning state and county—are putting these fish advisories on, not in languages that the people who were eating the fish [spoke]. And that was a really clear picture, and so then when this [PHP representative] comes and does a presentation, he's like, "Pregnant women can eat one ounce of fish a month." And so [audience members] are like, "What are they supposed to eat the rest of the month?" So that scared him, but he didn't educate the Spanish speakers. He's talking about fish, and they're thinking about the fish you buy in a store. Not fish you take out of the river!

In addition to severely misleading audience members, Jeri remembers that the presentation—to mostly Spanish speakers—was entirely in English, and that it obscured who would be implicated in paying for the cleanup. "He [the presenter] was speaking to Latino people, [but] he wasn't speaking in Spanish," Jeri recalls. "He's dumbed down his presentation, with the end of it saying, 'Well, you're the taxpayers. It's going to fall on you, so whether we spend a million or a hundred million, it's going to fall on you, so it's your decision.' And I'm like, 'Oh my God!'" Jeri understood that local residents and business ratepayers would likely be on the hook for some of the cleanup costs, given that the city was a PRP, but she also knew that the full tab was likely to be shared among dozens of mostly corporate entities. Jeri emphasizes, "It was a really stupid presentation. It was so dumbed down. It was *so* dumbed down." For Jeri, the presentation was nothing but a scare tactic to convince residents to advocate for a less costly cleanup.

Bob Sallinger, director of conservation at Portland Audubon from 1992 to 2022, echoes Jeri in recalling the deceptiveness of the PHP's outreach tactics via written correspondence with me in 2021–2022:

> This was a very sophisticated effort to manipulate public opinion as major decisions around the cleanup approached. Notably, some groups including Audubon actively opposed and confronted this effort. I recall it being challenging because many groups, including frontline [EJ] groups that were relatively unfamiliar with Superfund, were initially receptive to this outreach. This was happening at a time when very few groups were focused on the river and especially the industrial river and even fewer knew anything about Superfund. The folks behind this effort presented themselves as simply trying to provide public information and education, but it was actually a big PR campaign for polluters, designed to build their credibility with the commu-

nity and to reduce concerns about the contamination. It came at a time when
groups like Audubon and [Willamette] Riverkeeper were also ramping up
public involvement efforts around Superfund. I can remember some really
challenging meetings where groups that were new to the issue were very hes-
itant to accept that this campaign was intentionally designed to deceive them.
It wasn't received as "Portland nice" for groups like Audubon to call this out
for what it really was. We actually took a lot of heat, but in the end I think we
and others did a good job of exposing what was really going on and the campaign was abandoned. This campaign was led by some of the most aggressive
anti-environmental businesses in Oregon.

The anti-environmental businesses involved in deceiving community
groups around Superfund had their hand in various other schemes as well.
In fact, the ratepayer theme would emerge down the line again as a quiet but
powerful fulcrum around which the cleanup planning process would pivot.
When PHP representatives mentioned concern about "ratepayers" being stuck
with the cleanup bill in their presentation to Latinx residents, they were not
just talking about ordinary residents who paid sewage and water bills for their
homes. They were chiefly concerned about corporate ratepayers—many of
them PRPs—that paid one of the highest rates in the United States for incom-
ing clean water and outgoing discharge. At the time, the Portland Water Users
Coalition (PWUC) was embroiled in a lawsuit against the city and the Bureau
of Environmental Services, filed on behalf of utility ratepayers that alleged illegal expenditure of ratepayer revenue. The PWUC included several PRPs, including Siltronic Corporation, Vigor International, and Harsch Investment.
Kent Craford, a lobbyist behind the lawsuit, explained in a 2014 interview with
the *Oregonian* that he was simply "speaking up for both residential and big industrial users. Water and sewer rates . . . affect everyone" (Theen, 2014).[2]

A Call for New Grassroots Involvement

Although outreach to diverse groups was a source of pride for the PHP, Jeri
Jimenez and others expressed extreme skepticism about the process. For Jeri,
the last straw came when one of the PHP's presenters advised a majority Span-
ish-speaking audience, many of whom likely consumed resident fish from the
Portland Harbor on a regular basis, to essentially imagine away any possibility
of bodily harm coming from the toxic sludge at the bottom of the river. "Don't
think of them as chemicals," Jeri recalls the PHP's representative saying, in reference to the deadly toxins subsumed in the sediment that qualified the Portland Harbor for federal Superfund listing. He suggested the audience instead

think of these pollutants as "little bugs in the mud." Jeri could not believe what she was hearing: "My biggest concern was, they're out there, flimflamming communities of color, and [the PRPs] spent a whole bunch of money to create a lie that [they] think will work."

PRPs were not only lobbying community of color groups; they lobbied politicians at all levels of government, hard. For instance, Vigor Industrial led a tour with Oregon senators Ron Wyden and Jeff Merkley and representatives Earl Blumenauer and Kurt Schrader in August 2012. Then in November of that year, all four elected officials signed a letter to the EPA that a local reporter described as sounding "very much like a press release from the harbor companies" (Mesh, 2012). The political lobbying had an outsize effect. City officials, for instance, began echoing a PRP talking point that the EPA was dragging its heels on getting to a record of decision. "This was pure gaslighting," notes Bob Sallinger. "The PRPs in fact were stalling the process, including producing reports that were deceptive and inaccurate." The EPA eventually fined a group of PRPs for producing inaccurate and deceptive materials—although the fine was revoked. "Industry's line," Bob explains, "was that Superfund process was dragging on forever harming their businesses when in fact it dragged on because they intentionally stalled the process. The interference of politicians had a real chilling effect on EPA—they were absolutely and overtly concerned that if they were too aggressive, the delegation would come after them."

Upon hearing of the PHP's deceptive presentations, Jeri immediately called Cassie Cohen at GWPDX. Jeri felt that with a home base in Albina, Portland's historically Black neighborhood, and given that Cassie had developed relationships in years past with several grassroots groups, GWPDX was uniquely positioned to convene frontline community members around the Superfund site cleanup. GWPDX's board was majority Black, and unlike most other social and EJ-focused organizations in Portland, GWPDX's work concentrated on community-controlled remediation and reuse of brownfield sites, and the board supported working collectively with other frontline communities.

One of GWPDX's early projects in 2010, for example, entailed facilitating the transformation of a lead-filled residential lot into a safe community garden. An Albina neighborhood house had burned to the ground, and dangerous lead paint residue remained in the soil where the structure once stood. GWPDX worked with Oregon Sustainable Agriculture Land Trust (OSALT), an organization that "holds farmland and urban gardens for the purposes of research and education on sustainable agriculture," to navigate land acquisition and cleanup permits (OSALT, 2016). GWPDX then led a community remediation and redevelopment planning process and worked with Black youth and elders to build and maintain the Emerson Street Garden on the site.

When Jeri called, Cassie immediately made the connection to the Superfund cleanup. "We [Groundwork] did brownfields work, and Superfund cleanup is kind of similar, kind of related," Cassie explains in a 2015 interview. In particular, GWPDX was familiar with the paradoxes involved with environmental remediation in gentrifying neighborhoods. Given the swiftness with which the development of green amenities, such as community gardens, was contributing to rising rents in inner Portland and cities across the United States, Cassie knew that without specific provisions to mitigate displacement—such as community-controlled development, community benefit agreements, and permanently affordable housing—Black and Indigenous communities, as well as other communities of color and lower-income white households, were at risk of being fully excluded from inner-Portland neighborhoods. Grassroots groups would need to insert themselves into the cleanup process on their own terms in order to ensure a thorough remediation that actually benefited those who had already been displaced and others at risk of future displacement.

Cassie recalls the catalyst that inspired her to call other community leaders, alerting them to the toxins that lingered in the Portland Harbor: "Really, it was just two people, two environmental justice oriented people that came to me saying they were concerned." Jeri was one of those people. The other was a federal-level staffer, who recalls in a 2015 interview, "It just seemed like there were a lot of voices that were not at the table. Because it's such a long drawn out legal process, it's so hard for a community member . . . it's really hard to figure out how to have meaningful involvement."

Thinking back to her first impression after speaking with these two key government employees—"inside activists"—in the spring of 2012, Cassie explains: "The PHP was reaching out to [BIPOC] groups, and they were paying them. It seemed like a public relation campaign that the PRPs were facilitating." Like Jeri and the federal staff member, Cassie was particularly concerned that, since the PRPs were the ones framing the issues during the focus groups, members of impacted communities were being exposed to only one perspective: that of the polluters, whose primary interest lay in keeping cleanup costs as low as possible. Recognizing a clear need for grassroots groups to insert themselves into the cleanup process on their own terms, Cassie began alerting representatives from other community organizations—separate from the PHCAG, given Jeri and EJAG's experience several years prior. People from a wide variety of groups began to convene to discuss what a coalition of frontline communities might look like.

A Coalition Takes Shape

While the polluters' outreach campaign was wrapping up in early 2012, PHCC was just getting started. Cassie Cohen, Jeri Jimenez, and a few dozen people soon gathered at a coffee shop in the back of the former Talking Drum Bookstore in Albina. Jeri describes the crowd: "We had a full room," recalling that leaders from Black, Indigenous, Latinx, Eastern European, and other groups attended. Analysis at Talking Drum painted a critical picture of the PHP's communications. "The general sentiment about those focus groups was kind of shock at how bad the contamination was—people didn't realize [the extent of] it. And concern, and that they wanted to do something about it, and that they didn't trust the PRPs to keep facilitating these outreach and engagement plans," explains one participant.

It was in this meeting that a clear picture of the polluters' outreach process began to unfold, and local leaders started to collectively connect what was at stake for their communities in the cleanup of Portland's waterways and riverfront land. While the polluter-led outreach campaign's official report portrayed the PHP as operating with the best interests of "the public" in mind, dialogue at Talking Drum painted a different picture. One participant remembers, "[The outreach campaign] seemed like this huge wave of greenwashing that didn't have any community voice in it, that was really just being paid for and well marketed and advertised by folks whose voices were already really well represented in the whole process." Those in attendance at that first meeting started thinking about mounting a community-led outreach campaign of their own. "[Discussion] was sort of like, 'What do we do? What's being done?'—an assessment of the situation," recalls another attendee.

While the majority of those assembled expressed criticism of the PHP's outreach campaign, there was some disagreement among meeting participants about the implications. "Some people were like, this seems like a buy-off. What's happening here? And then others were like 'No, this is great. We need to be involved in this one way or another,'" remembers Jeri. One leader from a prominent Black-led organization, in particular, voiced approval for the PHP's campaign, citing the PHP's outreach as just the first step in what promised to be a valuable opportunity for Portland's Black community to be engaged in a high-profile environmental issue. The organization ultimately declined continued participation in the group that would become PHCC.

From Jeri's perspective, however, there was more to the story. "Oh, [they] had to say that [statement approving of the PHP]," Jeri explains, "to save face." As reported in local media at the time, the PHP had paid $20,000 to the Urban League, $10,000 to Latino Network, and $12,500 to Immigrant and Refugee

Community Organization for participating in the outreach (Mesh, 2012). Yet, rather than focus criticism on the PRP's misleading presentations, the media condemned community-based organizations for taking money from polluters. *The Willamette Week* quoted Jeri, airing her own critique of the three community groups that accepted payment: "I was shocked to hear that the groups I work with were taking money from these people. . . . That was alarming, to think that somebody's spending a lot of money so they don't have to spend a lot of money" (quoted in Mesh, 2012). Program leaders were upset that she had called them out publicly. Jeri reflects on the controversy: "They weren't our community engagement people. They took the money because they were a jobs program and then [they] got called out. . . . I'm like, 'Whatever, you did the wrong thing!' . . . People were pissed at me, and I'm like, 'Get over it, you shouldn't have taken money from them.'" While Jeri was disappointed in the community groups' decisions to accept payment from PRPs, she is clear that her main ire was reserved for the PRPs themselves. "But of course, for the *Willamette Week*, that's the part they want to play on," she laments.

Despite being critical of the PHP, leaders from a few other larger organizations serving BIPOC communities were also resistant to joining the coalition. One organization's executive director told Cassie that the harbor cleanup just was not a high priority compared with other urgent matters. Cassie remembers him saying, "I think it's great what you're doing, but we have too much else going on. Definitely, when the time comes, we can put our name down as endorsing." Cassie surmises that lack of resources fueling long-standing conflicts, as well as personality differences with others involved, may have influenced some organizations to pass. She summarizes her conversation with leaders of the handful of groups declining participation in PHCC: "'Your organization's constituents are the ones most affected by the polluted fish, and it sounds like when you had the focus group that people were concerned and interested and wanted to be involved or to know more about it. And do you have plans to follow up with those folks? Or can we help?' For whatever reason— maybe I just didn't press hard enough, or—it just didn't happen." Jeri offers another perspective: "Because most of those organizations have a list of what they're supposed to do, what they get funded for . . . if there's anything that's not what they get funded for, then they don't participate. That's pretty common. . . . Most of those groups [that declined participation] . . . were social service agencies, not social justice [groups]. They're paid to provide services, not to cure the system."

In April and May 2012, Cassie and GWPDX board members also reached out to representatives from the six tribes with treaty rights to the harbor area, to ask for advice on whether there was a need for a grassroots community-based effort. They contacted the Confederated Tribes of the Grand Ronde Community of Oregon, Confederated Tribes of Siletz Indians, Confederated Tribes of the Umatilla Indian Reservation, Confederated Tribes of the Warm Springs Reservation of Oregon, the Nez Perce Tribe, and the Confederated Tribes and Bands of the Yakama Nation. The tribes by and large declined participation in PHCC, Cassie explains, because they are sovereign nations and have a formal government-to-government relationship with the EPA. Nevertheless, several tribal representatives have continued to be in communication with PHCC following those initial conversations. One person from the Umatilla Tribal Council, for instance, attended an early meeting. Cassie remembers his assessment: "We don't know what our role . . . would be, but keep us on the email list." And the Grand Ronde Tribe agreed to support PHCC through its Spirit Mountain Casino Community Fund, awarding crucial funds to PHCC early on.

Later, the Yakama Nation in particular came to take on a key leadership role in pushing the EPA to require a more robust cleanup plan, with representatives working in close coordination with PHCC. Davis Washines, Yakama elder, longhouse leader, and former executive chairman of the Yakama Nation's General Council, describes the Yakama's reasons for getting involved in harbor cleanup in a 2022 interview: "We have a right, by treaty, which under the Constitution is the supreme law of the land, to go and continue to gather food where we've always gathered it. But not only that, for it to be free of any danger of contaminants. What's the point of gathering something you can't use?" Davis goes on to explain why the Yakama decided to engage with PHCC: "Our message is about the places we live, the places we call home," he says. "That's what it's about. And so we want to fully engage with people that are willing—maybe you don't have to buy into everything that we say—but at least we have a common denominator that says 'we are concerned about the environment, we are concerned about what's going to happen to future generations.'"

Crucially, the dozen or so mainly small grassroots organizations that came to form PHCC represented diverse backgrounds and geographies. Jeri offers a summary: "What was interesting was, leaders from those communities came. The [larger] organization staff didn't come, but *leaders—the people on the ground*—came." Some were affiliated with smaller nonprofit organizations, whereas others were part of grassroots groups with few formal designations. Jeri reflects on the organic process of assembling such a wide variety of participants:

> We had several meetings, we talked to different funders and everything else. . . . So [GWPDX] did organizing to bring all these groups together, to get people from all these different walks of life. And pretty soon you're bringing in

Eastern Europeans, and all these people are going, "Of course the river's the most important thing to us, of course water's important to us, of course having fish is a cultural thing for us and a spiritual thing for us." So you brought together all of these people who historically have a much deeper understanding with the land than many Americans do. And so it was just the perfect group of people, and to go organize and to say, "Hey, wait a minute, you haven't talked to these people. You say you're done but you haven't talked to these people, and they're right here!" And they're concerned, and we're telling you, "You have to stop what you're doing and talk to them." It was brilliant, and to keep moving on that and finding more people, and even if you're not finding people, the stories that are going out are hitting people's ears, and they know it's true. The African American community—my husband's family lives on Albina near Beech—they always, always fished in that river.

Most groups, such as Wiconi International, the Czech School of Portland, and Wisdom of the Elders, had memberships of between twenty and a hundred people. Two, the East European Coalition and Right 2 Survive, joined on behalf of several hundred people, although their core leadership teams delegated to PHCC remained small. Ultimately, a dozen organizations, give or take, representing diverse perspectives on the contamination and cleanup, came together to form the Portland Harbor Community Coalition.[3]

A handful of mainstream environmental organizations also showed up right from the beginning. Portland Audubon, notably, had a long-term commitment to restoring the river for people and wildlife and saw connecting with PHCC as critical to this effort. Prior to 2010, Audubon was one of the only organizations working intensively on harbor issues. Bob Sallinger reflects on the evolution of community engagement around the harbor since then:

> The North Reach [of the Portland Harbor] has always been a battle against naked greedy capitalism. For the first twenty years that I worked on these issues, it was a pretty lonely battle against corporations that cared little for the community or the environment. There were very few conservation groups or social justice groups that were concerned about the health of the Portland Harbor in the 1980s, '90s, and early 2000s. Many groups simply wrote off the Portland Harbor as a polluted industrial wasteland. Portland Audubon was one of the only big conservation groups with an urban agenda, and we spent a lot of resources trying to engage the community on river issues. There were some huge battles over the river during this time period over issues like West Hayden Island, North Reach River Plan, the Big Pipe, and the river and community would be in far worse shape today had we not fought those battles.
>
> There is sometimes a tendency to look back today and view that work

through the perspective of what did not get done or was not involved, and that is both fair and important as we move forward. At the same time I think it is also important to recognize that we were working to engage community with the river, that we were advancing important conservation and social justice goals, stopped some really bad things from happening, and laid some of the groundwork for a more inclusive approach today. Between 2010 and 2015, we saw a massive influx of groups into the river discussion. A growing interest in climate change, racial and social justice, recreational access, and the importance of urban conservation in general shifted the way the community began viewing the challenges and opportunities associated with the Portland Harbor. I hope it was also the result of some of the seeds that we planted in prior years as well.

There was suddenly a lot of groups and coalitions orbiting Portland Harbor. PHCC was perhaps the most interesting because it was trying to create new and different internal and external power structures. This from my perspective is a really exciting evolution. It helps advance a much more equitable and holistic vision of what our river could be, especially with regards to communities that have been historically marginalized. It is also much more complicated as we try to integrate complex agendas and move forward together.

While it took PHCC members, Audubon, and other groups time to build trust with one another, eventually an alliance formed that would be critical to challenging polluters and mainstream sustainability boosters alike.

PHCC's Diverse Concerns

Over the next four years, PHCC, Audubon, the Yakama Nation, and others came to center analysis on the urgency of removing contaminated sediment from the river, so that it might become safer to eat resident fish. Nonresident fish that migrate to the ocean, such as salmon, live beneath Portland's iconic bridges for only a portion of their lives. In contrast, resident fish, such as catfish, carp, and bass, spend their whole lifespans in the harbor, eating a daily diet of the benthic organisms living in the mud at the bottom of the river. These organisms, in turn, eat a host of other highly toxic substances buried in the river's sediment—including polychlorinated biphenyls (PCBs). Banned by Congress in 1979, and one of the most potent of the over one hundred contaminants found in the harbor, PCBs are odorless, tasteless, man-made chemicals that were used in the manufacture of transformers, electrical equipment, thermal insulation, plastics, paint, motors, hydraulic systems, and other household and industrial goods for decades. PCBs do not break down over time. The PCBs in the Willamette have been bioaccumulating in the bodies of small organisms and resident fish, and in the bodies of people who eat resident fish, for generations. Those who do subsist on fish from the harbor face significantly elevated risks of developing cancer: the Oregon Health Authority currently advises against eating *any* amount of resident fish—indicating a problem much more dire than little bugs in the mud. Indigenous people from dozens of bands and nations—including the Multnomah, Chinook, Clackamas, Tualatin-Kalapuya, and many others—have depended on the Willamette's bounty for generations upon generations. Black and white people have also now fished in the harbor for many decades, and more recent immigrants and refugees from throughout Eastern Europe, Central America, and Southeast Asia regularly consume the harbor's fish today. Pacific Islanders with deep ocean fishing traditions miss their primary food source and seek out fish in the local rivers. Fishing helps longtime residents and newcomers to Portland alike maintain cultural traditions and buffer against food insecurity.

In addition to demanding habitat that can support healthy fish and people, PHCC sought to ensure the utmost care in the removal of toxins. Diesel trucks carrying sludge away from the harbor should be required to use the most effective air filters available, to avoid further pollution of communities near the river, PHCC asserted. The coalition was also vigilant to preemptively advocate for those communities "elsewhere" that are too often the recipients of contaminated waste: dredged sludge should not simply be dumped in rural, low-income areas, coalition members began to urge.

Tied to healthy fish, people, and habitats, PHCC also demanded riverside land for "community use" and "public access," including for affordable housing, gardens, recreation, and undeveloped green space. With the exception of Cathedral Park in North Portland, nearly all of the Portland Harbor's riverfront land is inaccessible to the general public. Moreover, next to none of it is stewarded by frontline communities. PHCC explicitly sought to bring land under the purview of Indigenous and Black people.

The coalition also stressed that family-wage cleanup jobs and truly affordable housing near the river should go to local residents from communities who have carried the burdens of the harbor's contamination. Undergirding these demands was a concern for shipyard workers of various races and ethnicities, who were exposed to toxins over the years while scrubbing lead paint off ships and working in asbestos-filled spaces. Over time, PHCC became especially distressed about thousands of Black shipyard workers, many of whom originally migrated to Portland during World War II to work on the docks—but who were excluded from joining the Boilermakers Union, and who were exposed to highly toxic working conditions. Black families originally lived in Vanport, a city the Kaiser Shipbuilding Company constructed just north of Portland in the early 1940s, until a 1948 flood destroyed their homes. Following the disaster, policing, racial covenants, a real estate "code of ethics," and tacit agreements with realtors segregated Black people to Albina, an area closer to downtown. Banks redlined the neighborhood, stopping the flow of private capital, and the city systematically disinvested in hundreds of blocks. More recently, steady inflows of public and private money, and largely white gentrifiers, have displaced longtime Black Albina residents to the outskirts of the city, particularly to the less resourced east. Thus jobs and stable housing for displaced residents were among PHCC's central demands.

Additionally, PHCC articulated concerns for the hundreds of houseless people who make their homes in lead- and dioxin-laced soil on the riverbanks. Police regularly carried out sweeps—forced evictions—in commercial and residential areas throughout Portland, pushing people to dangerous margins of the city, including the Superfund site. Although PHCC worried about the health of those living along the river in toxic soil, the coalition also understood that the riverbanks offered slightly more stability for houseless people than almost anywhere else in the city. In other words, PHCC worried about how the harbor cleanup *itself* would threaten the lives and livelihoods of hundreds of already highly marginalized and vulnerable people who called the river home. PHCC therefore demanded that houseless people be given six months' notice prior to the start of any cleanup work. The coalition also sought funds for permanent, affordable housing for anyone forced to move due to the cleanup and more generally supported a citywide anti-sweeps and anti-displacement movement led by R2S that sought to stabilize vulnerable communities.

For all of PHCC's core participants, the river that cuts through the heart of Portland became a central unifying concern, and indeed it ultimately became the factor that stitched seemingly disparate groups together to work in solidarity during the four years leading up the EPA's June 2016 release of the *Proposed Plan* and beyond.

Conclusion

Traditional industries—and public agencies working on their behalf—attempted to skirt accountability for cleanup of the Portland Harbor from the outset, prompting local grassroots groups to take notice. In the absence of meaningful outreach by public agencies, the initial public involvement process was largely led by representatives of polluters and entailed facilitators telling participants that highly toxic substances were akin to benign bugs. Although PHCC evolved to fight for the benefits of a cleaned-up harbor more broadly, the coalition's origins are rooted in a classic EJ situation.

A dozen or so grassroots groups would eventually emerge to become core members of PHCC, with highly diverse but converging interests. A river cleanup centered on the lifting of fish consumption advisories, so that people could safely depend on the river for interrelated cultural and subsistence purposes, was of prime importance for PHCC at the outset. Coalition members also articulated a host of other concerns, as they learned more and more about the harbor and all of the facets of the city that intersected with the cleanup planning process. At PHCC meetings, people brought up concerns about paying for cleanup, displacement of unhoused people living along the riverbanks, and rising rents. On the surface, these might seem irreconcilable with PHCC's platform of a cleaned-up river. Rather than advocate for a less robust cleanup in order to keep housing costs low, however, PHCC folded multifaceted concerns into a holistic analysis that was uncompromising in its demands of a thorough remediation of the river—*and* one that would benefit, rather than exclude and displace, those most impacted by pollution.

What is crucial to understand about PHCC's origins is that strict categories of EJ, social justice, and "the environment" hold little meaning; PHCC members treat these areas as interconnected, inseparable concerns. In fact, when I asked coalition members about their understanding of the concept of EJ, some indicated little knowledge of the EJ movement writ large and offered a take that differs from what is commonly understood by the term. One PHCC member, for instance, explained that for her, EJ means "just taking care of your environment, so like, where you live, the air you breathe, the water you drink. It's justice for all the environments that can't take care of themselves or that the people can do a lot more for. I guess they don't have a mouth or anything to say, 'Hey don't do this to me.' We need to act upon it." This statement indicates that although PHCC leaders and supporters might have done more to help newcomers contextualize the coalition's work within the deep roots of the EJ movement more broadly, members also possessed an evolving openness to reading the contamination and cleanup of the harbor in inherently nonbinary ways. As we will see, this understanding emerged for PHCC members from both lived experience independent of PHCC and through collective learning at PHCC functions. In all cases, the coalition's conceptualization of environmental injustice was rooted in an evolving shared understanding of the harbor's history—a history that diverged from mainstream historical narratives of the harbor.

Nelson's Checkermallow
Sidalcea nelsoniana
Threatened

CHAPTER 2

A Peoples' History of the Portland Harbor

Today, Portland is a paradigmatic "sustainable city" in nearly every sense, with considerable influence on urban greening trends worldwide. River remediation and adjacent development is a central part of Portland's sustainability success story. In 2001, for instance, the city constructed a 1.5-mile-long esplanade for biking, walking, and wildlife viewing on the river's eastside, right at water level underneath the Interstate-5 freeway. Downtown workers can now take lunchtime strolls and runs, crossing multiple bridges linked to the esplanade and back. Commuters zip along the esplanade on bikes, connecting to the city's vast network of bike lanes—adding to Portland's reputation as the "bike capital of the US" (Duffy, 2014), among many other green accolades.

Yet, people who carry the burdens of Portland's toxic legacy today know that the city's green facade hides a murkier reality, one that sustainability-themed tours often overlook. To really understand conflicts playing out today, it is necessary to look back several centuries. The Portland Harbor, in particular, is home to a long history of "slow violence," that is, "violence that occurs gradually and out of sight; a delayed destruction often dispersed across time and space" (Nixon, 2011). The harbor is also home to a long history of resistance and survival. To understand why PHCC members and supporters are not celebrating the Portland Harbor as an urban recreational paradise, and to see the ways in which today's fight is part of a long lineage of activism for a more just future, it is necessary to examine the history of the harbor from below, through the lens of a "peoples' history." This perspective centers the experiences of those who have carried the burdens of pollution, exploitation, dispossession, and displacement for decades and centuries, and who have long fought for a more humane, holistic way of living.

Mainstream storylines emphasize the role of the Willamette and Columbia Rivers in putting "Oregon Country" on the map and making Portland one of the main urban centers of the Pacific Northwest. Such narratives also highlight how infrastructure improvements over the past half century have enabled a once-sullied river to newly become an epicenter of urban recreation and sustainability for all. PHCC's perspective complicates such accounts. As a central part of the coalition's activism, participants have produced a new, shared narrative about the history of the Portland Harbor. Like the stories told in local media outlets and official government statements, PHCC's version accounts for the river's industrial past and green present. But it puts these elements into a much more nuanced context. PHCC emphasizes the endurance of Indigenous people in the Willamette Valley over the last two centuries, despite exposure to disease, massacre, forced removals, and the destruction of traditional food habitat. The coalition also recognizes the survival of Black residents, notwithstanding shipyard workplace exploitation, exposure to industrial pollution, segregation, and serial displacement to, within, and from neighborhoods adjacent to the harbor over the last several decades. And the coalition incorporates the continued exposure to toxins of food-insecure subsistence fisher people, including immigrants, refugees, and others, despite water quality improvements. Finally, PHCC stresses that the lives of unhoused people of diverse races and ethnicities seeking shelter along the river are threatened when they consume contaminated fish, live in toxic soil, and experience serial evictions.

People with claims to these often-overlapping identities make up PHCC's core membership base and are buoyed by supporters from environmental organizations, labor and neighborhood groups, and other interested parties. As the coalition works to politicize the harbor's future, members draw attention to the racist, colonial past and present and to efforts to survive and thrive in order to ensure that frontline communities collectively steer and benefit from urban environmental cleanup. This ongoing history is the focus of this chapter.

Much of the history recounted here emerged out of a process of producing a communal narrative through coalition activities, such as sharing personal memories during introductory activities at monthly meetings. Memories and histories have also materialized via participation in culturally specific events organized by members, such as water ceremonies and cookouts, and through the collaborative process of creating popular education materials. As people learned from one another, a collective, shared history of layered stories developed, with the narratives of different groups becoming woven together in complex ways (see chapter 4, as well as Goodling, 2019). One of my own roles has been to help stitch these different narratives together in various mediums in collaboration with many others, including in a short film co-produced with PHCC members and local college students; in short pieces of writing, such as an op-ed published with PHCC organizer and journalist Donovan Smith in the local street newspaper, *Street Roots* (Goodling and Smith, 2018); and in a comic book created by local artist Stephen Christian, with support from several PHCC leaders. These public accounts of the coalition's shared history are all relatively short. The goal of this chapter is to expand on these versions to include more historical details, while maintaining the spirit of PHCC's collective narrative as it continues to evolve.

Those who have benefited from Portland's green urbanization process over the years may consider PHCC's narrative an "alternative" history. But for those who have lived some part of the story told here, there is nothing alternative about it. In *Black Geographies and the Politics of Place* (2007), Black studies scholar Katherine McKittrick and the late geographer Clyde Woods stress that Hurricane Katrina may well have exposed the way in which layers and layers of violence resulted in today's "homeless, the jobless, the incarcerated, the invisible labourers, the underdeveloped, the criminalized, the refugee, the kicked about, the impoverished, the abandoned, the unescaped" (2); in other words, those who "[occupy] the underside of democracy." Yet, the underside is "not the underside at all" (3), they emphasize. Rather, for people who are "forgettable, unseeable," the underside is actually "the everyday" (3). According to the logic of McKittrick and Woods, mainstream media accounts, government reports, and many historians' texts actually constitute the *real* underside, from the perspectives of ordinary people who are most affected by systemic violence. Perhaps accurate in their facts, such mainstream versions of history are remiss in their *essence*, as historian Roxanne Dunbar-Ortiz (2014) reminds us. McKittrick and Woods argue for the imperative of making visible the "erasure, segregation, marginalization, and mysterious disappearances" (4) that have occurred and continue to take place, in order to get not just the facts right, but to get closer to the *core* of the origin stories of U.S. cities and in turn the country as a whole, its people, and its lands. The stakes are high. This kind of a perspective might, McKittrick and Woods assert, "move us away from territoriality," what they define as "the normative practice of staking a claim to place" (4), and toward a more generous way of living.

Groups such as PHCC are working to undo a societal commitment to the entangled exploitation of land and people. In telling *this* version of the Portland Harbor's history here, PHCC, and I, are attempting to make "the everyday" as experienced by hundreds of thousands of people over the last three centuries and beyond more visible. Not as an underside, nor as an alternative, but as a coherent weaving together of the past, present, and future of the Portland Harbor, in a way that also connects people and landscape here to people and places afar. What has happened in the Portland Harbor is in step with a much larger project of settler colonial violence throughout the world, a project that rests on the genocide of Indigenous peoples and the theft of Indigenous lands, the theft of Black peoples and their labor, and ongoing violence on multiple fronts. Historian Katrine Barber (2019) explains that although settler colonialism may look different in different places, it shares some common elements, including "settler land hunger, extinguishment of Indigenous land rights (and people through physical violence as well as cultures through assimilation), and importation of immigrant laborers who were excluded from citizenship rights and expelled during periods when their labor was not critical" (386).

Perhaps even more important is to emphasize what McKittrick (2011:959) calls the "human relationality" of ordinary people collectively engaged in struggle, including paying attention to the life, joy, and strength that exists even in the midst of upheaval. The particularities of such dialectical processes are crucial to articulate in order to affirm the existence of those on the front lines of fights for a new kind of future. The version of the Portland Harbor's history told here no doubt remains incomplete, but it nevertheless makes every effort to bring forth the everyday as experienced by ordinary people.

This chapter elaborates on previous versions of PHCC's peoples' history, drawing on archival materials, secondary histories, media reports, oral histories, interviews, planning documents, and participant observation. Taking a chronological approach, it begins with attention to the Chinookan peoples and others who have inhabited the region for more than ten thousand years. It then articulates how white settlers invaded the area and introduced devastating diseases, massacred whole families in an effort to access resources, stole land, and forced Indigenous people onto reservations. Chinookans, Molallans, Tualatin Kalapuyans (Atfalati), and many others continue to resist such violence and remain in Oregon today, joined by Indigenous peoples from around the Pacific Northwest and beyond. Next, this chapter outlines waves of industrial development in the harbor, with an emphasis on the experiences of Black shipyard workers and their families fighting for fair housing and employment. The remainder of the chapter brings us to the present, focusing on the struggles of PHCC members: Black Portlanders and urban Indigenous people living and practicing traditions in the Portland area and beyond, immigrant and refugee fisher people, and houseless people of various backgrounds attempting to survive along the Willamette.

Wapato Valley Life

For thousands of years, approximately three thousand Chinookan people belonging to multiple bands and tribes, as well as Molallans, Tualatin Kalapuyans, Yakama, and many others, called Wapato Valley home. The northern end of today's Willamette Valley, Wapato Valley is located where the north-flowing Willamette River drains into the Columbia River and on out to the Pacific Ocean. The Clackamas band of the Chinook lived between Willamette Falls and the Willamette's confluence with the Columbia River. The Multnomah lived mainly in sixteen villages on Wapato Island (today's Sauvie Island), north of what would become downtown Portland. Additional villages were located along the Columbia near today's airport and just east of present-day Portland, and a few others were located near Willamette Falls, upriver from Portland on the Willamette. Dozens of additional Chinookan villages, including those of the Kathlamet, Clatsop, Kalama, and others, dotted the length of both banks of the Columbia River from near Celilo Falls downriver to the Pacific, and a few were located to the north and south of the Columbia's confluence with the Pacific, on the coast (Zenk et al., 2016).

Altogether, there were at least fifty-five documented Chinookan villages in the region, although a precise number is nearly impossible to ascertain due in part to a partial historical record and in part to the transience of many settlements. Some villages were inhabited year-round, some were seasonal, and some were occupied only for short stints. Moreover, while some sites may have hosted inhabitants for a generation or two, others were populated for centuries. Regardless of tenure, all known Chinookan villages were sited along rivers or other major bodies of water. Villages ranged from one to twenty-eight houses. Most permanent structures were built from wooden posts and rafters, with cedar planks attached to the walls and roofs. Less permanent structures entailed layers of bark slabs for walls and roofs, attached to structural poles (D. Ellis, 2013; Saleeby, 1983).

Notwithstanding the occasional flood, an abundance of resources, especially wapato, a potato-like root vegetable, made Wapato Island and the rest of the valley suitable for year-round residence. Chinookan stories hold that the camas bulb and Chinook salmon emerged in early spring. Next came game such as grouse, quail, "mudfish," chub, trout, eel, lamprey, and sturgeon, followed by wild strawberries, roots, and wild carrots. Blackberries, raspberries, huckleberries, serviceberries, crabapples, and chokecherries ripened in the summer and fall. Autumn was also an important time for catching Chinook salmon returning from the Pacific, collecting and drying wapato, harvesting camas root, and hunting for deer and elk in the surrounding hills and mountains. Other important staples in various seasons included shellfish, small game such as rabbits and birds, and various insects, seeds, grasses, and nuts, including acorns. *Illahee*, Chinook for a tiny fish also known as eulachon or smelt, helped sustain people throughout the valley and beyond, especially in the winter (D. Ellis, 2013; Saleeby, 1983; Spores, 1993; Whaley, 2010).

The word *Illahee* refers not only to a resident fish but also to the territory west of the Cascade Mountains in present-day Oregon and Washington (Whaley, 2010). An elaborate network of tribes linked by trade and kin stretched throughout *Illahee* and beyond, and many traveled throughout the Willamette Valley for trading, fishing, and wapato gathering on a seasonal basis, especially in springtime and likely in fall as well. Part-time groups that came to the Lower Willamette Valley included the Kathlamet and various other Chinookan bands from the Lower Columbia region. Additionally, the Tualatin Kalapuya (Atfalati), the Molalla, the Klickitat, and other Yakama bands and tribes traveled—and continue to travel—throughout Wapato Valley, and especially to Willamette Falls, for salmon and lamprey gathering. "We followed the seasons. We have prescribed specific reasons for being in different places at different times of year," explains Davis Washines, Yakama Nation elder. Governance of land and water throughout *Illahee* was largely according to usufruct terms: that is, various people *depended* upon a site or resource without *owning* it. Whole communities, whether neighboring or through kinship ties, had usufruct rights to fishing sites, camas fields, wapato-root ponds, shellfish beds, and other sources of food and shelter (Boyd and Hajda, 1987; D. Ellis, 2013; Spores, 1993; Whaley, 2010; Yakama Nation, n.d.).

Dispossession, Disease, and Forced Removal

With the arrival of white settlers came what Whaley (2010) calls "the collapse of *Illahee*"—though collapse has been far from complete, with thousands of Indigenous people fighting back and their descendants continuing to live throughout the region today. The first white settlers documented to have met Chinookan peoples were North American merchant sea captain Robert Gray and British explorer George Vancouver, who arrived separately at the mouth of the Columbia River, in 1792 (Coleman, 2019; W. Lang, 2013). Both Gray and Vancouver claimed "discovery" of the Columbia River—a claim that historian Kenneth Coleman (2019:417) describes as "absurd," given that the lower Columbia region was already a densely populated place. Vancouver sought colonial access to resources for Britain. Riding on the coattails of the Northwest Ordinance and under the banner of "manifest destiny," which asserted that the U.S. government and white settlers had free reign over land that had been inhabited by Indigenous peoples since time immemorial, Gray sought a claim to territory for the U.S. government, as well as otter pelts to trade with China and a safe supply point for fur trappers (Whaley, 2010). The arrival of Gray and Vancouver, as well as the famous U.S. explorers Meriwether Lewis and William Clark in 1804 and others in the decades that followed, opened the door for disease, theft, and murder to devastate Indigenous populations and was a precursor to the U.S. government's ratification of treaties that systematically eliminated access to resources and forced people off their traditional homelands (Barber, 2019; Boyd, 2013; Coleman, 2019).

European diseases likely arrived at the Portland Basin via trade routes between Chinookans and other tribes who connected with Euro-Americans in other areas even earlier than 1792, as well as two or three more times in the early to mid-1800s. Smallpox spreads much like the flu, by ingesting germs transmitted from an ill person, such as through a sneeze or cough. After a ten-day latency period, a rash typically develops on the extremities, which then turns into lesions. About a third of those infected in the area died within a month, while others survived and were then immune to reinfections. Malaria had an even worse impact on Lower Chinookans (Boyd, 2013). The 1825 establishment of the Hudson's Bay Company at Fort Vancouver, just north of the Willamette-Columbia confluence, catalyzed the unfolding of "one of the most catastrophic epidemics in American frontier history" (Bergman, 2008:40). Spread by mosquitos, "intermittent fever" began to appear at Fort Vancouver by mid-July 1830. Nearly everyone at the fort became infected. By September, Chinookans living in the area were also hit hard. Indigenous populations suffered much worse than settlers, in large part because of a lack of access to medicines. All told, approximately 92 percent of Chinookans died over the next few years, and in the Willamette Valley, disease reduced Indigenous populations from fifteen thousand to fewer than two thousand (Bergman, 2008; Boyd, 1999; Spores, 1993).

Disease may have conveniently removed a physical impediment to white settlement, but with an attitude that they had free reign over "uninhabited" territory, white settlers also engaged in calculated murder and theft of Indigenous lands (Estes, 2020). Animated by the promise of "free" land, large numbers of white farm families began to come west on the Oregon Trail by the 1840s. The 1850 Donation Land Claim Act (DLCA) granted white men and "half-breed Indian" men 320 acres each and married couples 640 acres (Coleman, 2019). White settler colonists then established a government to legitimize their land claims, at the same time banning Black people from Oregon.

Given the legislation's explicit focus on redistributing land based on race, historian Kenneth Coleman (2019:415) describes the DLCA as "essentially creating an affirmative action program for White people," one that was based on white supremacy. Geographer and ethnic studies scholar Laura Pulido (2024) defines white supremacy as "a set of attitudes, values, and practices emanating from the belief that white people and Europe are superior to people of color and non-European places." Critically, emotions of hatred and animosity are not necessary for white supremacy to exist. Rather, the thing that defines white supremacy, legal scholar Frances Lee Ansley (1989:1024) stresses, is the "political, economic, and cultural system in which whites overwhelmingly control power and material resources. . . . Relations of white dominance and non-white subordination," she explains, "are daily reenacted across a broad array of institutions and social settings." In other words, white supremacy produces outcomes that are most favorable for white people, and white people believe consciously or unconsciously that this is the way it ought to be. Coleman (2019:415) illuminates the legacy that the early white supremacist land "giveaway" would have in Oregon: "The issuance of free land," he explains, "resulted in a massive economic head start for White cultivators and initiated a long-standing pattern in which access to real estate became an instrument of White supremacy and social control"—including in subsequent eras of Portland Harbor development. Figurative and literal erasure of Indigenous people "enabled squatters—settlers occupying lands without legal title—to envision themselves as the rightful owners of land already held and used in common" (417), privatizing land that previously had been governed according to usufruct terms. Even "ordinary acts of fencing and plowing fields" became technologies of subjugation (Barber, 2019). Following a blueprint begun by Hudson's Bay Company colonial fur trappers at Fort Vancouver and elsewhere, settlers would also go on to engage directly in "shocking acts of violence" (Lewis and Connolly, 2019:369), including inflicting physical injury, murder, and trauma, in order to secure land and resources.

Soon after the institution of DLCA, the U.S. government ratified treaties that formally eliminated access to resources and forced Chinookans and many others off their traditional homelands, displacing people to reservations around the region. U.S. government representatives engaged tribes in two rounds of treaty making. In 1851, Anson Dart, the superintendent of Indian affairs for the Oregon Territory, sought to make the best land available for white settlers by moving western Oregon tribes east of the Cascade Range, to the Umatilla area. The Umatilla and western tribes protested, however, pushing Dart to write treaties that "guaranteed each local tribe a permanent reservation within its traditional homeland" (Lewis et al., 2013:320). Ultimately, Dart negotiated nineteen treaties with western Oregon tribes (Kentta and Lewis, 2010), but Congress refused to ratify them because white settlers complained about living adjacent to reservations (Lewis et al., 2013).

In 1853, Joel Palmer took over for Dart, and he also attempted to move Oregon tribes to a single reservation, east of the Cascade Mountains. Again, the proposal failed, in part due to Indigenous acts of resistance. The Takelma, Shasta, and Athapaskan people of southwest Oregon, for instance, severely disrupted the U.S. government's plans for the region during the Rogue River War of 1855–56 (Tveskov, 2017). Palmer then sought to establish one reservation for coastal and Willamette Valley tribes in western Oregon, later called the Coast Reservation. Palmer ultimately purchased land from white settlers with assistance from the U.S. Army and established a reservation centered in the Grand Ronde Valley and extending far beyond (Lewis, 2016). In winter 1855, tribes signed the Willamette Valley Treaty, ceding most of the Willamette River drainage to the U.S. government (Lewis et al., 2013).

Soon after, reservation construction began, and by spring 1856, U.S. government officials forcibly moved approximately two thousand people from the Columbia River, Willamette Valley, Cascade foothills, and upper Umpqua and Rogue Valleys to what would become the Grand Ronde Reservation, as well as to the Siletz Reservation further south (Lewis et al., 2013; Wilkinson, 2010). Many people hid, resisting displacement for several years (Lewis, 2016). On June 30, 1857, President James Buchanan established the Grand Ronde Reservation by executive order, as part of or adjacent to the Coast Reservation.[1] Various acts of Congress throughout the late 1800s and early 1900s tinkered with the boundaries of the Grand Ronde and Siletz Reservations, removing hundreds of thousands of acres over time. For instance, the Dawes Allotment Act of 1887 forced the Siletz Tribe to turn over 191,000 acres to homesteaders. In 1895, some land in the Grand Ronde Reservation was split into allotments, and the rest went up for sale to the public in 1901. Over the next few years, the U.S. government forced Willamette Valley Chinookan Tribes, as well as Umpquas, Molallas, Clackamas, and Rogue River Tribes and individual Klamath and

Klickitat tribal members, off their homelands and to the Grand Ronde Reservation. Making few efforts to maintain kinship ties, the federal government sometimes indiscriminately sent members of the same families and tribes to different locations (Kentta and Lewis, 2010; Lewis et al., 2013).

It was common for members of various bands and tribes to form new identities and alliances throughout this violent process. Moreover, off reservation, Grand Ronde and Siletz tribal members assimilated into rural Oregon life throughout the late 1800s and early 1900s. Many people worked on nearby farms, picking hops, berries, and beans; others became loggers. Periodically, people traveled to their ceded homelands to fish, gather, and visit relatives. Particularly important off-reservation activities included fishing in Oregon City at Willamette Falls and on the Columbia River. Although technically illegal, tribal members had informal agreements with state law enforcement officials until at least 1950, allowing them to fish in accustomed places irrespective of treaty rights (Lewis et al., 2013). Importantly, the Yakama Nation, with a home base upstream along the Columbia River and stretching into the eastern foothills of the Cascade Mountain Range in Washington, has maintained treaty rights to harvest fish at all "usual and accustomed places" since the Treaty of 1855, including at Willamette Falls. With regard to fishing, the phrase "usual and accustomed places" refers to "every fishing location where members of a tribe customarily fished from time to time at and before treaty times, however distant from the usual habitat of the tribe, and whether or not other tribes then also fished the same waters" (*United States v. State of Washington*, 384 F. Supp. 312 [W.D. Wash. 1974]; see also Yakama Nation, n.d.). Yakama members continue to travel to Willamette Falls every June and July to collect *asum*, also known as Pacific lamprey or eel, for subsistence and ceremonial use (Yakama Nation, n.d.).

Portland Harbor Destruction, Development, and Disagreements

The violent attempted erasure of Chinookans and their kin enabled white Euro-American settlers to establish the Portland Harbor as a main hub for the exportation of grain, lumber, and other commodities and later as a primary site of wartime shipbuilding. Access to the Willamette and Columbia Rivers was a key motivator in the theft of land and development of the region, generally, and of the area that became the city of Portland, specifically. Historian William Lang (2010:97) emphasizes how settlers in Portland have relied on the Willamette for three main uses throughout the twentieth century: as a shipping channel, as a place of aesthetic beauty and recreation, and as a sink for "urban detritus." The mouth of the Willamette is approximately 100 miles upriver from the Pacific on the Columbia River, and downtown Portland sits another 14 miles upstream on the Willamette; this relative proximity of Portland to the ocean put the city at an initial advantage over Washington's main port cities of Seattle and Tacoma, given that they are 144 and 175 miles, respectively, from the sea. By the 1860s, Portland shippers had begun to export produce and raw materials out of the Willamette Valley, including metals, wheat, wool, lumber, and other materials. As the city developed bridges in the central area in the following decades, shipping docks, freight terminals, and other infrastructure became concentrated further downstream on the Willamette, to the north (Abbott, 1983; Hillegas-Elting, 2018; W. Lang, 2010).

Early settler colonial developments along the Willamette also occurred a dozen miles upstream from Portland, adjacent to Willamette Falls, the forty-foot basalt cliff where Indigenous peoples have fished for salmon and lamprey for generations. Following construction and operation of smaller sawmills beginning in 1829, the Crown Paper Company and Willamette Falls Pulp and Paper Company established larger mills in 1889. Later, in 1908, the Hawley Pulp and Paper Company built another mill. Taking advantage of the hydropower offered by the falls, these mills went on to operate for more than one hundred years (W. Lang, 2010).

A series of public investments throughout the late nineteenth and early twentieth centuries enabled further destruction and development of Portland's harbor. By 1872, the U.S. Army Corps of Engineers began dredging and clearing debris to make the Columbia-Willamette channel navigable for larger vessels (W. Lang, 2010:98). Beginning in the 1890s, the state-created Port of Portland Commission focused on dredging the final stretch of the Willamette. In 1912, Congress cemented the Columbia-Willamette channel when it authorized development and maintenance of a massive navigation channel that began at the ocean bar at Astoria, stretching upstream to Portland's harbor. The corps also built several dikes, and the Port of Portland built additional terminals. The Commission of Public Docks spent $30 million from property tax revenues on terminals, dry docks, and a modernized grain elevator. Additional investments brought in huge cranes, storage bunkers, and other infrastructure. Notably, the Port of Portland and Corps of Engineers undertook a massive effort to straighten out the Willamette near Swan Island, a marshy area on the river's east bank just north of downtown Portland. Uncurling the river made it easier for larger ships to navigate, and it also enabled creation of a modern dry dock facility adjacent to Portland's industrial district (MacColl and Stein, 1988; W. Lang, 2013).

While public and private investments lubricated infrastructure development, local officials remained preoccupied with what they perceived as a key impediment to harbor profit-making in the early 1900s: people living on boats, or old ship skeletons commonly referred to as "scows," up and down the water's edge. A late nineteenth-century article in *The Oregonian* (1890:498, quoted in Blalock, 2012:126) describes the scene at the turn of the century in detail: "Old skeletons of mighty ships—or shallow river crafts—lie white and dry on the embankment. Scant trees, usually shaking in the river breezes, of such deciduous growth as balm or oak, lend grace to an eerie looking shore. There are various river crafts tied up or moored along, or hauled up on the sand, some of which are occupied by families whose cook stove smokes ever curl and blow, and whose red and white garments washed and hung out to dry, ever flap in the breezes."

In 1910, approximately five thousand people lived in scows and other makeshift shelters up and down the Willamette within city limits. Like today, the river's bounty of fish and relative solitude enticed people struggling to get by to seek refuge along the banks of the river. Also like today, state agents frequently evicted people from the waterfront in an effort to protect profits and tax revenue. Around the peak of riverside inhabitance, Joseph Simon, Portland's mayor from 1909 to 1911, ordered scows and their residents removed. In December 1909, Portland City Council members unanimously passed an ordinance that made it illegal "for any person to keep, anchor, moor or maintain, or permit the keeping, anchoring, mooring or maintaining of any boathouse, house boat, scow house or scow dwelling used for human habitation within the harbor limits of the City of Portland" (quoted in W. Lang, 2010; see also MacColl and Stein, 1988; Aurand, 2015). The vote came after tensions mounted between shipping businesses located near the Stark Street dock and those living in the vicinity, "who had been accused of dumping debris, managing floating whorehouses, running thievery rings along the waterfront, and generally behaving in an unsightly manner" (W. Lang, 2010:96). Mayor Simon's recruits set some shelters on fire, and the mayor directed workers to move others to cheap plots of then-rural land six miles east of the river, in the Lents neighborhood (Blalock, 2012). Nevertheless, people continued to seek refuge along the Willamette in the decades to come. Numbers surged in the "Hoovervilles" of the Great Depression (J. Rose, 2016). Land use conflicts between property owners, the city, and people living unhoused that began during the 1920s and 1930s would emerge again in the early 1980s following the federal government cutting billions of dollars from affordable housing budgets, as poor people attempt to carve out space to survive on public land and officials attempt to protect landowners' property rights today (Western Regional Advocacy Project, 2010).

In the meantime, between 1900 and 1930 Portland's population nearly tripled, largely due to shipyard—and hydropower—investments. While local business leaders succeeded early on in developing the Willamette to their liking, upper stretches of the Columbia were slower to progress. Canals and locks constructed in the Columbia River gorge allowed some passage of ships, but shippers desired much better navigation to compete with the railroads. Large dams and reservoirs would enable more efficient "slack-water navigation," as well as hydropower. A series of attempts in the 1920s to build such a system failed to secure sufficient federal funds. But with the Great Depression and subsequent New Deal public works program came a new opportunity, and the Army Corps of Engineers constructed a massive dam forty miles upriver from Portland on the Columbia. The Bonneville Dam enlarged the Portland-area water network substantially, making it possible for the largest oceangoing vessels to navigate (W. Lang, 2010; White, 1995).

Ultimately, the dam's provision of hydropower enabled the Kaiser Shipbuilding Company to build a series of large shipyards downstream on the Columbia and just upstream on the Willamette. Henry J. Kaiser and his son, Edgar, first leased eighty-seven acres on the Willamette River in January 1941, and later that year they built another facility on Swan Island and a third in Vancouver, Washington. Beginning with a contract to build cargo ships for Britain, the Oregon Shipbuilding Corporation went on to produce massive Liberty ships, tankers, aircraft carriers, and more for the United States. Portland thus became an epicenter of World War II shipbuilding and shipbreaking (W. Lang, 2010; Lindner, 2019).

Portland's Black Migration, Fight for Housing and Labor Rights

Black Portlanders played a key role in the shipyard economy beginning in the 1930s, and their long, ongoing fights for housing, labor, and environmental justice are rooted in the Portland Harbor. In a paper documenting the history of Black communities in the Pacific Northwest from 1865 to 1910, historian Quintard Taylor (1979) explains that although a handful of Black people had migrated to Oregon starting in the 1860s, it was not until World War II that Portland's Black population grew to sizeable numbers, when thousands of people boarded trains to work in the Kaiser shipyards. Previously, an 1857 clause in the state's constitution excluded people of African descent from crossing state lines, under threat of the lash. Only in 1926 was this clause revoked, legally allowing Black people to live in the state.

Until 1910, most of Portland's Black residents lived near Union Station, where they worked, on the city's west side just north of downtown (McElderry, 2001). In 1913, when the Broadway Bridge opened, Black Portlanders began moving across the river. Although white people living in inner eastside neighborhoods began migrating further out to the new streetcar suburbs, a 1919 decision by the Portland Realty Board forbade realtors from selling homes in white neighborhoods to Black people, and many landlords refused to rent to non-white tenants. Most Black Portlanders settled along Williams Avenue, in what became known as the Albina district. Throughout the 1920s and beyond, Portland's Black community built vibrant churches, businesses, and community centers in Albina.

Around this time, the Albina area's housing stock began to fall into disrepair due to public and private disinvestment in the area. Improvements were sorely needed, but when the city had an opportunity to access federal funds for public housing thanks to the 1937 U.S. Housing Act, residents voted no. Local Black leaders such as DeNorval Unthank and others affiliated with the local chapter of the National Association for the Advancement of Colored People (NAACP) fought for a state civil rights bill that would end housing discrimination. Although they did not succeed this time around, efforts galvanized a local racial justice movement, with Black residents, newspapers, realtors, and groups such as the NAACP and the Urban League playing key roles (M. Lang, 2018; McElderry, 2001).

Following the construction of Bonneville Dam and the Kaiser shipyards in the 1930s and early 1940s, over twenty thousand Black people arrived in Portland to work on the docks, mainly between 1941 and 1943. "They came from the cotton fields, they came from other laboring types of jobs in the South, and some professional people came because they were interested in seeing what the West Coast [racial climate] was like," explains Kathryn Hall Bogle (1992:401), a racial justice activist, journalist, social worker, and the second Black woman to hold an office position in government in Portland. Many arrived on "Kaiser Karavan" trains from New York and other northern cities (Lindner, 2019).

The influx of Black residents, along with demands made by local Black leaders, prompted city officials to finally decide to build public housing. But by July 1942, the Housing Authority of Portland (HAP) had authorized construction of just 4,900 units—far short of the projected need for 37,000. Local white business owners who feared competition in the housing market, white laborers voicing racist sentiments, and white supremacist neighborhood groups that favored segregation slowed things down. In 1942, for instance, white Portlanders staged a rally protesting a proposed east side housing project for Black shipyard workers, and white employees of the Albina Machine Works and Shipyard publicly demanded that the project be called off (McElderry, 2001).

While several thousand Black migrants settled in Albina homes, others doubled up with fellow Black households that had previously settled in other parts of the city, moved into west side hotels now vacant due to the forced relocation of Japanese people, or slept in cars, churches, and other makeshift lodgings. Another wave of civil rights organizing emerged out of these precarious housing arrangements. This time, aided in part by the wartime-induced need for workers to reside in the area, activists succeeded in pushing HAP to build more public housing. Additionally, the Kaiser family sought funds from the U.S. Maritime Commission to build thousands of units just north of Portland, near the Willamette's confluence with the Columbia River. Vanport City would ultimately be managed by HAP, becoming the largest wartime housing project in the United States and the second-largest city in Oregon. From 1943 to 1945, more than forty thousand people lived in Vanport, set on 650 acres of floodplain in North Portland. Approximately 18 percent of residents were Black in the beginning; this number would increase to approximately one-third by 1948. As in Guilds Lake, a second HAP housing project, Vanport officials segregated Black residents to certain sections (Gibson, 2007; McElderry, 2001).

Approximately 96 percent of Portland's Black newcomers worked in the shipyards and other defense-related industries during the war, in relatively well-paying jobs. Compared with average family wages totaling less than $500 a year in the South, shipyard jobs paid close to $3,000 annually (Lindner, 2019). Yet, white workers not only attempted to limit housing options for Black workers and their families, but they actively ensured highly discriminatory working conditions (Lindner, 2019; Pearson, 1996; Polishuk, 2019; A. Smith and Taylor, 1980). Historian John Lindner (2019) describes the paradox: "Called on to build weapons for the 'war on freedom' abroad, Black workers were systematically denied the most elementary freedoms at home" (520). The unions were not much better. Black union membership grew to half a million overall in the United States between 1935 and 1940, and the International Longshoremen's and Warehousemen's Union (ILWU, now the International

Longshore and Warehouse Union) prohibited discrimination based on "race, religion, creed, color, nationality, or 'political affiliation'" in its constitution adopted in 1941 (Lindner, 2019). Nevertheless, ILWU Local 8—Portland's chapter—prohibited Black workers from fully joining the union well into the 1960s (Polishuk, 2019). The Boilermakers Union, which presided over the majority of skilled shipyard jobs during World War II and had nearly sixty thousand local members, likewise excluded Black people (Lindner, 2019). Bogle recalls that the first waves of those approaching the U.S. Employment Service office in Portland in search of work included Black people "who had worked as stevedores all their lives in the south," but who were excluded based on their race in Portland. "They could not be employed as longshoremen because the longshoremen's union in Oregon wouldn't let them join," says Bogle in an oral history interview (1992:402).

Bogle further emphasizes, "There was nothing to be done because the push was for *employment*, not for specialty employment for anyone in particular. . . . Black men just had to settle for [whatever they could find]" (1992:402). In the ILWU, Black workers were allowed to labor as "casuals"—day laborers—but were only hired if no (white) union card-carrying workers were available. Jimmy Fantz, a white longshoreman who worked to integrate the union in the 1930s, recalls the discriminatory practices that kept Black workers out. When one Black longshoreman, someone with ample experience gained working in the Gulf Coast, attempted to request a work permit from the union's executive board, for example, board members literally paid him off: they pulled cash out of their pockets and told him to try again in Seattle (Polishuk, 2019:553). Eventually, local 72 Boilermakers Union leaders met the letter of the law by instituting auxiliary unions that did not discriminate against Black workers. With no union hall, elections, or other provisions, however, these were nothing but a "fig leaf" that enabled the Boilermakers to claim they were within the law—and to fire Black workers who refused to join the tokenizing auxiliary for "non-union clearance" (Lindner, 2019).

Work conditions were extremely dangerous for Black laborers. Robert Fambro, a Black longshoreman, recalls the violent ways in which white workers attempted to force him and his colleagues out of the workforce: "One time they dropped paper on me in the hold. . . . I jumped . . . but a whole bolt of paper was sliding back and forth and it hit me just as I went to get up under the coal bin. I knew it wasn't an accident" (Polishuk, 2019:554). Another Black longshoreman, Linell Hill, likewise remembers the way he and his coworkers were treated: "It was a lot of institutional racism, subtle racism, outward racism, outward animosity" (Polishuk, 2019:556–557). Hill recounts specifics, saying, "Oh yeah, I was concerned with my safety. You had winch drivers, you had hold men, you had a lot of people that did try to put you in what we call the bite, put you in a precarious position to get hurt. . . . [And] there's a lot of other ways to get to you as opposed to just hurting you. Work practice, you know. There was work practice that make you do the majority of the work, you know, put you in the position to work the hardest. . . . You can do a whole lot of work and then the boss'd come back and tell you to tear it down." Hill emphasized the demanding nature of the job: "A lot of the guys that they didn't harass out of here, black and white, they worked 'em out of there. I mean it was *hard* work, real *hard* work then. Everything was hand mucking" (Polishuk, 2019:557).

Additionally, people were exposed to extremely toxic substances while working in the shipyards, such as lead and asbestos (Pearson, 1996). PHCC member Wilma Alcock frequently recounts stories of her parents chipping lead paint off of ships during the war years. My own uncle, Paul Walters, tells similar stories of blasting lead paint off ships with high-powered hoses, only to let the debris fall into the water, as late as the 1980s (Portland Harbor Community Coalition, 2015). As local EJ activist Jeri Jimenez recounts in the previous chapter, diesel emissions from harbor-related and freeway traffic in the adjacent Williams Avenue district would also later come to severely affect many Black shipyard workers and their families in cumulative fashion.

Union exclusion and hazardous workplace (and residential) conditions were not unique to boilermakers and longshore workers: the local truck drivers', electrical workers', and laundry workers' unions all similarly excluded Black people. Bogle explains the surprise that Black southerners encountered upon arrival: "They did not allow black people to join the union, and that again amazed the black men who had driven trucks and all kinds of vehicles in the South, but were not allowed to do that here just because they were black. . . . It was extremely upsetting and frustrating for some of them to find out that the one kind of work they were accustomed to doing and were accepted to do in the South was not permitted here. This was [supposed to be] the land of freedom!" (Bogle, 1992:403).

Beginning in late 1945, as the war slowed down, one-third of Portland's Black residents were laid off. Some people left the city altogether, but thousands remained. They were now settled in a new place with few prospects for non-war-related work, and Vanport provided an important source of stability. As early as 1944, however, local officials began quietly making plans to close down Vanport and force residents out. "This was not permanent-type housing," explains Bogle (1992). "There were many complaints that the walls were thin and the structures weren't really finished." The shoddy construction would go on to become a huge liability a few years later.

Civil rights activists fought back in the spheres of both housing and labor. In 1942, seventy-five Black workers at Kaiser's Vancouver shipyard penned a resolution, declaring: "We, the Negro people employed by the Kaiser Company, maintain that under a false pretense we were brought from east to west to work for defense, and we demand, within due process of law, the following rights: (1) to work at our trades on equal rights with whites; (2) to go to vocational school or to take vocational training on equal rights with whites" (quoted in Lindner, 2019). But it would be several years before their demands were met. Following a series of local actions and protests in 1942, and aided by national-level protests that resulted in President Franklin Roosevelt's Executive Order 8802, which banned discrimination in defense industries, Black shipyard workers and the local NAACP chapter eventually won an important victory against Local 72 of the International Brotherhood of Boilermakers: in 1944, the Fair Employment Practice Committee ruled in favor of Black workers, and by 1945, Kaiser finally ended its practices of firing Black workers who did not join the auxiliary (Lindner, 2019). Much later, in the 1960s, ILWU Local 8 would finally allow Black longshoremen to join the union with full privileges. A combination of pressure from the international union, internal agitation by a handful of progressive white longshoremen, and Black workers, emboldened by the civil rights movement and 1964 Civil Rights Act, who filed a discrimination lawsuit, finally forced the change (Polishuk, 2019).

But other setbacks occurred in the interim. Kaiser laid off droves of Black workers as the war neared an end. And following heavy rains and snowmelt, on May 30, 1948, the dikes holding back the Columbia River catastrophically failed. Massive amounts of water poured into the streets of Vanport, toppling infrastructure and wrecking cars and houses in its path. In all, the Vanport Flood killed fifteen people and destroyed the homes of over eighteen thousand residents, including those of approximately six thousand Black people. The Red Cross, public agencies, churches, and others provided emergency relief in the form of temporary housing, trailers, and other measures. Many of the emergency units were extremely substandard, however, especially those assigned to Black residents. Moreover, local officials took the flood as an opportunity to eliminate much of Portland's public housing and at the same time bolster private real estate profits through a disaster capitalism scheme. Time and again officials and voters deflected opportunities to improve public housing stocks over the next few years (Gibson, 2007; McElderry, 2001).

Notwithstanding the efforts of civil rights groups to secure more resources for public housing in multiple places, the majority of displaced Black residents settled in Albina along lower Williams Avenue—adjacent to the harbor—and toward the north, along Mississippi Avenue at its base and rising up above the shipyards, turning into Albina Avenue after several blocks. That Albina became the center of the Black community is no accident. A 1957 report, "The Negro in Portland: A Progress Report, 1945–1957," authored by a local civic organization, the City Club, reveals that 90 percent of realtors refused to sell homes to Black residents in so-called white neighborhoods, fearing that Black residents would reduce property values and that their real estate businesses would suffer. White residents simultaneously established racist covenants, prohibiting the habitation of any non-white people in their neighborhoods. And insurance redlining systematically blocked mortgage lending in so-called high-risk areas where Black residents lived. By 1950, with Guild's Lake and Swan Island housing developments closed, two-thirds of Portland's non-white population "were channeled and compressed" into the Albina district, according to planning historian Karen Gibson (2007:10). Gibson succinctly describes the transition of the heart of the Black community from Vanport to Albina: "The flood that washed away Vanport did not solve the housing problem—it swept in the final phase of 'ghetto building' in the central city" (10).

As segregation became more pronounced, civil rights groups, including the Urban League and the NAACP, continued to fight for its end. Yet, following a script playing out in urban areas across the United States, Portland's white boosters, aided by local and federal government agencies, pursued "revitalization" schemes in an effort to produce profits following the shuttering of wartime industrial facilities and systematic disinvestment in Black neighborhoods (see Massey and Denton, 1993). Gibson (2007:11) recalls the kinds of structures that white-led institutions erected in an effort to social-engineer segregation and maximum profits: "Luxury apartments, convention centers, sports arenas, hospitals, universities, and freeways were the land uses that reclaimed space occupied by relatively powerless [Black] residents in central cities." Portland was no exception. In 1956, voters decided to build a coliseum in the hopes of attracting a professional sports franchise. Bulldozers destroyed businesses and 476 homes in Albina's Eliot neighborhood—where half the inhabitants were Black residents. Soon afterward, an additional several hundred homes in Albina were destroyed to make room for Interstate 5 and Highway 99. The city then applied for federal urban renewal funds, arguing for the need to raze "blighted"—Black—neighborhoods. Despite tireless organizing by Albina residents, the city destroyed several more homes to make way for a never-realized expansion of Emanuel Hospital and other developments (Gibson, 2007).

Urban renewal, unemployment, discriminatory practices by banks and landlords, and ongoing disinvestment by the City of Portland, enforced by a white supremacist police force, continued to make life very difficult for Portland's Black community (Serbulo and Gibson, 2013). With the civil rights movement gaining energy, and thanks to tireless work by Black-led organizations and steadfast perseverance by residents, Albina nevertheless became and remains an important place for Black Portlanders, materially and symbolically. In the 1990s, community pressure finally pushed the City of Portland to begin to invest in Albina. The Albina Community Plan, adopted by the Portland City Council in 1991, promised beautification of the district's streets and sidewalks, development of vacant lots, and loans for storefront improvements; urban renewal funds would subsidize the plan (Gibson, 2004; Gibson and Abbott, 2002). The city and private developers invested in bike lanes, parks, a light-rail transit line connecting Albina's west side to downtown, and other "sustainability" improvements.

But white, wealthier residents also began to purchase single-family homes in Albina in the 1990s, taking advantage of relatively low prices as a result of systematic public and private disinvestment throughout the preceding decades, in a process that Gibson (2007:20) describes as a shift from "redlining to greenlining." Earlier on, city officials had promised that increasing property values along the light-rail line would buffer existing residents against gentrification and displacement. But a tax-activist lawsuit against the Portland Development Commission (now Prosper Portland) that same year halted most precautionary anti-displacement measures (Scott, 2012). With few provisions to ensure that longtime Black residents would not be priced out of Albina, the city's investment benefits accrued mainly to an influx of white gentrifiers. What community organizer Matt Hern (2016:7) dubs "a deliberate, methodical effort" on the part of city officials, along with the foreclosure crisis, has resulted in the involuntary displacement of nearly ten thousand and counting Black Portlanders from Albina since 1990. Black people now live further from their jobs, businesses have lost customers and leases, congregants commute long distances for church, and many now live in neighborhoods with reduced public transit service, fewer parks, and less access to other services (Bates, Curry-Stevens, and Coalition of Communities of Color, 2014; Gibson, 2007; Goodling et al., 2015).

This is the historical context in which PHCC's Black members and the coalition's non-Black members, who have learned much of this history, are fighting for a cleaned-up harbor and the power to control what happens in the harbor's vicinity. PHCC members are working on behalf of their ancestors who worked in the shipyards and endured decades of white supremacist discrimination and segregation. Black Portlanders have long fought against such injustices, and today's grassroots leaders are following in the footsteps of activists of years past by fighting for economic opportunities and access to land in inner-core neighborhoods for the Black community, as well as better services in the city's outer eastside neighborhoods where many people have resettled. The Portland African American Leadership Forum (later renamed Imagine Black), notably, led a year-long community planning process to lay out a Black vision for the city, articulated in its "People's Plan." Centered on the concept of a Black Utopia as a symbol of hope, the plan outlines a vision for Portland's Black community that "taps not only into its legacy of resilience but is truly one afforded the opportunity to thrive" (Portland African American Leadership Forum, 2017). Black elders attending PHCC meetings still speak fondly of the Willamette River, recalling weekend outings to fish in the harbor. In more recent years, organizations serving Black youth have joined PHCC, keen to engage young people in fishing in healthy waters and take advantage of the green job opportunities that a thorough cleanup of the harbor might provide. Groups are also lured by the possibilities of producing food and teaching young people about ecology, engineering, and agriculture on community-controlled land near the river. With summer 2020 Black Lives Matter uprisings turning people out in larger droves than ever, it remains to be seen what possibilities lie ahead for the harbor and city at large, and especially its Black residents.

Indigenous Termination, Restoration

Black workers were not the only non-whites working in the shipyards under discriminatory and difficult conditions. Indigenous people, too, came to Portland to work on the docks. Many people arrived from nearby reservations, and others, including half of the Turtle Mountain Tribe of North Dakota— six thousand people—joined the war effort in Portland (Curry-Stevens et al.,

2011). Indigenous migration to Portland continued following the war as well, but for a different reason. A series of Termination Acts in the 1950s forced people off of reservations across the country, constituting "the culmination of over a hundred years of efforts by the federal government to eliminate Tribal claims to their lands" (Lewis et al., 2013:308). The Western Oregon Indian Termination Act allowed tribal members to purchase their own land—or to leave. "Few members had the resources to purchase their allotments" (Lewis et al., 2013:308; see also Lewis, 2009). Oregon's tribal members sold off much of their tribal lands that had remained west of the Cascade Mountains.

The Grand Ronde, whose membership includes many of those with roots in today's Portland area, was one of the first tribes to be terminated, in 1954. According to the federal government, tribes of Western Oregon "agreed" to termination. This highly problematic narrative conflicts with accounts of tribal members: "Elder stories of the period tell us that we did not agree to termination.... It seems clear from archival documents that the superintendent of Indian affairs in Portland, E. Morgan Pryse, manipulated the tribes and Congress to get the termination bill approved" (Lewis et al., 2013:308). Pryse submitted documents in support of an early termination bill, in 1952, in order to pass the 1954 bill. Moreover, Pryse reported to Congress that tribal leaders were unavailable to testify—but that "they had agreed in principle to termination" (308).

For those living at Grand Ronde, termination was "a terrible experience," to quote David Lewis, member of the Grand Ronde Tribe with Takelma, Chinook, Molalla, and Santiam Kalapuya ancestry, and his colleagues (Lewis et al., 2013:308). Tribal members "lost hope and faith" (308), and over the years they and their descendants suffered further loss of familial and cultural identities. In the generations following termination, it became more difficult to learn tribal histories and traditions, interrupting cultural continuity. Although some tribal members were able to purchase land from the federal government and remain in the Grand Ronde area, others moved elsewhere: "Many people, thrust into poverty, immigrated to the cities and disappeared among the many other wage laborers who were struggling to make a living" (2013:308–309).

In the 1970s, Grand Ronde tribal members began working to restore tribal designation. Finally, in 1983, the federal government agreed to reinstate the tribe. Over the next twenty or so years, the Confederated Tribes of the Grand Ronde developed services of all sorts necessary for its five thousand and counting members and began working "to restore selected rights to its ceded lands, the traditional homelands that were given up in signed treaties in exchange for a reservation and services" (Lewis et al., 2013:309).

Whether living on reservations, in Portland, or elsewhere, many people with deep ancestral roots in the region continue to visit Willamette Falls, the Portland Harbor, and the Columbia River, catching lamprey, salmon, and other fish. People also visit the harbor for canoe journey preparations, water ceremonies, and other cultural activities, as their ancestors have done since time immemorial. More broadly, Portland is home to the ninth largest urban Native American population in the country, with a population of over 45,000 people in the area, and more than 380 tribal affiliations, including more than 780 Chinookans—"descendants of the Portland Basin Cascades, Willamette Falls, and Wapato (Multnomah) peoples"—living in the greater Portland region (Boyd, 2013:249). Thousands of Indigenous people from the Portland metropolitan area and Columbia River Basin tribes consume fish from the Portland Harbor and nearby waterways, eating nearly ten times more fish than non-Native people (Columbia River Inter-Tribal Fish Commission, 1994).

Six tribes have treaty rights or other interests in the Portland Harbor area today, and they have formal roles in the cleanup and restoration process as sovereign nations: the Confederated Tribes of the Grand Ronde Community of Oregon, Confederated Tribes of Siletz Indians, Confederated Tribes of the Umatilla Indian Reservation, Confederated Tribes of the Warm Springs Reservation of Oregon, Nez Perce Tribe, and Confederated Tribes and Bands of the Yakama Nation. Five of the six tribes—all but the Yakama—as well as the National Oceanic and Atmospheric Administration (acting on behalf of the U.S. Department of Commerce), U.S. Fish and Wildlife Service (acting on behalf of the U.S. Department of the Interior), and Oregon Department of Fish and Wildlife (acting on behalf of the State of Oregon, were involved with the Portland Harbor Natural Resource Trustee Council at the time of writing. Formed in 2002, the Trustee Council is an entity responsible for assessing and restoring public natural resources—birds, water, fish, wildlife—in the Portland Harbor Superfund Site. The Comprehensive Environmental Response, Compensation, and Liability Act of 1980 (CERCLA) empowers trustees to "obtain compensation for harm to trust resources and to plan and carry out actions to restore injured resources through a process called natural resource damage assessment." The Trustee Council's legal authority for natural resource damage assessment activities in the Portland Harbor derives from "a wide variety of federal and state statutes and regulations, Tribal treaties, agreements and regulations, and land ownership" (Oregon Department of Fish and Wildlife, 2016).

Notably, the Yakama Nation withdrew from the Trustee Council in 2009, when their calls for a natural resource injury assessment of the Lower Columbia River, given downstream pollution from the Portland Harbor, went unheeded by the other trustees. The Yakama's advocacy for the harbor prior to 2002 was one of the main reasons for the EPA listing the site on the Superfund priorities list. Yet time and again, the Yakama have asserted that toxins in the sediment and surface water in the Portland Harbor do not stay neatly contained within the harbor's boundaries; they move downward into the Lower Columbia, where they poison salmon and other species. In a 2022 interview, Davis Washines, Yakama elder, articulates, "It's not just Willamette Falls, it's not just Portland Harbor, proper [that is contaminated], but the contaminants go out into the lower Columbia River and impact all the resources that have to migrate through that lower portion of the Columbia River." He continues, referring to salmon, lamprey, and other first foods, as well as tribal sovereignty, in explaining why the Yakama have taken their particular course of action: "These foods, they were here before us, and they volunteered, they stood up and said, 'We will take care of the people when they get there.' . . . What the elders taught us is that our sovereignty is what we are going to depend on [to survive]. . . . We have a responsibility as a government, not only to benefit the health and welfare of our people, but also to what is termed the natural resources, which are our first foods." In 2017, the Yakama filed a lawsuit (*Yakama v. Airgas USA, LLC, et al.*) "to recover assessment and response costs for injury to natural resources caused by Portland Harbor pollutants in the Lower Columbia River" (Yakama Nation, n.d.). For the Yakama, PHCC, and others, it makes sense to extend natural resource damage assessment boundaries downstream.

Conserving the River, Building a Green City

Despite the violence experienced by Indigenous peoples and Black Portlanders through the settlement and industrial development of Portland's harbor, the city has gained a reputation as an urban green paradise. Yet, this greening process, too, has inflicted great harm on Indigenous and Black people, as well as many others who rely on the harbor for sustenance. The roots of Portland's greening stretch far back, over a century. Starting in the 1920s, just as the shipbuilding industry was gaining steam, public health experts, sanitary engineers, conservationists, and well-to-do anglers began a fight to clean up the Willamette. The main concerns of these early environmentalists revolved less around generalized shipbuilding operations, however, and more around municipal sewage effluence and toxic discharges from the pulp and paper mills that lined the river. Activists worried about the harmful effects of such contamination on commercial fishing, as well as on tourist and recreation-centered fishing, business, and swimming (Hillegas-Elting, 2018).

The harbor's origins as a place for white settlers to recreate emerged largely from the influence of John Olmstead, famous landscape designer Frederic Law Olmstead's son. Historian William Lang (2010) documents early efforts to green the city by Olmstead and others. Olmstead, Lang explains, identified Guilds Lake, a four-hundred-acre wetland on the west side of the Willamette across from Swan Island (and eventual home to wartime housing, as we have seen), as an ideal site for parklands. Efforts to develop the planned greenspace coincided with plans to host an exposition in commemoration of the one-hundred-year anniversary of the Lewis and Clark Expedition. To date, the city had largely concentrated on constructing docks and industrial infrastructure, while neglecting to set aside land for parks or other recreational uses. The Lewis and Clark Centennial and American Exposition and Oriental Fair offered an opportunity to shift priorities. From June to October 1905, eight hundred thousand people attended the fair, centered around an "engineered lake environment that re-cast the wetlands into a movie-set landscape" (W. Lang, 2010:100).

Other notable riverside recreational opportunities were developed around this time, including Oaks Amusement Park, built by the Oregon Water Power and Railway Company south of downtown on the river's east bank. Oaks Park included roller coasters and carousels, skating rinks and river swimming areas. Other public swimming infrastructure of this era included an area on the Columbia River established by the Portland Electric Company, as well as a forty-acre amusement park and pool called Jantzen Beach, on Hayden Island in the Columbia River. Trolleys ushered visitors to and from these recreation sites.

Part of an ongoing process of "uneven development" (N. Smith, 2002), conversion of industrial land to recreational spaces provided a way for industrialists to hold on to land and cut losses while awaiting more profitable business opportunities. William Lang (2010) describes the relationship between recreational and industrial uses as "symbiotic": "Riverside recreation areas, even those that provided substantial economic return to private developers, always remained susceptible to higher value use, especially as industrial land" (101). Investors purchased parcels of the wetlands developed for the Lewis and Clark Exposition, for instance, for manufacturing. By 1913, developers had transformed twenty thousand feet of riverbank along the exposition site from marshy parkland into a modern industrial stretch.

In 1924, the city began to come to terms with the complications of constructing a downtown district adjacent to the river, namely the frequent flooding of riverfront businesses. In 1929, the city completed development of a 5,400-foot seawall that would serve as a buffer between land and river. The city also constructed a sewer interceptor that helped divert waste from the river and laid plans to create an esplanade for recreation and picnicking. The esplanade would not be constructed until several years later, following development and then removal of a riverside highway. Despite such infrastructure improvements, a 1934 report authored by scientists reported on the continued impacts of urbanization on local habitat: "From the standpoint of fish life, there is an absolute barrio of denuded water . . . where oxygen loving forms of life cannot exist" (quoted in W. Lang, 2010:106). A year later, the Columbia River Fishermen's Association threatened to sue Portland for dumping sewage into the river, endangering commercial fisheries. Indeed, E. coli bacteria were detected at dangerous levels in the late 1930s.

In a detailed account of early efforts to clean up the Willamette, historian James Hillegas-Elting (2018) documents how, in 1938, advocates succeeded in establishing the State Sanitary Authority, which mandated that pulp and paper mills upriver from Portland stop dumping waste into the Willamette. Then, between 1947 and 1952, state-level officials required the City of Portland to clean up its act, resulting in the city spending $15 million (the equivalent of nearly $140 million in 2017) on a wastewater treatment plant and other infrastructure improvements. In 1967, the U.S. Coast Guard filed complaints about filth in the river with the State Sanitary Authority. Around the same time, a local TV anchor, Tom McCall, brought the river's health to the public's attention. Elected as Oregon's governor in 1967, McCall started the Willamette Greenway program in an effort to remediate the river. McCall's efforts enabled the State Sanitary Authority to better enforce regulations on the pulp mills further upstream from Portland.

These initial river remediation efforts helped put Portland on the map as a leader in the nascent environmental movement. Portland landed in the national spotlight when *National Geographic* highlighted local stewardship of the Willamette in its cover article (Starbird, 1972). That same year, parts of Oregon's administrative framework informed creation of the federal Clean Water Act (Hillegas-Elting, 2018). Portland began to gain substantial credibility as a leader in the green urbanist movement throughout the 1970s and early 1980s, when Oregon's Land Conservation and Development Commission adopted fourteen goals; one of these goals mandated that local jurisdictions institute urban growth boundaries. Intended to protect farms and forests from urban sprawl, the urban growth boundary concentrates services such as roads, water and sewer systems, parks, schools, and fire and police protection within urban areas. Portland's adoption of a *green* growth strategy that has entailed development of miles of bike lanes, acres of urban parks and green spaces, and scores of LEED-certified buildings through the 1990s and early 2000s came in the context of the state's urban growth boundary system, thus cementing Portland's reputation as an exemplar of urban sustainability (Knox and Florida, 2014; Slavin and Snyder, 2011).

Notwithstanding substantial efforts to remediate the Willamette throughout several decades of the twentieth century, however, the river's condition remained in peril. In written correspondence in 2021–2022, Bob Sallinger, conservation director at Portland Audubon, explains that remediating the river had been a lonely fight prior to the 2010s:

> It is important to note that urban natural resources received much less attention prior to 2000 than they do today. Under Goal 5, for instance, the State of Oregon was responsible for inventorying natural resources in the urban environment. The state, however, did not see much value in urban natural resources back in the 1980s and 1990s. In the 1980s Oregon Department of Fish and Wildlife came to Audubon (because we were the only conservation group with an urban conservation focus at that time) and offered us $5,000— to do all the urban natural resource inventories. Audubon staff and volunteers walked the North Reach and the rest of the river mapping all those natural resource values. This was the first wildlife habitat inventory of the Lower Willamette. These inventories were required under state land use planning law. Audubon, which had a strong urban conservation program, saw this as a high priority and has remained actively engaged with the industrial harbor in the ensuing decades. Our approach was driven by a philosophy that all people should live in a healthy environment and have access to nature where they live. It was that ethic that took us into some of the most degraded areas in Portland. It would not be until later that we and the community would come to recognize that protecting the environment in urban areas can lead to displacement.

Inventorying wildlife habitat barely began to scratch the surface. In 1991, environmental organizations brought forth a lawsuit, prompting the city and state to enter into an agreement to spend more than a billion dollars on a system to keep raw sewage out of the river.

In 1996, an organization called Willamette Riverkeeper formed, with a mission to protect and restore the river. In 1999, the National Marine Fisheries Service listed two local fish species under the Endangered Species Act. Then, in December 2000, the EPA designated a ten-mile stretch of the Portland Harbor as a Superfund site. Superfund designation emerged less as a result of compromised water quality and more out of concern for toxins, including polychlorinated biphenyls (PCBs), heavy metals, pesticides, and other dangerous industrial byproducts that remain buried in the soil and sediment today.

Whereas the harbor's soil and sediment remain highly contaminated, continuing to compromise the health of fish and those who consume it, the water quality by and large has improved in recent decades. The "Big Pipe" project, begun in 2001, is a key part of the river's water-focused conservation story. The Big Pipe constitutes two pipes, actually: one 4-mile long, 14-foot wide tunnel 70 feet below ground on the west side of the river, and one 6-mile long, 22-foot wide tunnel 150 feet down on the river's east side. While regulation of the pulp and paper industry following World War II made a substantial difference in water quality, it was not until 2011 that this new bi-pronged sewer project would more fully eliminate waste streams. For decades, the city had allowed sewage and stormwater runoff to mix and flow into the waterway; Portland has a combined sewer system that integrates sewage and stormwater, which leads to "combined sewer overflow" (CSO) during heavy storm events that exceed the system's capacity. Enlarging the pipe increases the system's storage size, thus reducing the need for CSO discharge. Sewer overflows into the harbor now occur approximately four times a year—a substantial reduction from the fifty or more overflow events that happened annually prior to the Big Pipe construction (W. Lang, 2010; Tomlinson, 2013).

The Water's Fine!—But Don't Eat the Fish

As a result of such environmental improvements over the last century, and especially the last two decades, the opportunity to pursue urban swimming and kayaking in the Willamette River has become a key feature of the city's sustainability success story. For the past decade or so, "riverlution" boosters, including the city's elected officials, have deemed the city's main urban waterway a perfect place to cool off on hot summer afternoons. As the introduction to this book illustrates, in spring 2016, Portland's mayor-elect Ted Wheeler even delivered his ballot via a mini-triathlon, swimming across the Willamette, biking along the waterfront, and walking to the ballot box. Thousands of residents likewise annually take to the river each July, donning fluorescent bathing suits and toting bright yellow inner tubes and floating coolers, for a highly celebrated "Big Float" event. Organized by the Human Access Project since 2011, and vocally and financially supported by Mayor Wheeler and the Bureau of Environmental Services, the Big Float epitomizes Portland's image as an urban recreation paradise in mainstream sustainability circles.

The carefree fun of the Big Float, with little acknowledgment by organizers and revelers of the histories of settler colonialism and white supremacy that continue to shape the harbor, however, also puts into stark view the disconnect between mainstream histories of the harbor and the experiences of PHCC members and so many others. Prior to one well-publicized swim, Mayor Wheeler remarked, "Today we're going to swim in the water, the water quality is very good. We're not going to stop and eat mud on the bottom of the river" (quoted in Acker, 2016b). Echoing this blasé sentiment, the Human Access Project's website pronounced "Come on in—the water's fine!" in its promotion of Big Float events. For those who rely on the river for fish, and for those on whose backs the river's industrial past and green present were built, such proclamations ring insensitive at best. They are especially hollow given that Wheeler clearly understood the gravity of the harbor cleanup prior to coming into office; in an interview at a grassroots-led event with PHCC members Donovan Smith and Laquida Lanford in 2016, Wheeler placatingly stated, "[The Superfund site cleanup] is the biggest issue that will impact Portlanders, and nobody knows anything about it today."

It is largely because of PHCC, working in solidarity with the Yakama Nation and organizations such as Portland Audubon, the Oregon chapter of the Sierra Club, Williamette Riverkeeper, and others, that residents most affected by contamination have begun to learn about the harbor. In addition to Black and Indigenous people who fish in the river, members of immigrant and refugee groups from around the world rely heavily on the harbor for sustenance, as do newcomers from Pacific Island communities. Over the last several decades, large numbers of people especially from Eastern European, Southeast Asian, and Central American countries have arrived in Portland and surrounding municipalities. Members of these groups and others travel to the harbor and other nearby waterways to fish, with motivations ranging from addressing food insecurity to continuing cultural traditions. A 2012 study drawing on a telephone survey of licensed anglers reported that about 7,800 people consumed resident fish from the Portland Harbor in the previous year. Licensed anglers with the most people reporting resident fish consumption were Eastern Europeans: 38 percent acknowledged eating resident fish, which are particularly susceptible to contamination since they spend their entire lives in the harbor (as opposed to salmon, for instance, which travel to the ocean and back). The study did not account for non-licensed anglers, and it is estimated that about 13.5 percent of those fishing in the Portland Harbor do not have licenses (Sundling and Buck, 2012). Reports from Department of Fish and Wildlife officials, local social service providers, and culturally specific organizations indicate that many unlicensed fisher people are likely to be immigrants, refugees, or newcomers; many are unaware of the dangers of consuming resident fish or have few other affordable sources of protein. Like Indigenous and Black Portlanders, Portland's members of these groups also face housing instability, contributing to household food insecurity and compounding challenges for people who have fled conflicts and poverty in other places (Curry-Stevens et al., 2010).

Another group today that is severely burdened by pollution in the harbor—as well as by efforts to remediate it, absent specific provisions that account for housing and police violence—is Portland's houseless population. The mayor, river boosters, and many others also erase those with nowhere else to live in their assertion that the river is fine. Catalyzed by the federal government's decision to reduce spending on affordable housing programs by nearly 80 percent between 1978 and 1983 (Western Regional Advocacy Project, 2010) and the rise of real estate as one of the primary profit-making sectors in the United States, unhoused people have once again settled along Portland's waterways in large numbers, as they have throughout the twentieth century and especially during the Great Depression. An estimated thirty-eight thousand people experienced homelessness in the tri-county area in 2017, with Indigenous and Black people disproportionately represented (Zapata et al., 2019). People's lives are threatened when they consume contaminated fish and live in toxic soil, compounded by experiences of police violence. In a cycle that plays out in cities across the country, houseless people experience sweeps—evictions—in commercial and residential areas, which push them into toxic spaces such as the Superfund site; exposure to hazards is therefore intimately linked to criminalization and police violence (Goodling, 2020). As the city evicts more and more houseless people from inner-Portland neighborhoods, the river maintains its draw for those seeking some semblance of stability. PHCC members worry, however, that riverbank sweeps will intensify in the years to come, as federally mandated Superfund cleanup progresses and urban development continues apace, at the same time as ongoing exposure to toxic soil and fish continues to impact those living unhoused due to cleanup delays.

Ongoing Legacies of White Supremacist Contamination and Cleanup

Pollution—and its remediation thus far—have thus had highly uneven, racialized impacts. Today, a growing number of the city's roughly six hundred thousand residents lack regular access to Portland's sustainability hallmarks, such as fresh and healthy food, safe neighborhoods, convenient transit, and stable housing. The causes of these disparities stretch back centuries, as we have seen. The Oregon Donation Land Act prioritized the land-owning dreams of white settlers at immense expense to Indigenous peoples and at the exclusion of Black and other non-white people. Well-paying wartime shipbuilding jobs that offered workplace protections were accessible only to white union members. Benefits from more recent public investment in housing and green infrastructure without concomitant anti-displacement provisions have accumulated mainly for the city's majority white population. The list goes on. In fact, Portland's sustainability successes have come at a direct cost to its less affluent residents, disproportionately Black and Indigenous people and other people of color—whose families have also suffered from years of exposure to pollution on the docks, in segregated neighborhoods, and in the local food supply. Descendants of those who had made the banks of the Willamette their home for thousands of years, and those who were exposed to shipyard pollution and suffered exploitation on the docks, are now by and large excluded from living in the inner-core neighborhoods most likely to boast green amenities.

In response to Black Lives Matter uprisings of summer 2020 focused on anti-Black racism and especially police violence against Black communities, river booster Human Access Project leaders issued an apology of sorts, albeit late, superficial, and lacking in analysis of larger structural violence: "We need to think bigger—to find better ways to increase river awareness among BIPOC communities and help them access and experience our river." Likewise, City of Portland leaders have recently become somewhat more aware of uneven impacts emanating from status quo urban greening at large. In laying out a twenty-five-year vision for the city, municipal planners explicitly framed the 2012 Portland Plan through a lens of social equity (City of Portland, 2012) and, thanks to strategic, ongoing organizing by grassroots groups and community organizations, including PHCC and its members, incorporated several anti-displacement provisions in the city's comprehensive plan that will guide development until 2035 (Bates, 2019). Yet, these efforts fall far short of truly responding to demands of marginalized communities, and groups such as PHCC know that there is great risk of falling back on old models without sustained outside pressure. This is especially evident as new waves of well-to-do white residents move to Portland and cadres of longtime white Portlanders adopt a "not in my backyard"—NIMBY—approach to growth, stifling the construction of more affordable housing and contesting the presence of houseless people that they fear will devalue their property.

Discrepancies between discourse promising social equity, alongside environmental improvements and economic growth, and actual outcomes for the city's Indigenous, Black, immigrant, refugee, and lower-income white communities have fueled a grassroots movement of people—including PHCC members—working to ensure that marginalized residents shape and benefit from Portland's so-called sustainable development. PHCC is a diverse, cross-class, cross-race grassroots coalition that is focused on jobs, housing, and human health—but first and foremost it demands robust environmental improvements as part of broader social and environmental justice outcomes. The health of the river, itself, is the coalition's overarching concern, but within a broader context of demands that cleanup benefits actually accrue to those who have been most burdened by pollution, industrial development, and displacement. PHCC's multipronged analysis speaks directly to the dialectics of urbanization: at the same time as the river is a site of present-day neoliberal greenwashing, it is also the basis of a more just, green future.

As the coalition works to reshape an urban landscape and the social relations that govern it, PHCC builds on the efforts of previous generations of change agents. At the same time, PHCC and so many other groups are forging a new path forward, in a new revanchist green urbanism era, and in a context of unprecedented housing and climate crises. Descendants of the original peoples of this land, many of whom continue to fish, gather, and live in these same lands today, have joined PHCC. Descendants of those who labored in the shipyards and who continue to fight for more housing, labor, and environmental justice have also joined PHCC. So, too, have people who have been directly and indirectly forced off their homelands by U.S. imperialism and who are creating new homes in the Pacific Northwest, including from Mexico, Iraq, and many other places. Finally, descendants of white settlers who colonized and terrorized Indigenous peoples, and who have therefore benefited from the theft of this land and the labor of enslaved people of African descent, are also PHCC members and supporters; some continue to benefit greatly from present-day sustainable development, while others have received fewer material advantages but nevertheless retain the privileges afforded by their white skin.

Such complexity is only legible in viewing the history of the Portland Harbor through a much broader lens that encompasses ongoing white supremacy, colonialism, settler colonialism, slavery, and uneven development—and that empathizes with fights to undo such structures. There is nothing exceptional, explains historian Katrine Barber (2019), about stories of Oregon that emphasize westward expansion as the basis for American national identity; nor, I argue, is there anything exceptional about stories of the Portland Harbor emphasizing conservation efforts as the basis for Portland's green identity. Oregon, Barber emphasizes, was just one piece of a much larger story during a "transformational period of mass migration, nation building, worldwide economic boom and bust, and establishment of a color line that reshaped the nineteenth-century globe, the outcomes of which reverberate around the world today" (385–386). Millions of white people, and especially British, Irish, German, and American migrants, settled throughout the world between 1815 and 1924; Oregon's history, therefore, occurred within a much larger settler colonial context. Likewise, the Portland Harbor's history occurred within a much larger settler colonial, racial capitalist, white supremacist context. It is crucial to consider this framework in recounting the harbor's past, and in understanding the constellation of present-day organizing efforts.

Golden Paintbrush
Castilleja levisecta
Endangered

CHAPTER 3

Our River, Our Future

More-than-Local Grassroots Activism

People are often moved to get involved in social movements out of concern for a particular issue or set of interrelated issues, whether or not they are impacted personally in an immediately tangible way. Climate change and fossil fuel dependency, police brutality, food insecurity, housing instability, and labor injustice are just a few key issues driving participation in today's organizing spheres. People also join social movements to become part of something greater than themselves and to connect with community. Other times, people get involved due to tangible, material reasons: they are hungry or at risk of homelessness, for instance. Over the years, many PHCC members have come to their first meeting with a friend who has already joined up, curious to learn more about the river they have crossed so many times but perhaps never really visited. After attending a meeting or two, they stay connected because their communities subsist on fish, and they become concerned about health impacts of pollution as they learn more. Or they engage because they are more generally concerned about economic justice issues and hear that green cleanup jobs may emerge in the harbor. Some show up to PHCC meetings after seeing a social media post: they want to dismantle everything having to do with the oil industry, or they care about ensuring more public access to riverfront land, or they are involved with the Mní Wiconi—Water Is Life—movement and see PHCC as a way to connect on such issues locally. Still others have joined because the coalition offers a chance to gather with like-minded people, to connect with community. For many, it is a combination of factors that draws them in.

Moreover, many who join social movements invoke a particular place, or locale, in their involvement. While people come to PHCC for many reasons, inherently woven throughout their motivations is a connection to a particular place—to the landscape of the river and harbor. In fact, the river itself has been a unifying motivator for nearly all coalition members. "Place attachment" entails an affective bond, an emotional connection, between people and place.

People typically come to intimately know a place by spending time there, deepening their personal and ancestral ties over years, decades, centuries. We therefore might expect that those pushing hardest for a cleaned-up harbor would be those living closest to the river. After all, place attachment and time spent in a given locale often precede work to preserve or improve a particular place.

But, for many, place attachment develops *despite* physical separation from or forced migration to a place. Although land relations may be "taking place in space," asserts Black studies scholar Katherine McKittrick (2006), they are also complicated by "subjectivities, imaginations, and stories." Symbolic relationships, then, rooted less in a physical connection and more in intangible linkages to land, water, and other landscape features, can contribute to shared meanings of a place—which in turn propel collective efforts to defend and shape the future of a place (Low, 1992). In fact, few PHCC members actually live near the Portland Harbor today. Most hail from throughout the city of Portland and surrounding areas, and some even travel hundreds of miles to the harbor for fishing, water ceremonies, picnics and cookouts, music festivals, canoeing, and kayaking. And it is not only the Willamette River, generally, or the Portland Harbor, specifically, that people cite in articulating the pull of the river. Rivers in other parts of the world, too, drive coalition members' participation, regardless of current residence. The Willamette River, and rivers more generally, connect people to PHCC regardless of their place of residence today, and regardless of their own ancestry.

This chapter addresses why PHCC members have gotten involved in cross-class, cross-race grassroots organizing for a more just sustainability, with particular attention to the role of place and landscape—and especially urban rivers—in such work. While PHCC's efforts are resolutely place-based, it is not only a time-oriented connection but also a symbolic, relational, more-than-local place-based connection, with PHCC members' work today coming into conversation with people and rivers of other times and places. The subjective-spatial complexity of PHCC's membership and resistance efforts is fundamental to grasp in order to understand who is shaping the Portland Harbor from below. In addressing the wide variety of motivations involved, and especially the complex place attachments invoked in harbor organizing, this chapter interlinks people, place, and space today, in the context of the deep history outlined in the previous chapter and the more just, green future about which PHCC members and many others dream.

Community Relationships and Commitments

Many people join movements because of the community connections that pull them in and emerge through collective work. Organizing takes place sitting around kitchen tables, attending events at libraries and schools, marching shoulder to shoulder at protests, and talking in late-night strategy sessions. Social movements are inherently collective, putting people in touch with others aspiring toward a common goal. They are *social*, and many people crave this kind of connection (Dubet, 1994, 2004; Rutland, 2013). Moreover, such organizing-focused relationships are often inherently place-based: people live in proximity to one another, or they care about the same landscape and forge their relationships around its care or stewardship.

Coalition members cite community connections and PHCC's relationship-based model as one key reason for joining up. In fact, in nearly all cases, groups that joined the alliance at the outset did so because one or more of their members had an existing relationship with Cassie Cohen or Jeri Jimenez, two people instrumental in the coalition's founding. A longtime EJ activist in the Portland area, Jeri initially became involved in the harbor cleanup around 2000. She then spent a decade focusing on other EJ issues but turned her attention back to the harbor in 2011, when comrades notified her that polluters were misleading grassroots groups, and public agencies were shirking responsibility to engage people in the Superfund cleanup planning process. Jeri called Cassie, the director of a local chapter of a youth-focused EJ organization. Cassie would go on to steward the coalition from its inception in 2012, up through 2020 and beyond.

Ibrahim Mubarak, founder and leader of the houseless-led group Right 2 Survive, recalls the fundamental influence of Jeri and Cassie on the decision of his organization to join PHCC in a 2015 interview. Ibrahim had known Jeri for years: "How I heard first about PHCC was through Jeri, and she was talking with Cassie and they figured out it would be a good connection, seeing as Right 2 Survive is a houseless direct action advocacy group, and they were finding a lot of houseless people on the Willamette. And so I went and talked with Cassie and we made the connection, and it felt really good because a lot of people, they were afraid to talk to the houseless community because of the stereotype that they hear." It was a combination of knowing unhoused people who made the harbor their home, coupled with personal relationships with PHCC leaders, then, that prompted Ibrahim and Right 2 Survive to get involved.

Indigenous groups also got involved through existing connections and networks, many of which were based in relationships to the land and river. One particular elder encouraged Cassie to get in touch with several smaller Indigenous-led groups in the Portland area in 2012, and the Portland Youth and Elders Council, the Portland chapter of the American Indian Movement (AIM), Wisdom of the Elders, and Wiconi International joined right away as founding members. As with Right 2 Survive, relationships were key for Wiconi, a faith-based organization "geared towards Native Americans that pushed the conversation about decolonization and about our role in the community," according to JR Lilly, Wiconi's interim executive director at the time, in a 2015 interview. JR explains how his relationship with Jeri was central to Wiconi's initial involvement: "I was invited by Jeri to come to a—she just said a community meeting and that it was important that I be there. And since Jeri is part of the Native Community, whenever an aunt or an uncle asks you to do something, you just do it." Wisdom of the Elders joined because Cassie and the organization's director had worked together over the years and had developed a mutual respect for one another. Leaders of Wisdom of the Elders (2023)—an organization that "records, preserves, and shares oral history, cultural arts, language concepts, and traditional ecological knowledge of exemplary Native American elders, storytellers, and scientists in collaboration with diverse institutions, agencies, and organizations"—found affinity with people at PHCC, who were concerned about the fate of local land and waters.

Several other local groups connected as well, many by word of mouth through community leadership networks. Cassie knew one of the founders of the East European Coalition (EEC) from her earlier days working with an immigrant and refugee rights group and called him. Another EEC leader encouraged Cassie to contact the Czech School of Portland, which also joined the coalition early on. Impact Northwest, an organization that supports low-income and houseless people in Portland, heard about the fledgling alliance via EEC, and people started attending meetings. Asian Pacific American Network of Oregon and the Iraqi Society of Oregon also joined up in those early days, as did Líderes Verdes, a neighborhood-based EJ group located nine miles east of the harbor. Several youth, adults, and elders from Portland's Black community likewise participated, through the EJ-focused work of Groundwork Portland and other channels.

At the heart of the relationship-oriented reasons for connecting with

PHCC, for many, has been a more generalized desire to serve their communities, now and in the future, through stewardship of the land and water and education about coalition activities. One member of Líderes Verdes says simply, "I participate because I like helping," gesturing to the river in the background behind her. Mañuela, also from Líderes Verdes, frequently talks about fishing in the Portland Harbor with her children before she knew about the health risks. She was horrified to learn about the contamination and now works to let others know: "The more we are informed, the more we can inform our communities." Another Líderes Verdes member explains, "I've been living here for a long time, and I didn't know that the water was polluted. It's surprising to me, because my children like to go swimming [in the Willamette]. And I'm also here to learn more and share it with my neighbors." Rodney, from Right 2 Survive, recalls helping his mother haul construction debris to houseless people when he was growing up, for fires to keep warm. Now, as an adult experiencing homelessness himself, he continues that tradition of community support: "I get a lot of satisfaction from helping people no matter what it is, so from when I was fifteen until now it has always been like that. You need a shirt, I'll give you my shirt. It may be a little stinky but you can have it."

A leader within Portland's Black community explains: "I'm helping bring people to PHCC, so that they can inform themselves about what is going on as far as pollution. And so that they can spread that information among their communities." Another participant, who also works with an organization serving Portland's Black community on issues of wellness, explains her relationship-oriented, place-based commitment to PHCC in this way: "I joined this group and decided to do this work because of the generations that came before me, the generation of people that are here now, and those that are still to come, who will have to fight the issue of poisonous water and air." In mentioning previous generations, she is referring to her ancestors who arrived in Portland to work in the shipyards, and who were exposed to environmental hazards in the workplace and in the home while being segregated, only to be later displaced. Such histories, described in depth in the previous chapter, help account for the entanglement of people- and place-oriented relationships in drawing participants in to PHCC.

Subsistence and Shelter

Hinted at in statements of general concern for community health, many individuals and groups joined PHCC because of a reliance on the Portland

Harbor for basic sustenance and survival. Food and shelter, especially, are place-based: such material elements needed for life come from *somewhere*. When people lack food and shelter, or water, conditions are ripe (though far from inevitable) for joining forces with others in an effort to enact change. Contamination in the harbor has rendered one particularly important food source, fish, unsafe to eat. One participant, from the EEC, explains, "[There are] a lot of [Eastern European] fishermen out there, who don't know about why you cannot fish there from the river; that's why we got involved." A Líderes Verdes member likewise expresses concern about the health of their community members who rely on the river to feed their families: "The water is very polluted. We nor our children nor our grandchildren are able to eat the fish. And that's why I like to participate."

Wilma Alcock, a Black elder who would go on to sit on PHCC's Steering Committee, reflects fondly on her childhood when she first joined the coalition around 2014. She grew up eating fish from the Willamette alongside hush puppies, potatoes, onions, and salad on weekly outings to the river with her family. Fish provided vital sustenance, and the whole process of fishing and cooking outdoors in a beautiful place was a source of leisure and comfort in a time of intense racial discord during and following World War II:

> We fished all up and down the river, wherever there was a bank you could get to. . . . It was a pastime and a feeding. We ate fish probably once a week because it was just healthy for you. . . . We weren't Catholic but we ate fish on Friday. . . . And we also would be out at Sauvie Island and after I got older, [my parents] had a little trailer, it was called a Teardrop, and it would attach to the back of a car. There was a place for a stove, and a place to sleep, and they would catch fish out in the river. We would use clean water and clean [the fish] and use salt and pepper and cornmeal and fry it in that black cast iron skillet. Oh my god, there was nothing any better than that . . . Fresh fish, you can't get any fresher than that. (PHCC, 2015)

When she joined PHCC, Wilma knew that many Black Portlanders continue to rely on the harbor for a combination of food and cultural sustenance, and she frequently recalled her own fond memories of spending time on the river as a child. She continues to speak at her community's gatherings and events to share with others what she has learned through PHCC about the harbor's pollution and cleanup-planning process—and what she knows from her life experiences on the river.

Another PHCC member, Mike, from the houseless-led group Right 2 Survive, recalls growing up in Portland in the 1960s and cutting steelhead that his father caught in surrounding rivers into one-inch thick steaks. His family added slices of lemon, salt and pepper, and onion rings, and "hobo cooked" the fish over campfires, in aluminum foil packets. A concern for the health and safety of fellow houseless people living along the river today, some of whom are not aware of the dangers of consuming toxic fish and others who eat it because it is one of the few truly free sources of protein offered by the land, drove this person's participation in PHCC from the outset.

Subsistence fishing is not the only survival-related motive for working with PHCC, especially for advocates of the houseless community. According to the group's website in the mid-2010s, Right 2 Survive is a "direct action group that educates both houseless and housed people on their civil, human, and constitutional rights," that works to "bridge the gap between housed and un-housed people by clearing away misconceptions and stigmas associated with houselessness and empower houseless people to stand up for themselves when their rights are violated". Right 2 Survive and its members joined PHCC out of a concern for the confluence of ways that harbor contaminants affect the health of people living unhoused and seeking refuge in the harbor. Lisa Fay, one of Right 2 Survive's leaders, summarizes an assemblage of threats to those taking shelter along the river in a 2015 interview:

> [PHCC] noticed what we already knew, that there were many houseless people that lived along the river, and that were being impacted with every aspect of their daily life along the river, health issues, environmental issues. They were worried about their health. They knew that there were toxins in the river. They knew they couldn't drink, or cook from the river. They knew that they shouldn't—although in many cases they didn't have a choice—clean their clothes from the river. They used the river to bathe and were concerned that that was an extra health risk being brought in through their pores.

In addition to toxic fish and water, houseless people also grappled with concerns about the riverbank soil, in which some grew vegetables and made their homes: "They've been drinking that water, growing vegetation on there, where the soil gets toxic water, so they eat toxic vegetables," explains one Right 2 Survive member. Dioxin and lead lurked in the soil in many places where people pitched their tents in the harbor. Without great care, dust from the soil could get into people's food as they ate, and on their clothing and into their tents. Ingesting soil with dangerous contaminants is a risk factor for all sorts of health problems, particularly for those with underlying ailments.

For houseless advocates, then, as well as many others, concerns about food, water, shelter, and health attracted them to PHCC. These building blocks of life are fundamentally place-based: they come from somewhere, and for many, that somewhere is the Portland Harbor.

"Something That Actually Benefits the Displaced People"

Yet, with the exception of people living unhoused, nearly no one who joined PHCC in its early days actually lived within walking distance of the harbor. Members often traveled great distances to fish in the harbor or visit the river. For many, inspiration to join PHCC therefore revolved around highly complex place or landscape attachments, which in turn are interconnected with concerns about various issues such as food, housing, jobs, and health care, as well as desires to connect with community. Environmental social scientists Lynne Manzo and Patrick Devine-Wright (2014) help elucidate how "place attachment" entails an affective bond, or emotional connection, between people and place. People care about a place and want to have a hand in shaping its future. People typically come to intimately know a place by spending time there, deepening their personal and ancestral ties over years, decades, centuries. The site of one's birth or childhood, the region where one's ancestors originated, or a place of significance due to a particularly moving experience that occurred there forges connections to land or water through emotional, physiological, familial experiences. Such connections in turn undergird the core of a group's collective identity and guiding values. As historian Roxanne Dunbar-Ortiz (2014) explains, origin narratives do especially powerful work to connect people to place and landscape.

But many PHCC members experience place attachment to the harbor despite not living in proximity to it. Some have never lived near the harbor. And many PHCC members and their ancestors *used* to live near the harbor, but years and centuries of violence and displacement prevent them from accessing the river today, as chapter 2 reveals. Ongoing settler colonialism and racial capitalism undeniably disrupt place-based relationships in multiple, complex ways. When people are forced to migrate due to violence—forced off their ancestral homelands, for instance—generational ties to a place become disrupted. Or when oil companies lay pipelines, perhaps where a landfill and other toxic industry had already located, the cumulative effects can mount for nearby residents and complicate peoples' feelings about a place. Yet, such disruptions and scars on the landscape can also take on symbolic meaning, motivating people to fight for improvements to, or for the preservation of, place— whether near or far. Writing about the Iñupiaq Eskimos in Shishmaref, Alaska, for example, Elizabeth Marino (2015) explores a community's conviction to care for and about a place even as that place is disappearing due to climate change and sea level rise. She emphasizes how people care for a place that was once, but can no longer be, home. Moreover, when people move, they carry memories of previous homelands with them, all the while forging new relationships to new places that motivate care in a conjoined way. Place attachment, then, can develop *despite* severance of physical ties to a place.

Feelings of attachment can also develop beyond, and even in spite of, one's tenure in a given place. Black people of diverse ethnicities in the United States, for instance, reveal that people do not simply feel that they "emerge from" land, on the one hand, or are "foreign" to it, on the other. Instead, they articulate a sense of "*becoming* of the land," independent of state-based citizenship or legal property claims (Tuck et al., 2014:68). Although land relationships—geographies—may be "taking place in space," then, they simultaneously intersect with "subjectivities, imaginations, and stories" (McKittrick, 2006:xiii). A symbolic relationship based not solely on a physical connection but rather on something less tangible can contribute to shared meanings of a place (Low, 1992).

Place attachment to the harbor is thus made more complicated by the histories of dispossession and displacement outlined in the previous chapter, and these histories inspire attention to myriad issues beyond fish and pollution. For members of Portland's Black community, jobs and housing, for instance, are inseparable from the health of the river, and this nexus of concerns motivates participation in PHCC. A community health worker in the Black community explains her motivation for working with PHCC: "I am here to make sure that we facilitate and leverage this Superfund site into something that actually benefits the displaced people who have been suffering not only from the toxins, but from the job loss, from displacement in housing, education, employment, children, the whole nine yards." Overarching and interrelated social and EJ issues in the harbor and beyond, including intergenerational health, workforce development, housing, and more, are motivating factors for many PHCC members whose people no longer live near the harbor but feel tied to it nevertheless.

A reverence for the Willamette River drives participation for Wilma, who was quoted above, for instance, despite the serial displacement her community has experienced. In a 2015 interview, Wilma explains the linkage between the work of healing the river and healing her community, fragmented by displacement:

> My hope is that [the river] gets back to where it once was where it can be life sustaining for people. Because really, actually, progress just—it doesn't sustain people, it just—well, ok, progress, if I'm talking about progress when

you're displacing something and putting something else, it usually doesn't last. . . . I said, "Portland has never had a ghetto, so now they are building one." And they said, "Where?" and I said, "Williams and Vancouver [Avenues], all of those, they are building a ghetto." "They're not building a ghetto. They are putting in all those new buildings and things," dah, dah-dah, dah-dah. Give it twenty-five years, those are going to be housing that people with no income and little income will be living in. Because [developers] will go on to the next cherry.

Contrasting the "progress" of city building with the restoration of a landscape and waterway that could actually support human life, and in particular the health and spirit of the Black community, Wilma's statement encapsulates the collective thinking of many PHCC members: development, green or otherwise, is futile without attention to life-giving elements of the landscape, such as the river. At the same time, river remediation is in vain if only white people of means steer the process and benefit from the outcome, especially if profits come at the expense of those who have suffered from pollution, displacement, and other forms of oppression. North Williams Avenue and North Vancouver Avenue, former hubs of the Black community and main thoroughfares through the formerly disinvested neighborhood, are now ground zero for gentrification and displacement in Portland. When she says that they are building a ghetto there, Wilma is referencing the seesawing of capital investments into and out of neighborhoods. Private developers, often lubricated by public subsidies, invest in so-called blighted neighborhoods where they can acquire land cheaply—only to eventually abandon such places a few years later in favor of profit-making opportunities in other places. Such "uneven development" (N. Smith, 2002) and gentrification characterize the vast majority of market-led city building today, as it has for several decades now.

Complex spatial concerns were similarly key motivators for Indigenous groups joining PHCC. In a 2015 interview, JR Lilly explains the more-than-local scalar connections for Wiconi. Although small in numbers, Wiconi's concerns were expansive, linking spirituality to international and local environmental justice issues alike and tying the past to the future:

A large part of the organization was around Christian faith, however, it wasn't exclusive to that. [We emphasize] all areas of spirituality and the sacred. So even in the Sun Dance, there are different elements of teaching that are . . . involved in it. So there's this big overarching conversation of, how do you—what degree, what percent of ceremony needs to be traditional, and what percentage of it needs to move forward and evolve, and grow with the changing times and elements. When you are carving a pipestone, do you use traditional methods of doing it that takes hours, or can you just use a drill? And what is traditional about it and what is not traditional about it? So a lot of those conversations we were pushing. . . . And we were trying to find some areas to focus on. What role does Wiconi have in Portland—we have such an international and national reach—but what are we doing here locally? . . . But we also were trying to bring the local issues—bring more awareness of it because we have a huge following just around the world and the nation. . . . So when we heard about Portland Harbor, and the challenges, like that there is no environmental justice [element being recognized], that [could be] part of our scope of what we were doing. So I proposed to the board that we get involved more. They agreed, so we began talking with Cassie. We became a core partner.

Moving in another direction, leaders with the Portland chapter of the American Indian Movement (AIM) put recovery of the Willamette at the heart of their participation, even though AIM members are scattered across the region. AIM leads seasonal water ceremonies on the banks of the Willamette and nearby waterways. People travel from as far as Umatilla, Pendleton, and Yakama to attend ceremonies, some following in the footsteps of ancestors who seasonally migrated to the Willamette Valley. Others, such as members of the Purepecha community, originally from Michoacán, Mexico, and who now live in Woodburn and Hubbard, often drive forty miles north to dance in AIM's ceremonies. "People can be healed, rivers can be healed," explains AIM leader Art McConville (Nez Perce, Cayuse, Umatilla) succinctly (PHCC, 2015).

For the Yakama Nation, an ally of PHCC's, the Portland Harbor and especially Willamette Falls are critical to their identity and survival—despite the reservation's location more than a hundred miles northeast, in present-day Washington state. "The treaty we signed 167 years ago guaranteed our right to go and harvest our foods wherever," explains Yakama elder Davis Washines in a 2022 interview. "In the legal terms, it's called usual and customary places. Although we were confined to a reservation, we were promised the ability to go to wherever we traditionally gather food. We recently returned to Yellowstone for buffalo, as an example." Yakama Tribal members continue to harvest lamprey at Willamette Falls, in particular. "We don't have any other place to go," Davis continues. "We can't pick up and move to some other place. This is where we believe our creator had put us and so we're here to stay." This enduring rootedness informs the Yakama's perspective around collaborating with PHCC on the harbor's cleanup: "Portland's always going to be there, and the citizens are always going to be there. So we have to be able to try to understand one another and be aware of the things that are important to all of us."

In addition to issues of place attachment made complicated by the past, for houseless people, the prospects of *future* displacement tied to harbor cleanup and development have motivated involvement. Right 2 Survive leaders know all too well that throughout the city, police serially force houseless people to pack up and move in the name of environmental remediation. "Move to where?" Right 2 Survive members ask. Advocates fear that as harbor cleanup gets underway, remediation, like sustainable development, will similarly become a convenient excuse to conduct sweeps with even more urgency along the river. Right 2 Survive member Loretta Pascoe articulates the contradiction that people living along the river face: "People along the river need a safe place to go, and we need to be able to afford to get that [housing] so that we can be away from the river while the cleanup is [taking place]" (PHCC, 2015).

More-than-Local Place Attachments

As members reflected on joining PHCC in the early days, many were motivated not just by their connection to the Willamette River, often in spite of displacement, but also by an affinity for rivers in other parts of the world. Participants made connections between their conceptions of rivers worldwide with the tangible goal of improving the Willamette River. In this way, members have taken historical more-than-local place attachments and inscribed them onto their work with PHCC.

Abudulhadi "Hadi" Mohammed, a leader with the Iraqi Society of Oregon, puts the river itself at the center of his organization's concerns about the Portland Harbor in a 2015 interview: "Nobody, no rules or [regulations] . . . told companies not to harm the river and what is inside the river, like fish. Even the plants, when you water the plants with pollution, they die." Like other Iraqi Society members, Hadi identifies intimate parallels between the Willamette River and waterways running through his home country:

> I remember in my country, we have two rivers: Tigris and the Euphrates. Old rivers, yes. They come from Turkish mountains, very clear water, very clean, and one of them passes into Syria lands, Arab country, and passes into Iraq. When [the river] reaches the south of Iraq, it is polluted heavily. Many diseases. The water becomes bitter or salty, not good to drink, or not good to water even the plants. So, it continues even now, when you see the river now

the color of the water becomes green or brown. Many living things or creatures disappear.... So now every family has a filter at home. [Otherwise, people get] diarrhea, and different diseases because it is full of germs.

Scientists, doctors write in the newspaper or go on TV and ask the government to please see what happened to the rivers, they are full of pollution. But no one here [in Iraq] acts to change it. They are busy in their personal things, and they drink pure water—bottled water, or they have systems [so the pollution doesn't affect them].

Hadi goes on to explicitly connect rivers of the Middle East and the Pacific Northwest: "I make a comparison between the Tigris and Euphrates and Willamette. We are suffering the same thing, like you, maybe worse. So I think they [should] take care, the government, if they warn people or notify them, 'Please, you have to take care of the rivers', not for Portland only, for all American states."

Similarly, Irina, a member of the East European Coalition, was concerned about the Willamette River because of her experiences growing up far from the Willamette Valley. Speaking about the Neva River in Saint Petersburg, Russia, Irina says, "I watched the river of my birth city and how it was polluted. From age five or six to age twenty, I saw sand getting dirtier, water getting more oily. There were no warnings." The daily ritual of drinking tea and serving it to visitors is what really brought the problem of the polluted river to the forefront for Irina. Her family's friends and relatives lived all over the region, including in what is now Ukraine and Moldova. They came to visit periodically. When they arrived, Irina's family served them tea. "The tea we drank as a little girl was really good," she recalls. But relatives came from Uzbekistan, Kazakhstan, and Tajikistan, which lie on the Silk and Tea Route from China, Irina explains: "They brought really good green and caravan teas" and gave them to Irina's family, as gifts. But by the time she was a teenager, St. Petersburg's tap water—from the Neva—had taken a turn for the worse. Irina remembers, "I was embarrassed to give [our guests] tea. The water tasted terrible. ... The water did not allow us to enjoy the flavors." Irina connects her experience with this profound shift in drinking water quality to her work with PHCC: "I do not want Portland to go this direction," she says.

Hadi and Irina, as well as many other PHCC members, therefore invoke the rivers of their home countries in their work with PHCC. It does not matter that the Willamette was a relatively new river for them and fellow newcomers to Portland; the attachments they have developed elsewhere actually transferred to form a foundation for developing a deep attachment to the Willamette relatively quickly.

Conclusion

Some PHCC members worried about whether their children could safely cool off or play in the Portland Harbor, and they joined up when they realized that fellow neighbors have similar concerns. Others long wished they could afford to live in the neighborhood where their families had raised children and grown old for many generations, near the river, and participated in PHCC activities because housing affordability is one of the issue areas with which the coalition is concerned. Still others wanted to be able to eat the fish they caught without concern for their health—whether they lived near the river today or had ancestral connections. For nearly all PHCC member groups, a medley of issues both near and far from the river—from jobs to housing, spiritual connection to sustenance, and intergenerational concerns to the health of the river itself—was woven throughout their involvement in PHCC. Coursing through all of these issues and relationships is the spiritually sustaining, "life-giving" Willamette River, and rivers of the world more broadly. By and large, place attachment develops through spending time in a given place, whether a beautiful coastline, a particular neighborhood, or a nearby corner market. For PHCC members, time is indeed a key ingredient in many peoples' feelings of place attachments and decision to fight for a cleaned-up harbor. Yet, place attachment has also developed and motivated efforts to join PHCC despite physical separation from the harbor. Many people have developed and maintain a sense of connection to the harbor even if they have never lived near the river. Despite hailing from disparate geographies made more complicated by past and ongoing dispossessing and displacing violence, the Willamette River serves as a convergence point for PHCC participants.

Linkages between place attachment and social movement participation, as we have seen here, are therefore complex and multidimensional. Attachments to place—to a harbor, a tree, mountains, neighborhood, sites of everyday and spectacular life alike—sometimes form a basis for mounting powerful challenges to oppressive regimes (see also Finney, 2014; Safransky, 2018; Wolfe, 2006). Shared meanings then become the basis of a group's efforts to defend and shape a place's future. In fact, Black Geographies scholar Katherine McKittrick argues that it is through "redefining and refusing to fully accept traditional geographic limitations" (2006:83) that grassroots groups actually assert their political visions. These kinds of complicated relationships to place can only be understood by closely attending to the stories of those that inhabit or otherwise feel deep connections to a place, explains Black geograhies and EJ scholar Tianna Bruno (2021).

This examination of PHCC's more-than-local, relational place attachments sets the stage to understand the complexities of PHCC's grievances and demands. It also lays a foundation to examine why the coalition's vision of how to redress grievances diverged so sharply with the public agencies' understandings. In later chapters, I contrast PHCC members' and public agency officials' conceptualizations of place. But first, I examine more closely the process by which PHCC members developed the coalition's shared historical narrative.

Bradshaw's Desert Parsley
Lomatium bradshawii
Endangered

CHAPTER 4

Producing a Peoples' History
of the Portland Harbor

During the Environmental Protection Agency's summer 2015 public comment period, the formal time set aside for people to influence the cleanup plan for the Portland Harbor Superfund Site, one PHCC representative explained the coalition's persistence in pushing public agencies in this way: "We're looking at this as not just an eleven-mile stretch. We see this as a 300-year plus thing. I understand how federal and state budgets are made. But we're not looking at this as a bureaucrat. We're looking at it as life and death. . . . We're the ones that have to live with the pollution." Their reference to the long term, to seeing the cleanup as a "300-year plus thing," hints at the role of history and memory in coalition members' broader understandings of who has been impacted by pollution and how, as well as what should be done to redress injustices. A collective process of learning history—and producing a new, shared historical narrative—has played an important role in PHCC's efforts to repoliticize the harbor's cleanup in order to bring about a new future.

The previous chapter illustrates some of the ways in which place attachment to the river, and rivers of the world, undergird the commitments of PHCC members. The connections to the harbor that motivate involvement have become organized into something larger and more powerful than any one individual and contribute toward new narratives that are shaping the river's future. Yet, while the river helps bring people together around the Portland Harbor in an interlinked material and symbolic sense, such a convergence has not happened automatically. Social movement undertakings do not appear magically out of structural conditions, nor are people predisposed to activism. Rather, agents of change who are working to transform the landscape and power relations, whether in so-called green cities or elsewhere, engage in what social movement scholars call "micromobilizations" (Hunt and Benford,

2004). They hold community meetings, learn from each other, form alliances, stage protests, write op-eds, submit public testimony, create political artwork, attend policy meetings, and produce counternarratives. Indeed, there is a *process of becoming political*, which entails interrelated collective identity formation and participation in collective activities (Rutland, 2013).

At the heart of such activities is learning and work, including *memory work*. Remembering, sharing, and collective learning are necessary to bring disparate histories together and make connections, especially across lines of race and class. Engaging with such histories has long played a crucial role in anti-oppression organizing, in part because marginalized groups' experiences are often written out of mainstream historiography, justifying colonial and racist rule. In undertaking their own historiography—"the writing of history" (Choudry, 2015:68)—members of marginalized groups collectively lay groundwork to imagine and shape a different future.

This chapter addresses the process by which PHCC members have put their own memories and histories and connections to the harbor into conversation, to develop an outline of the collective historical narrative of the harbor recounted in chapter 2. PHCC's "peoples' history" of the harbor emerged over a multiyear politicization process, which entailed interrelated collective identity formation and participation in coalition activities. PHCC's historical narrative is not simply an additive one, however, with Indigenous history stapled to Black history stapled to immigrant history, and so on. Rather, it is a joint story of many histories woven together that has come into being through dialogue and collective action, and it continues to evolve. As PHCC works to ensure that frontline communities collectively steer and benefit from urban environmental cleanup, the coalition draws attention to the racist, colonial past and present, in order to politicize the harbor's future. PHCC's new, shared history did not emerge overnight. How did the coalition's collective historical narrative come into being, and to what ends? How do disparate cultural memories become a shared narrative? What is the role of a collectively produced historical narrative in cross-class, cross-race grassroots organizing within a context of ahistorical, depoliticized sustainability discourse?

This chapter first provides an overview of the role of cultural memory—popular understandings of the past—in social movements. It then illustrates the process through which PHCC's collective history has evolved, drawing on brief vignettes focused on coalition meeting icebreakers, culturally specific events organized by coalition members, a short film produced with the support of local college students, and strategic engagements with public agencies. It ends with a discussion of the vital role of the shared production of history within grassroots efforts to redress generations of dispossession and displacement, with a particular focus on what this looks like in a context of ahistorical sustainability discourse.

Microprocesses of Socio-Ecological Change

As we saw in chapter 3, people engage in social movement work for a variety of reasons: to meet a metabolic need (e.g., food, shelter, safety); to build relationships and honor community connections; to address a concern over a particular social or EJ issue. Woven tightly into peoples' motivations for getting involved is often a deep connection to place and landscape. Linkages between place attachment and social movement participation are complex and multidimensional, given histories of displacement, dispossession, migration, and more. Adding to this complexity, people are never fully formed, nor internally homogenous, political subjects; notwithstanding the motivating reasons for joining up at the outset, social movement participants go through an ever-evolving process of becoming political. One's resources and objective interests, social circles, and core dispositions are always in flux, independently and in relation to one another. At the same time, how people become positioned as political subjects is also heavily influenced by the enduring logics of white supremacy. While racism, colonialism, and xenophobia "preclude easy solidarity" (Pulido, 2018:311) between disparate racial and ethnic groups, it is within and against them that political subjects are "made and remade," ever changing, managing several "discordant, even contradictory, logics of action" (Rutland, 2013, citing Dubet, 1994:22).

In diverse social movement groups, this individual change process occurs in relation to work with others, in part via formation of a collective identity. Collective identity entails "an individual's cognitive, moral, and emotional connections with a broader community, category, practice, or institution" (Polletta and Jasper, 2001:285). This "shared sense of 'we-ness'" (Snow, 2001) emerges through micromobilizations—*work*—that people initiate to prepare for and undertake collective action (Hunt and Benford, 2004). In iterative fashion, a sense of collective identity informs engagement in social movement activities, and active wrestling with the contradictions of working across lines of difference has the potential to strengthen a group's collective identity. Whether formal or informal, "collective learning" is therefore a key activity for diverse grassroots groups, such as PHCC, because of its fundamental role in collective identity construction (Kilgore, 1999). Collective learning "occurs among two or more diverse people in which taken-as-shared meanings (including a vision of social justice) are constructed and acted upon by the group" (191). In collective learning scenarios, each participant contributes different understandings developed through their life experiences to the collective process, rendering the whole more than the sum of its parts.

I want to be careful not to oversimplify the challenges of working across difference, however, particularly around land-based organizing in a racial capitalist, settler colonial context. While collective learning offers no guarantee of more democratic processes, nor materially different outcomes, pedagogy and social movements scholar Deborah Kilgore (1999) nevertheless argues that because people learn primarily by resolving contradictions, it is precisely the *presence of difference* that can push collective learning to transpire: social actors "produce meaning in the face of conflict" (199). Collective learning that starts with participants' own lived experience helps prime people to incorporate new ideas into existing schemas, strengthen relationships between participants, and build commitments to the group (Choudry, 2015; Freire, 1970; Horton and Freire, 1990). These ingredients are crucial (even if not a guarantee) for solidarity to develop (Hunt and Benford, 2004).

The Uses of History in Grassroots Movements

Tapping personal memories and group histories through collective learning endeavors can contribute to social movements in layered ways. Invoking the past is one way of asserting "We were there," cultural geography scholar Carolyn Finney (2014:66) explains, ultimately allowing "for more control and power in deciding (collectively?) who we were and who we *are*." Sociologist George Lipsitz (1988:241–242) similarly argues that eliciting a collective memory of the past can also serve as a "critique of the present," sometimes enabling oppressed groups to "fashion a counterhegemonic struggle" despite seemingly insurmountable challenges. Jointly remembering the past can also help social movement participants maintain a sense of "movement continuity," thereby strengthening collective identity and resolve (Gongaware, 2010), particularly when events of the past "convey triumph over oppression" (Harris, 2006:20). In addition, "group-based memories" can inform cooperative action by "operating as a retrospective lens where insurgents can articulate grievances, cement group loyalties, establish goals, evaluate new events, and reflect on the possibility for successful cooperation" (22). In fact, Gaye Theresa Johnson (2008) suggests that Black and brown people organizing in Los Angeles, for instance, "have consistently envisioned futures that include each other's memories and histories, even when it wasn't always a conscious choice."

Crucial to consider are the *mechanisms* that facilitate a diverse group's "memory repertoire" (Harris, 2006:22) becoming a useful tool in fighting for a more just future. Feminist social movement scholar Chela Sandoval (2009) asserts that "differential consciousness" is precisely what has allowed "third world feminists" to effectively work together in solidarity across lines of difference to challenge mainstream, white conceptions of feminism. Differential consciousness involves reading "the current situation of power" and selecting "the ideological form best suited to push against its configurations" (348). Strategically shifting from one ideology to another requires intimate knowledge of one another's vantage points, as well as flexibility, strength, and grace, in order to form alliances with others—even when individual "readings of power" (348) might be contradictory. Rather than fully give up one's own ideology, participants instrumentally and temporarily assume each other's principles. Sandoval explains, "As the clutch of a car provides the driver the ability to shift gears, differential consciousness permits the practitioner to choose tactical positions, that is, to self-consciously break and reform ties to ideology" (348) in order to work cohesively across differences. Laura Pulido and Juan De Lara (2018) go a step further, drawing on American studies scholar Christina Heatherton's (2012:xvi) notion of "spaces of convergence"—sites where "disparate radical traditions [are] forged into alliance, leading to new models of political mobilization and the subsequent creation of new political theory." Examining convergences of Black and Latinx EJ organizing, Pulido and De Lara (2018:83) argue that radical imaginaries are relational rather than bounded; distinct radical visions actually converge to form "entirely new forms of opposition" through social movement organizing around EJ.

Re-historicizing to Repoliticize the Sustainable City

Mainstream green urbanism discourse tends to gloss over the disparate impacts reified by sustainability paradigms. Urban sustainability storylines suggest that all will automatically benefit from expanded green space, bike lanes, farmers' markets; from reduced carbon emissions and water pollution; and from a taken-for-granted decision-making process. Such discourse also tends to focus on the present and future: never mind how we got here; what is important is that the next chapter leaves the world a better place, and that we aren't too uncomfortable making that happen. It is not that groups such as PHCC are not concerned about the future—on the contrary. Rather, agents of change attempting to work through a racial justice lens realize that it is impossible to ensure a more just way forward without also reconciling the racist, colonial past and present.

Similar to the ways in which radical feminists strategically utilized what may appear to be conflicting ideologies as a means to an end, the process of producing a shared historical narrative and the narrative itself have enabled PHCC members to work together across lines of race, ethnicity, and class to challenge universalizing and ahistorical sustainability discourses. This new historical narrative emerges out of, at the same time as it has helped to create, a space of convergence. The centrality of a *process* of producing history and, in turn, evolving consciousness for PHCC participants contrasts with standard EJ narratives, which often imply a sort of "aha moment" in which sudden cognizance of toxicity prompts people to act (e.g., Gibbs, 2011; McGurty, 2007). Instead of solely engaging in the discovery of facts, PHCC members have worked collaboratively to piece together their own and each other's stories. In the process of learning from one another, participants have gained consciousness about how systems of oppression intersect, which has shaped the group's course of collective action.

That is not to say that internal and external conflicts have never threatened to derail the coalition's work. But PHCC's mode of historically rooted collective learning has opened space for a wide variety of issues to come to the fore, from inhumane treatment of houseless people to access to land and living-wage jobs as reparations for displaced Black residents. Serving as a sort of clutch, PHCC members strategically invoke various historical threads tied to these priorities, and sometimes the coalition's historical narrative in its entirety, at different moments.

PHCC's Production of a Peoples' History of the Harbor

The "peoples' history" outlined in chapter 2 corrects conventional narratives of the river's cleanup. But where did this peoples' history come from, and what ends has it served? Since 2012, PHCC members have convened on a near-monthly basis. In addition, PHCC has hosted hundreds, perhaps thousands, of evening meetings, culturally specific events, panel discussions, festivals, marches, water ceremonies, river walks, strategy sessions, and other happenings. Given that PHCC members speak with such fondness for the river, it is not surprising that it is the basis around which a collective identity has formed for the diverse coalition. But there is labor involved in turning these motivations—which are entangled with participants' personal histories—into a collective identity and commitment to sustained action. Some of the work, or micromobilizations, this process has entailed for PHCC has included icebreakers, production of a short film, and collective testimony writing. Such activities have helped transform individual affinities for the river into a shared, collectively produced history of the harbor that informs political consciousness-raising and collective action.

Member Meeting Icebreakers

Since PHCC's inception in 2012, coalition members have held a meeting nearly every month, almost always on a Thursday evening. Meetings take place in various spaces, including a community center basement, the lobby of a church, and the local Sierra Club chapter office. At most meetings, organizers use PHCC funds raised through grant writing and donations to purchase a meal for all to share: *panuchos* from PHCC member Mañuela's Yucatecan food truck; green curry from the Thai restaurant down the street; pizza delivered from Domino's. Occasionally, the coalition hosts a potluck, in which members bring whatever they are able to contribute. Highlights have included Iraqi food prepared by members of the Iraqi Society of Oregon and smoked salmon caught in nearby waters by Dishaun, PHCC member and founder of a local organization that introduces youth to fishing.

In addition to foods that reflect the heritages of coalition members, members know they can nearly always count on PHCC organizers to facilitate an icebreaker at the beginning of meetings. Common in community organizing and other popular education settings, icebreakers are designed to do just what the name implies: they break the ice by helping people get to know one another, and they prepare participants for whatever topic will be discussed during the meeting. At PHCC gatherings, icebreakers often involve a round of introductions, in which whomever is leading the meeting invites each person to share their name and pronoun and a response to a particular question. Some questions might prompt people to connect the topic of the harbor to their own personal experience: What brought you here tonight? What is your earliest memory of the Willamette? Others provide space for participants to reflect on a recent event: What is one word that comes to mind when you think about the EPA meeting last week? And others open dialogue about participants' hopes and dreams: What is your vision for the future of the Portland Harbor? Sometimes, especially when there are new faces in the room, organizers invite participants to turn to a partner to respond to the prompt. Facilitators then invite people to introduce their partner to the larger group.

Questions such as "What is your earliest memory of the Willamette?" in particular open space for participants to learn about each other's past and present connections to the river. In response to this prompt in May 2014, one participant, originally from Oaxaca, Mexico, where there are no rivers as large as the Willamette, recalled that when she arrived to Portland she felt scared to cross the city's dozen massive bridges. "*El río era tan hermoso, y grande!*"—the river was so beautiful, and big!—she recalled. An interpreter who PHCC hires for nearly all functions translated this—and all— words spoken at the meeting, repeating Spanish phrases in English and English phrases in Spanish.[1] A second participant, who grew up in Portland and had experienced homelessness off and on for the previous ten years, recollected hunting and fishing along the river as a boy. Another person, from a local Indigenous-led group, remembered swimming in the Willamette as early as 1967. A formerly houseless person recalled seeing raw sewage discharging into the river prior to expensive sewer and stormwater infrastructure improvements; she was living outside at the time and felt threatened.

Following this memory-focused icebreaker, the group went on to discuss an expansive array of harbor-related topics. First, the group heard a report back from someone who had attended an EPA meeting, as well as a short "EJ 101" presentation from Alex Lopez, an environmental geologist who had recently begun attending PHCC meetings. Alex suggested that one tactic PHCC might pursue was to demonstrate to EPA officials how harbor contamination disproportionately impacts houseless people, Black and Indigenous folks, and immigrants. One participant, attending his first PHCC meeting that day, responded, "You have the haves and the have-nots. I know what you're talking about!"

The conversation evolved from there, with reports from participants who had recently attended meetings with city officials and union representatives. Then Rose, from PHCC member organization Wisdom of the Elders, gave an update on a potential film project she was pursuing that would give various tribal perspectives on the harbor. "The Nez Perce, from Idaho, are connected historically," she stressed. "Their ancestors came to the Willamette, traveled hundreds of miles. The Yakama, Warm Springs, Siletz: same thing. We want to get this Native perspective visible to the general public." Rose went on to describe another harbor-focused video project, led by Native American Youth and Family Center and Groundwork Portland's "Green Team" youth. The youth would go on to interview several people connected to the coalition and post short videos on PHCC's website.

One attendee then discussed an upcoming Canoe Journey, a tradition in which the urban Native community welcomes and feeds those traveling down the river. The group leading the effort was currently fundraising and making a traditional canoe in preparation, with twenty-five people meeting every other week. Next came brainstorming for a PHCC-led community education event about the harbor pollution and cleanup. "What level of language will it involve? Can any person off the street understand?" one person inquired. Finally, another person gave an update about cleanup of one especially polluted site, Willamette Cove, where dozens of houseless people made their home. Many more questions than answers emerged in response: Who's in charge of Willamette Cove: the state Department of Environmental Quality or the EPA? People are camping and swimming, despite major health concerns and warning signs; what should we do? One person lives on a boat there; maybe they can help monitor pollution with the coalition? Should we plan a protest?

The simple icebreaker focused on personal memories laid a crucial baseline for such disparate topics, from government processes to fundraising, multimedia projects to soil testing, to cohere for this diverse group of people over the course of the meeting. Pedagogy experts refer to introductory activities such as icebreakers as crucial for activating prior knowledge. By triggering thinking along certain lines with the "earliest memories" question, PHCC members became primed to more easily integrate new information and experiences into their understanding than they might have with no warmup. Such icebreaker questions do important relationship-building work as well. PHCC facilitators nearly always arrange chairs in a circle, so that those in attendance sit facing one another. In this way, people are able to more easily *see* each other and *hear* each other. Hearing about early memories helped participants learn very specific details about each other's lives, giving human context for subsequent technical and strategy discussions.

Importantly, PHCC prioritizes paying a trained interpreter for most meetings, so that people who speak different languages are able to learn and work together. Monolingual and bilingual English and Spanish speakers have been the most common attendees, and those who speak Arabic, K'iche', Russian, and Czech have often attended as well. Indigenous people also occasionally introduce themselves or share stories in their native languages, including Diné. In part due to the commitment to translation, but also just because it takes time to hear from each person, it often takes a solid twenty or thirty minutes, and sometimes even longer, to work through PHCC's icebreaker exercises. These are not intended as brief feel-good activities to rush through prior to the "real" meeting; in other words, icebreakers that often tap participants' memories account for a full 25 percent of time spent together in a standard two-hour meeting, making it an important part of the *substance* of the meeting, and of the coalition's shared work.

Reflecting on the kinds of learning that happens at PHCC meetings including through such activities, one participant, a member of Right 2 Survive, describes the impact. He explains that although he has learned much from guest speakers who the coalition sometimes invites to meetings and from the EPA or other public agencies, he has learned the *most* from fellow members: "Other coalition members that came to the PHCC meetings, they've had input, they've attended other meetings as well and bring it to the table at the PHCC meetings. So, it's not as much of what I've learned as much as what all of us learn and bring *together* so we all have a greater understanding of what's going on with the Superfund site and what's going on with the river and the banks, and what DEQ [Department of Environmental Quality and the EPA] is doing about it or not doing about it." This participant emphasized the word "together": that learning happens collectively, from ordinary people coming together from many different walks of life, as opposed to learning from relying on so-called authorities.

Producing a Short Film

PHCC has made learning and dialogue about each other's personal histories more public as well, including in a short film that undergraduate students and I helped produce in 2015. While brainstorming ways to communicate about the Superfund site in coalition members' own words with PHCC members, I suggested that undergraduate students in my upcoming course at Portland State University (PSU) could assist PHCC with creation of some kind of popular education materials. The course was entitled "Justice, Environment, and the City," making PHCC an ideal organization with which to engage. One student in the class was majoring in film. When PHCC members heard this news, people were excited about the possibilities. Together we decided to produce a short film—*A People's View of the Portland Harbor*—that would communicate four things: a brief history of the harbor and Superfund site from PHCC's perspective; a brief overview of the origins, mission, and membership of the coalition; PHCC members' main concerns about the contamination and cleanup process; and PHCC members' hopes for the future (PHCC, 2015). We decided it made the most sense for PHCC members to interview one another, rather than for students to conduct interviews; that way, the sharing and hearing of each other's stories would be built into the filmmaking process itself, in addition to being featured in the final product.

One foggy Saturday morning in spring 2015, thirty PHCC members convened on the banks of the Willamette River, at Cathedral Park, to interview one another for the film. Most people had been attending PHCC functions for some time, while a few new people also showed up. We set up one table with a spread of lunch provisions: sandwich fixings, chips, fruit, chocolate cookies. On another table, we set out markers and butcher paper for younger children to draw. Older children practiced casting in the grass with a hookless fishing rod. Meanwhile, adult participants, and later a few of the older children, brainstormed interview questions and practiced telling their stories. When everyone felt ready, PSU students filmed the interviews. We ensured that everyone who participated was featured in the film, even if it resulted in redundancies.

The end product is a twenty-two-minute, documentary-style film that loosely covers the history outlined in chapter 2, in coalition members' own words. About a dozen interview clips make up most of the film's contents, and Faduma Ali, one of PHCC's community organizers, narrates additional historical details. Visually, the film is composed of footage of interviews, integrated with photos and film clips of people working in the shipyards, fishing in the river, and participating in PHCC functions. Spanish and English subtitles run along the bottom. Acoustic guitar blues riffs, recorded in a single-room-occupancy hotel bathroom by a formerly houseless PHCC member, purr in the background.

Throughout the film, interspersed between clips of interviews, PHCC member Wilma Alcock intermittently reads from poems she wrote about the river and her experience as a child in Portland's Black community during the war years. Wilma articulates connections between her family's move to Portland from Lawrence, Kansas, to work in the shipyards in the 1940s and her community's experiences with workplace racism:

> We are the Black Migration who left a place we knew to descend into a place we didn't know.
> To experience the same, but different.
> To adapt to change, whether weather, or our attitude;
> to blend, and begin again, and not quite blended
> but like whole milk that separated into cream and less bodied full milk.
> However hostile the environment, we endured by the weekend
> with Friday night dancing, and spiritual prancing on Sunday,
> to leave our slights on the floor, enabling us to push onto Monday once more.

> Hard to verbalize our dilemma, but with a grunt and an "umph" and a stare, as we stepped forward to work harder with less reward than the others that were there.

As Wilma speaks, sepia-tone images of segregated neighborhoods from Portland's not-too-distant past flash on the screen. Later in the film, Wilma recalls fishing in the river as a girl, when her parents worked as "chippers," shaving lead paint off of ships in the shipyards. This is the same lead that currently sits at the bottom of the harbor, bioaccumulating in the flesh of catfish, carp, and bass—and in turn in the bodies of those who rely on the river for sustenance.

Wilma's family was one of thousands of Black households segregated in the Albina area and then forced to move to make way for urban renewal projects in the decades that followed. Her community now faces displacement yet again. Wilma reflects, "It's been a gradual taking over. . . . It's very subtle, but once you *really* see the pattern, it's not subtle; it's very planned out." Her father ultimately died of mesothelioma, likely a result of cumulative exposure to contaminants in the shipyards, his neighborhood, and elsewhere. Wilma talks about the violence, suffering, and premature loss of life that her family has endured: "You can't take back someone's life, and it doesn't even come out until the person is dead. My dad was dead by the time they really started saying mesothelioma is caused by asbestos and all of this. And he suffered. . . . It just makes me so angry, because his environment killed him." Wilma's father and thousands of others came to Portland to work in the wartime shipyards. The Boilermakers Union excluded them, industrial corporations motivated by wartime profits exposed them to harsh toxins, and city officials ensured their segregation and serial displacement. Driving home the weight of this history, Wilma talks about the *reparations* that would only begin to redress past and present wrongs: "It's almost like, you know, the slavery thing, where they should pay us. It's almost the same thing. . . . It's not going to happen, but something should happen—they took so much." She also shares fond memories of her family catching fish and frying them up on the beach as a girl. Such remembrances paint a fully human picture, one that honors suffering and joy alike and that makes a strong case for true reparations.

Another person featured multiple times in the film is Roy Pascoe, a mixed Indigenous and white person with roots in Idaho and the Puget Sound area, who had experienced homelessness off and on for decades. In one clip, Roy, gesturing to the harbor a hundred steps behind him, articulates the challenges of living on the riverbanks after being laid off from his job: "We lived on the river for quite a while, and it had its many challenges. The river goes up and down with the weather. We had the rain to battle with, the snow, the police, the parks, our stuff being stolen from us." Later in the film, Roy discusses the direct impacts that depending on the harbor for shelter and sustenance have had on his body: "We [found] out about a year or so ago that the river's completely contaminated. A lot of pesticides, leads, mercuries. . . . I've fished out of these rivers. I've eaten out of these rivers. . . . Once we found out the river was contaminated . . . we found it more complicated. . . . I just recently beat cancer. I don't know that [the cancer] wasn't because of [living along the river]. . . . There are a lot of cancer-causing agents that are in these rivers." A year after filming, however, lung cancer caught up with Roy. He died on May 16, 2016.

The juxtaposition of such stories in the film, from Wilma, Roy, and others, has had multiple impacts. Featured on the coalition website's main landing page, *A People's View* has enabled PHCC to succinctly communicate a harbor history that counters mainstream storylines to the general public. It has also provided a foundation for new coalition members to connect, enabling newcomers to learn the complex past of the harbor from multiple perspectives and more quickly integrate into coalition activities. Crucially, the actual filmmaking project contributed to the "making and re-making" (Rutland, 2013) of participants, through learning each other's stories, helping make editorial decisions, and watching the finished product. PHCC members have watched *A People's View* at least a half dozen times at meetings, especially when new members were in attendance. By highlighting cumulative and intergenerational trauma, the personal histories of Roy, Wilma, and others have helped PHCC members link seemingly isolated incidents to oppressive systems.

One example of how the film has helped members integrate each other's histories into their own understandings of the harbor, at the same time as PHCC introduces a more complete narrative of the harbor's history to outsiders, came in spring 2016. PSU instructors invited PHCC members and me to show the film and connect with local undergraduate students in an interdisciplinary undergraduate course focused on politics, planning, and activism around urban rivers. During discussion afterward, one speaker, a white person who was unhoused at the time, described how he has learned from Indigenous, Black, immigrant, and refugee PHCC members who rely on the river for fish. With the support of an interpreter, another speaker, a Latinx woman who had never experienced homelessness and who was not involved in activism prior to joining PHCC, then eloquently summarized the triple burden of toxic exposure, police violence, and displacement that houseless people living in the harbor face. She also explained how displacement has impacted Portland's Black community for generations, severing physical connections to the harbor but not emotional linkages. Her synthesis of intersecting issues for multiple, overlapping groups served as a powerful demonstration of the type of cross-race, cross-class understanding that has unfolded through the coalition's activities. In turn, the film inspired students in the class, who went on to work on several projects in support of PHCC, including hosting neighborhood meetings and translating materials into Spanish. Three students from the class later participated in PHCC functions for several years, and instructors from the course have since moved on to new universities but still use the Portland Harbor and PHCC as a case study in cross-race, cross-class EJ activism.[2]

The film has contributed to a more complex, collective understanding of how different groups' histories weave together, and of how exposure to toxins, food insecurity, unstable housing, displacement, police violence, and many other issues intersect. Multiple histories co-exist in the film's single narrative, in conversation with one another. By bringing attention to cumulative and intergenerational trauma, these personal histories help link individual stories to oppressive systems. They also form a foundation for the resistance efforts underway, providing a basis for conversations around reparations and more.

Taking Action Based on Stories, Not "Distant Statistics"

The shared historical narratives that have evolved out of meetings, events, informal dialogue, filmmaking projects, and so many other activities help convey a much more complex story of the harbor than do mainstream storylines. PHCC's shared history-making process, together with the content of the coalition's shared narrative, have laid groundwork for the coalition's course of action.

In early 2016, when it became clear that City of Portland officials would not meaningfully engage impacted communities in the harbor planning process without escalated tactics, forty PHCC members and supporters gathered on the front steps of City Hall for a rally and press conference. Afterward, the group took turns directly addressing city officials. A dozen members took turns speaking about their communities' historical and present-day connections to the harbor. Edward Hill, who took over at the helm of Groundwork PDX in spring 2015, summarized PHCC's position for city officials:

> This is . . . about communities not only taking part in the [decision-making] process but also actually becoming a part of the river—becoming again integrated into the river. For African Americans that were here during the war and now are being moved around the city, it's been historically a problem. For

Latino and Chicano populations, who have used the river or been near the river, it's a problem. For First Nations People, for Native Americans who were here originally, not having access to the river has been a problem.

Edward's statement recaps in short form the historical narrative around which the coalition formulated its demands that spring. Bolstered by a local news article empathetic to the coalition's cause (VanderHart, 2016), the coalition's public-facing stance, centered on the complexity of the harbor's history and the ways in which it reverberates today, made an impact. Soon after showing up to City Hall, the City of Portland agreed to release over $65,000 in grant funds to support community organizations' Superfund-related outreach to underrepresented groups. While PHCC's work was far from over, and while the amount of money put forth paled in comparison to both the profits gained on the backs of PHCC members and their ancestors and the cost that a thorough cleanup would require, members considered this a short-term victory.

A few months later, the coalition's official testimony letter submitted to the EPA included a version of PHCC's shared historical narrative of the harbor, which stood in stark contrast to the complex graphs and charts on display at EPA public hearings. A loose team of about ten PHCC members and I were charged with writing the letter. We went through dozens of iterations, reading each out loud at meetings, sharing scribbled notes across coffee shop tables, and tracking changes on a shared Google document. Not surprisingly, the final version tied together the histories of impacted communities: "Many of our people face cumulative and intergenerational impacts from Portland Harbor pollution, and some of these harms are compounding pre-existing harms. Decades and centuries of displacement away from the harbor area also means that impacted communities cannot be easily mapped and tracked—which means that not all impacts can be measured."

In asserting that "not all impacts can be measured," we sought to emphasize that although no studies have directly linked higher cancer rates to the river, the consequences of industrial development on vulnerable communities are nevertheless real. For one thing, PHCC lacked the substantial resources required to mobilize such quantitative data. Moreover, because impacted communities are dispersed across countless zip codes, and because people suffer from cumulative and intergenerational impacts, the coalition could not have simply hired a geographic information system (GIS) expert to map disproportionate impact. But producing a historically rooted narrative and communicating it via public testimony was within the coalition's means. The coalition thus demanded that the EPA make decisions based on historically rooted stories, rather than "distant statistics" (Finney, 2014). Cultural geographer Carolyn Finney explains the power of calling upon stories—memories—in fighting for change: "Memory also constitutes a body of knowledge for the individual, and community memory becomes a way its members claim and own their past, particularly when their narratives are relegated to the margins of social and cultural importance" (132). In foregrounding memories and histories during engagements with public agencies, PHCC's groups gained power.

In addition to PHCC's collaboratively written letter, individual PHCC members submitted letters that drew on personal and collective histories. One person wrote: "I grew up here in second generation family of (extended 79 members in tribe from both parents) Portlanders. Mama, Vi Suart, will become 100 on April 16th 2017, having been born 4/16/1917, making me now 64. . . . We won't let Schnitzer clan or these, any of these, corporations 'off the hook'—they should be prosecuted for criminal activities!!!'" Another wrote: "I am 73 years old and was born and raised in Portland. I have eaten fish from the river for years. I have many health problems and want to know if the water and fish have poison in them." And yet another argued: "The river is more than a symbol of the city. People have lived off of the river for centuries, and the current state of the river is a shame." This is just a small sample of the kinds of historical references that ultimately informed the EPA's official plan for the harbor's cleanup.

PHCC's collective historicized learning over the previous four years proved indispensable for the coalition's ability to articulate grievances and make demands to hold the City of Portland and EPA accountable to marginalized groups during the crucial 2016 public comment period. And because of the foundation built over the years via shared history making, the coalition was prepared to act, both inside and outside of formal public participation channels, when the need and opportunity arose. Foregrounding collectively produced histories during confrontational engagements with public agencies helped PHCC and its members gain ground. In 2017, the EPA released a Record of Decision that doubles the volume of sediment to be dredged from the river compared with earlier plans. While far from perfect, PHCC considered this decision a modest victory. EPA officials publicly stated, to a room of local public agency officials, EPA staffers, polluters' representatives, and community leaders, that public outcry—which was mobilized largely by PHCC, in tandem with conservation and other community groups including Portland Audubon, Willamette Riverkeeper, and the EPA's formal Community Advisory Group—substantially influenced the agency's decision to strengthen the cleanup plan over earlier versions. Regardless of forthcoming fights to maintain PHCC's legitimacy in the eyes of public agencies, the shared history that PHCC members produced in the years leading up to the EPA's public comment period laid crucial groundwork for diverse coalition members to work together in solidarity.

Conclusion

PHCC has embarked on a deliberate process of collectively producing a shared historical narrative. In turn, this new history has played a key role in the formation of political consciousness and as the basis of political action aiming to reshape a paradigmatic green city. This is not merely a story about the *discovery* of facts, but rather the collective *production* of historical facts that correct mainstream narratives—and form a basis for reenvisioning the future. Paulo Freire (1970) asserts, "Dialogue is the encounter between men, mediated by the world, in order to name the world." Linking personal histories to violent planning and policy decisions—sharing personal histories in order to name the world—has helped PHCC members stitch together a critical analysis of class- and race-based environmental injustice, laying a foundation for collective action. While PHCC has not entirely given up on public agencies' willingness to act on members' behalf, the coalition also sometimes operates in a more confrontational, or oppositional, way in its engagements with public agencies, as we will see in the chapters to come. Fundamental to this more conflict-oriented approach has been the politicization of the coalition's members and supporters. The collective production of history has been at the core of this politicization process.

The case of PHCC helps drive home the importance of attending to the microprocesses involved in social movements, in order to avoid fetishizing activist work and taking the hard work of political subject formation for granted; indeed, it is in paying attention to the mundane details of the day-to-day events, such as icebreaker questions at the beginning of meetings, that we can see the ways in which shared historical narratives facilitate collective action for a more just future. While long-term impacts remain to be seen, the case of PHCC sheds light on how a shared history-making process has unfolded to counteract mainstream sustainability narratives that perpetuate a white-washed version of history. It illustrates how a new, collective history has helped stitch people together across difference, contributing to fights for a new, truly green peoples' harbor.

PART II

Challenging the (Green) Growth Machine

White Rock Larkspur
Delphinium leucophaeum
Endangered

CHAPTER 5

Greenwashed Greenwashing

Challenging the Sustainable City's
Classic Growth Machine

As the capacity to generate a profit through industrial activities has waned in recent years, growth machine coalition actors have turned to the arts, the "creative class," and smart, green growth strategies to stimulate development (Gould and Lewis, 2019; Logan and Molotch, 2007; While et al., 2004). Bicycle infrastructure, LEED-certified buildings, urban waterfronts, and other green-themed initiatives entail the "selective incorporation of ecological goals in the greening of urban governance" (While et al., 2004:551). One hallmark of such sustainable city development is depoliticized—"postpolitical"—discourse, used to advance the interests of green-themed developers, sustainability-minded entrepreneurs, and environmentally branded corporations. Urban geographers highlight how sustainability boosters often invoke an Armageddon-like narrative, that all city residents will suffer without environmental improvements and green development, putting sustainability agendas "beyond contestation" (Davidson and Iveson, 2014:545). They define the postpolitical city as one that is governed "'through a stage-managed consensus' . . . whereby certain ends become 'common sense' and disagreement from these ends is depoliticized (i.e. rendered as deviant rather than political)" (544; see also Swyngedouw 2007, 2009; MacLeod, 2011). Cities need immediate action to remediate pollution—not political debating—so-called green city leaders say. Technological solutions emerge as the neutral answer to multipronged challenges, opening space for green-themed initiatives to (temporarily) generate new rounds of capital accumulation with few obstacles.

Postpolitical discourse that renders disagreement with green planning and policy as deviance forecloses space for alternative perspectives and solutions to surface, especially ones that involve a redistribution of resources and power (Swyngedouw, 2007, 2009). For instance, in Harlem, sustainability discourse that appealed to eco-conscious residents and implied a "technocratic, politically neutral approach to solving environmental problems" shut longtime lower-income residents out of the planning process for a new park (Checker, 2011). While stifling dissent is not unique to the green city (McCarthy, 2013), the conceptual "fuzziness" of sustainability discourse imbues it with a particularly powerful tendency to foreclose contestation (Gunder, 2006). In essence, the slipperiness of the concept allows decision-makers to appeal to a wide variety of people, without actually making any real commitments.

Yet, instead of fixating on the postpolitical tendency of sustainability discourse on its own merits, geographer James McCarthy (2013:22) suggests that more attention is needed on the "structural questions about the recurring ways in which capitalist modernity consistently creates and frames environmental 'problems' and 'solutions.'" I propose that, in so doing, we might better understand the *ever-evolving* relationship between liberal, depoliticized discourse (sustainability-themed or otherwise) and the pursuit of profit via urbanization processes.

Given Portland's position as a prototypical green city, we would expect to see sustainability postpolitics alive and well in the harbor. Indeed, for the first few years of the coalition's existence, local officials thoroughly depoliticized the cleanup, even going so far as to fully eschew a public participation process of any sort. Yet, something somewhat unexpected went on to unfold in the Portland Harbor. Rather than *green* growth boosters pushing local government to tailor a cleanup to their development expectations, *classic* growth machine actors have continued to exert a strong influence on public agencies to push forward with a watered-down remediation plan. While government agencies have been the main entities with which PHCC interacts, and although green growth entrepreneurs influence all manner of policies in the city, polluting corporations continue to heavily mediate the harbor cleanup and development process. In other words, while green growth may remain part and parcel of the classic, polluting growth machine, the *discourse* differs in ostensible sustainable cities—with implications for grassroots groups' strategies for pushing back. Classic growth machine actors make no pretense to being equitable, whereas green development actors purport to having people's (and the planet's) interests in mind. As a result of the way in which City of Portland officials portrayed the cleanup, implicitly using postpolitical sustainability discourse, at first PHCC thought it was up against mainly green-branded actors and pursued a strategy of trying to get environmentalists and sustainable development boosters to become more EJ focused. But as things unfolded, it became clear it wasn't just sustainability boosters that PHCC needed to look out for; polluters were even more of a force with which to be reckoned.

By early 2017, PHCC realized one main mechanism by which polluters influenced city officials. A series of lawsuits filed on behalf of polluters appears to have dampened any impulse the city may have had to engage residents around the harbor cleanup. I therefore argue that despite sustainability's neutralized discourse perpetuated by green growth actors, it is imperative that those concerned with bringing about a more *just* sustainability not overlook the classic growth machine politics that continue to drive uneven development processes—even in paradigmatic sustainable cities, such as Portland.

By first examining the relationship between sustainability discourse and growth regimes (green, greenwashed, or otherwise) in broader historical context, it is then possible to sharpen analysis of where current urban growth regimes might be vulnerable to challenges from below. After all, sustainability fixes, like other attempts to avert crisis, are tenuous, prone to fracturing (Hackworth, 2007; Harvey, 1989; While et al., 2004; see also Long, 2014; Temenos and McCann, 2012). And as with other kinds of fixes, a green development approach is "capable of holding for a time, though not necessarily resolving" (While et al., 2004:551) tensions arising between profit-seekers and labor, property owners and tenants, economic growth proponents and environmental and social justice activists. Examining PHCC's experience engaging with public agencies opens space to interrogate the (green) growth machine operating in the Portland Harbor from the vantage of those fighting for a more just cleanup, to see where cracks may be wedged open toward more just ends. The case of PHCC can serve as a cautionary tale for similar groups working in other cities, helping grassroots organizations understand the behind-the-scenes actors attempting to undermine social and EJ advances in green cities.

In this chapter, I first describe some of the coalition's interactions with City of Portland officials, highlighting the process that triggered PHCC members to lose faith in the city's willingness and ability to meaningfully engage residents. In so doing, I uplift the role that ordinary people, politicized in part through the cross-race, cross-class historical learning process described in earlier chapters, play in holding government agencies accountable to those who have carried the burdens of pollution and are least likely to benefit from urban greening. I then focus on a series of lawsuits filed on behalf of polluters, which likely exerted much pressure on the city to eschew a robust public participation process. The chapter ends with a discussion of what the case of PHCC reveals about sustainability postpolitics: whereas a depoliticized process has indeed unfolded in the Portland Harbor, traditional industry remains just as much behind this postpolitical state of affairs as newly emerging green boosters. It is crucial, therefore, that groups such as PHCC, and their allies within local government, are attuned to inequities pushed by classic growth *and* sustainable development actors alike.

From "Portland Nice" to Oppositional

During the time between the harbor's listing as a Superfund site in December 2000 and the EPA's release of the *Proposed Plan* in 2015, City of Portland officials did little to meaningfully engage impacted communities—or any residents, really—in the cleanup planning process. The coalition spent considerable energy attempting to push city officials to institute a public participation process that would recognize PHCC's members and account for their needs in the cleanup from 2012 to 2015. In late 2015, the city at first seemed prepared to finally support PHCC's work engaging underrepresented communities. But by winter 2016, it became apparent to coalition leaders that dissemination of a public opinion poll would be the city's main form of public engagement around the Superfund cleanup—a clear indicator of the city's tokenizing treatment of marginalized groups in these years, and a sign of depoliticized sustainability discourse, more broadly. PHCC therefore shifted from pursuing change through mainstream participatory channels to taking a more oppositional stance, launching a "name, blame, and shame" campaign that called the City of Portland out for violating civil rights laws. The coalition submitted a letter to the city alleging infringement on the rights of those least likely to benefit from a status quo cleanup and showed up en masse at City Hall, demanding that officials do more to authentically involve the public and especially underrepresented groups. PHCC's shift to taking a more explicitly confrontational approach resulted in the City of Portland allocating resources that helped support the coalition's work through the EPA's public comment period. While the longer-term outcomes of this strategy remain to be seen, in the short term, the coalition gained recognition and resources that enabled more sustained engagement with the EPA at the regional scale.

Bob Sallinger from Portland Audubon offers critical historical context within which PHCC emerged and fought for a more just cleanup in the mid-2010s. In the 1990s and early 2000s, he explains in written correspondence in 2021–2022, the city's approach was dominated by business interests on the river. They excluded not only frontline communities but the community in general. In part, this dynamic was shaped by Oregon's land use policies (especially Goal 9), which prioritize that cities maintain a twenty-year supply of industrial land over other goals such as environmental protection. The land base that is zoned industrial in Portland is aggressively guarded by industrial developers, business interests, the Port of Portland, and many labor groups. Bob also notes that many groups avoided industrial land-related battles over the years, either because they did not see the value in these lands ("it is an industrial wasteland") or because they "did not want to get crosswise with power elites or . . . to be seen as against jobs and growth." He continues: "I cannot tell you how often I was told by politicians and NGOs, including social justice NGOs, that the North Reach [of the Willamette] was not a battle they wanted to fight because they were afraid of being painted as anti-job. I think that stifled progress for a very long time. There are many institutional, legal, social, and political barriers that have been put in place over decades to exclude that public from being real participants in the evolution of Portland Harbor."

Early Communications: A "Tricky Situation"

From the coalition's inception, PHCC leaders were well aware that the EPA's Record of Decision (ROD) would ultimately dictate the terms of the cleanup from an ecological standpoint. The ROD was the document the EPA would produce following an official public comment period focused on the *Proposed Plan*. Submitting comments or giving testimony on the *Proposed Plan* was the main sanctioned way the public could sway the harbor's future. PHCC leaders also assumed that the City of Portland's official position on the cleanup would likely influence the EPA's course of action to some extent. Additionally, it became clear that the city and other local agencies, rather than the EPA, had jurisdiction over what would happen along the waterfront *following* remediation. Starting in 2013, coalition leaders were therefore in touch with city officials, pushing them to begin a public involvement process. In particular, PHCC leaders hoped that the city would provide some funds for the coalition to conduct outreach, to complement the city's community engagement work. This approach would simultaneously support PHCC's efforts and help the city meet its own public involvement obligations, mandated by both federal Title VI statutes and the city's own policies. The EPA would accept written, oral, or video testimony submitted via email, online portal, postal mail, or in person at formal public hearings. To ensure that all people can meaningfully participate in this process, the EPA and any entity receiving federal funding, including the City of Portland, are governed by Section 601 of Title VI of the 1964 Civil Rights Act. This statute states: "No person in the United States shall, on the ground of race, color, or national origin, be excluded from participation in, be denied the benefits of, or be subjected to discrimination under any program or activity receiving Federal financial assistance" (U.S. Department of Justice, n.d.). Furthermore, EPA's Section 602 regulations prohibit activities "which have the effect of subjecting individuals to discrimination." In other words, it is the outcome of the participation process—not simply the intent—that matters.

At first, coalition leaders met with city staff in what was then the Office of Healthy Working Rivers (OHWR). Since OHWR was under the purview of the mayor, PHCC leaders and members also periodically met with staff in Mayor Sam Adams's office and, later, the office of Mayor Charlie Hales. When responsibility for the cleanup changed hands yet again, this time shifting to the Bureau of Environmental Services (BES), PHCC representatives met with the commissioner, the late Nick Fish, and his staff.[1] Cassie Cohen, PHCC's cofounder, recalls in a 2016 conversation:

> From the beginning, we were always asking: "Has the City sent something out? Any updates? How are you [the city] letting people know what's going on, or asking for input?" This went on for years. "This is a huge decision about a critical element that everyone should have access to—the river—but people are in the dark about it. Why the void in communication?" It kept going. Two years out from when they said the comment period would happen— the end goal—still nothing. Oh my god. One year out? Nothing. Six months? Still nothing.

In addition to the City of Portland's own public involvement policies, three other important reference points factored into PHCC leaders' assumptions that the city would conduct (or at least contract with another entity to lead) a robust public involvement campaign that solicited input from underrepresented communities. The first was a report commissioned by the OHWR, which detailed economic outcomes from different cleanup scenarios. "We continually reminded them [city officials] of research conducted by EcoNorthwest on the positive economic development impacts that a thorough cleanup would result in," one coalition representative remembers. PHCC leaders assumed this was the kind of win-win that city leaders often sought in politically fraught circumstances. Second, since PHCC's cofounder, Cassie, had worked for the city and had served on the city's Public Involvement Advisory Council from approximately 2008 to 2011, she was familiar with the City of Portland's public engagement obligations and its growing capacity to design and conduct outreach in a way that meaningfully involved vulnerable groups. "I helped write the rules for how each bureau should be tracking public involvement," Cassie explains. She expected the city to follow those rules. Finally, PHCC participants were aware of the city's track record in catering to green development interest groups and figured the Superfund cleanup would follow past trends. Taken together, these factors indicated to coalition members that the City of Portland would advocate for a thorough cleanup and would engage its residents in a good-faith effort to ensure this outcome. PHCC leaders further reasoned that although it might likely require a fight to gain traction, the coalition's concerns for jobs, housing, and other issues could surface through the city's public involvement process.

Starting in 2012, coalition representatives conveyed to city officials that the coalition was prepared to assist the city with outreach, especially by leading communications with underrepresented groups. Elected officials and their staff members indicated eagerness to work with PHCC, in due time. By 2014, however, city officials began reminding PHCC representatives that, as a potentially responsible party, the City of Portland was on the hook to help pay for the Superfund cleanup. Discussions insinuated that the city was leery of anything that might increase its liability to pay for remediation. When pressed by PHCC representatives, officials acknowledged that, as a public agency, the city had a responsibility to keep its residents informed. Nevertheless, they continually emphasized that this dual role put the city in a "tricky situation," implying that they were in no hurry to conduct public outreach. PHCC leaders maintained the perspective that the city was responsible for engaging its residents in the cleanup process and held out hope that it would eventually happen. Cassie recalls that at some point the coalition learned about how BES— the same bureau of staff working on the Superfund—had been doing outreach to fisher people eating contaminated fish from the Columbia Slough, a tributary to the Willamette, in large part due to pressure from Willamette Riverkeeper, an environmental organization. "BES had robust outreach materials and surveys and engagement of people around the fish there," Cassie remembers, "but nothing to show for the Portland Harbor. At some point that came into our consciousness, and we were like, 'What the hell?'"

Yet after years of inaction, in June 2015, conversations with city finally became somewhat more concrete. Commissioner Fish's office encouraged PHCC to submit a memo outlining the coalition's plan to continue engaging frontline communities around the cleanup, as well as a budget requesting funds from the city to carry out the work. His office also indicated that the city would be especially keen to see what sorts of community economic development ideas PHCC might propose. City staff further suggested that the commissioner might be willing to help sponsor community events, such as the upcoming Willamette River Revival Festival that PHCC was co-organizing with the EPA's officially appointed Portland Harbor Community Advisory Group.

PHCC leaders got the message: couching PHCC's request for city funding in terms of workforce development and community celebrations would be the most likely route to garnering monetary support for the coalition. PHCC leaders submitted a memo to Commissioner Fish, as requested. In addition to outlining components of a workforce development plan, communications explicitly referenced the city's Title VI civil rights responsibilities: "PHCC views City support of green jobs development and training as one substantial way that the public sector can steward not just . . . Portland's environment, but also its people. Support of PHCC's efforts will also assist the City with meeting its federal Title VI obligations related to the Superfund Site, ensuring that marginalized groups have an opportunity to meaningfully participate, influence, and benefit from cleanup" (copy of PHCC memo shared with author).

But the memo had little immediate impact. A city staffer called PHCC representatives in the first week of July, encouraging them to check back again in six to nine months. In the eyes of PHCC members, the city was yet again evading its public involvement responsibilities.

Back in 2012, the EPA had announced that it would release the Record of Decision in 2014 (Profita, 2014). Delays pushed the timeline back several times. Nevertheless, by early summer 2015, less than a year away from what would ultimately become the official public comment period, PHCC leaders and members found it unacceptable that the city had *still* done no outreach. They worried that the city and the EPA would hear Portland's (green) growth boosters loud and clear during the comment period, and that these voices would muffle those demanding an environmentally friendly cleanup, and especially one that also considered important social and EJ issues.

At this point, in early summer 2015, PHCC's future was unclear. The coalition's funding had run out. There was no money to continue paying an organizer's salary. No resources for childcare or bus tickets for people to attend coalition meetings. No funds for printing or other basic costs. GWPDX, the organization that had stewarded PHCC and served as its fiscal sponsor from its inception, was also out of funds. Four PHCC leaders' families welcomed new babies into the world that year, and organizers had less capacity than before. One key PHCC leader was facing a no-cause eviction, and another was battling stage-four lung cancer. Houseless-led PHCC member group Right 2 Survive was devoting significant attention to negotiating a city-mandated relocation of Right 2 Dream Too, the unsanctioned rest area the group ran for unhoused downtown residents, as well as continuing to battle the city's relentless sweeps of houseless people from the city's inner-core neighborhoods and surrounding green spaces. More generally, PHCC member groups were totally overwhelmed by a housing crisis that was making it nearly impossible for working-class and even middle-class households to afford rent in Portland; BIPOC communities, whose members made up the majority of PHCC's constituents, were particularly hard hit. It is no surprise, then, that the coalition lost momentum.

While PHCC's activities slowed way down, the city continued to operate on its own timeline and according to its own priorities. In August 2015, Commissioner Fish's office invited PHCC leaders to a meeting. The commissioner explained that the city had finally changed course in terms of its decision to conduct a public engagement campaign around the cleanup. He explained the shift this way: with Michael Jordan now at the helm, BES had a new and "very competent" leader. Furthermore, a "ratepayer scandal" surrounding the city's provisions of sewage and water utilities had died down, taking pressure off BES. It was now time for BES to strengthen partnerships and "support equity," the commissioner explained. Commissioner Fish asked what economic development, employment, and other brownfield-related opportunities PHCC foresaw. PHCC representatives conveyed the coalition's overlapping concerns about jobs, job training, housing, the city and EPA community engagement processes, and more. Anything related to food, health, and sustainability had his deep commitment, Commissioner Fish stressed. The meeting concluded with enthusiastic but loose conversation about solidifying points of contact with BES, figuring out a communication plan, and including a range of voices in the planning process.

Following the meeting with Commissioner Fish, I huddled with fellow PHCC representatives in City Hall's lobby. Although the conversation seemed to indicate a substantial shift in the city's willingness to take responsibility for funding public engagement, several points remained unclear. We agreed that the commissioner seemed to be feeling us out, trying to figure out where PHCC stood in terms of shifting the burden of cleanup costs to ratepayers, in particular. In mentioning the "ratepayer scandal," Commissioner Fish appeared anxious that the city might be expected to pick up more than its fair share of the cleanup tab, and that the city might even be sued for unlawfully charging residents for something not directly related to providing sewer and water services.

In 2011, the late former city commissioner Lloyd Anderson led ratepayers in a lawsuit against the city alleging that officials had used water and sewer funds for inappropriate expenditures, including park construction and Hurricane Katrina assistance. At issue was that ratepayer dollars paid directly to the Water Bureau and Bureau of Environmental Services can only be used for the operation of those bureaus—not the city's general operations, which are funded by property and business taxes. For more than four years, the battle waged on in the courts.

Did officials worry that more public involvement would somehow increase the city's financial liability? On this point, PHCC members were clear: residents—and therefore the city—should not pick up more than their fair share of the tab. "The polluters should pay to clean up the mess," flatly stated one PHCC member in a follow-up discussion. Little did we know at the time, but this was just one small piece of the ratepayer lawsuit story, to which I will return shortly. And yet, PHCC maintained that the city still needed to engage residents and especially impacted communities.

As we talked in the City Hall lobby, I sat down on the heavy wooden bench and fanned my face with my notebook. I was nearly nine months pregnant, and taking the bus all over the city to attend PHCC-related meetings during the hottest summer on record in the Pacific Northwest was taking its toll. I apologized for not contributing more during the meeting, particularly in helping set concrete next steps before the meeting concluded. We were all exhausted. Nevertheless, we agreed that this was a "sure opening" to secure some funding from the city for PHCC to continue to facilitate impacted communities' collective action, while simultaneously holding the city accountable for its public outreach obligations—regardless of whether we agreed with the commissioner's rationale for turning to public engagement so late in the planning process. It seemed that the commissioner's decision to finally conduct public outreach at this juncture hinged entirely on a political calculation. He was still worried about the ratepayer scandal and would justify doing or not doing public outreach based on what was politically expedient. But given the precariousness of PHCC at the time, we did not feel that we were in a position to question motives. We laid out our plan: within thirty days, the coalition would prepare an updated proposal outlining priority areas for PHCC, as well as a revised budget, ready to send to BES.

In retrospect, given that officials never made any concrete promises, we should not have been so confident that the city's support would be forthcoming, and also we should have anticipated the strings that would come with public funding. Additionally, we should have been more conservative in estimating our own abilities to maintain open communication with BES through the fall, much less sustain consistent contact with coalition members, given that so many people within the coalition were spread very thin at the time. In fact, from June through November 2015, no general PHCC member meetings took place. This lull points to the fragility of what organizers had begun in earnest in 2012 and sustained for over three years. It also points to the importance of paying attention to the *agents* of change involved in particular campaigns and movements, rather than only to structural components. In the Portland Harbor, ordinary people working together have been the unequivocal factor in interrupting the inertia of an otherwise status quo cleanup planning process, largely influenced by polluters.

The City's Survey: "Positive and/or Negative Impacts on Jobs"

Nevertheless, a few decisive events transpired in fall 2015. Perhaps things played out as they did in large part *because* the coalition momentarily lost cohesiveness; without organized outside pressure, the city's decisions went unchallenged. In a series of communications between PHCC leaders and the City of Portland and its contractors, city officials explained that they were contracting with Oregon Kitchen Table, a program of Portland State University's National Policy Consensus Center (NPCC), to design and carry out a public engagement process around the Superfund cleanup. Then, in November, PHCC received two emails, one from the City of Portland's Bureau of Environmental Services and one from the NPCC, identifying a PHCC leader as a stakeholder in the Superfund cleanup process and asking if he was interested in being interviewed "to explore a possible community engagement process around the EPA's preferred alternative cleanup plan for the Portland Harbor Superfund Site." Beyond these cursory communications, nearly all other developments that fall happened behind closed doors, without any input by or knowledge of frontline communities.

Then, in an email sent on January 12, 2016, Commissioner Fish officially invited PHCC to participate in a survey design process. The commissioner explained that the city aimed to "understand the community's perspective about tradeoffs in the proposed cleanup plan, and about Portlanders' top priorities for the cleanup." He continued, "We'll use a survey to do that, and what we learn through the survey will inform our official comments to the EPA." Commissioner Fish concluded:

> We have a limited timeframe to gather input, but we believe this is an important opportunity for Portlanders to participate in helping the City respond to EPA's proposed plan. We also hope our survey will help get the word out about EPA's process, so that more people understand how to weigh in on their own. . . . Because it is so vital to hear from a broad diversity of community members, [our contractor] will be contacting you separately to discuss the possibility of a contract to help with outreach and organizing efforts.

Despite PHCC's efforts to push the outreach conversation for years, the City of

Portland once again dismissed its own public involvement policies, turning to what would essentially amount to a public opinion poll to simultaneously educate residents and solicit input on the largest environmental cleanup undertaken in the city's history. Commissioner Fish's invitation implicitly communicated the city's perspective that not only would the survey suffice for engaging the public at large, but that it would be adequate for engaging those most impacted, namely EJ communities that had suffered from the effects of harbor pollution for generations.

At this point, PHCC members began to reengage with the coalition. Newborn babies were now at least a few months old, and collectively people had slightly more capacity. In particular, Cassie felt that she could not remain silent, even though she was no longer at the helm of GWPDX and had stepped back from PHCC to care for her daughter. Cassie caught that the commissioner seemed to acknowledge the limits of the survey in his email, noting the "limited timeframe." Given that the city knew that disparately impacted communities existed—but had largely ignored them, all the while engaging with polluters—Commissioner Fish's reference seemed especially egregious. For the first time in nearly a year, Cassie interjected in the conversation with city officials and their contractors working on the survey. Cassie noted that the survey's only job-related item implied that a thorough cleanup would have a *negative* impact on jobs. On February 7, 2016, she emailed the city's contractor:

> Jobs training/cleanup jobs attached to the Superfund site cleanup . . . is separate and unique from the issue of preserving existing Portland Harbor jobs. The City conducted an economic development report a few years ago, under the guidance of Ann Beier—Director of the Office of Healthy Working Rivers, that indicated the potential for greater job growth in correlation to a robust Portland Harbor cleanup, but this report was not well received by PRPs at the time, so it did not get publicized nor utilized. But it is a [sic] risky to insinuate to the public (whether intentional or not) that a robust cleanup will result in overall job loss. I am afraid leaving the questions as is will not give the public any choice to imagine the potential for a substantial increase of environmental cleanup jobs. Groundwork Portland as the lead, with the Portland Harbor Community Coalition already gave feedback to EPA 2 years ago that one high priority of community groups is to have EPA's Superfund Jobs Training for the Portland Harbor cleanup.

But Cassie's concerns fell on deaf ears. Despite her email taking issue with the framing of workforce development, the only reference to jobs in the final version of the survey sent out to tens of thousands of city residents was a Likert scale statement, which said, "It is important to me that the cleanup plan considers potential positive and/or negative impacts on jobs." What, exactly, would marking "strongly agree" on this statement indicate? A concern for the cleanup plan's impact on existing industrial jobs? Impact on future cleanup jobs? It was impossible for survey takers to know what was meant by this statement, and equally impossible for survey analysts to know to interpret responses. The survey was yet another example of failed public outreach.

Despite the scope and complexity of the cleanup, the city had marched forward with its survey-as-sole-public-outreach undertaking on the eve of the public comment period, leaving little time to follow up with other forms of engagement. In essence, the city's outreach process landed squarely on the "degrees of tokenism" rung of the classic ladder of public participation made famous by Sherry Arnstein (1969). It vacillated somewhere between "informing" and "placating" activity levels. And despite clear EJ implications, which obligate extra care in public participation processes, the City of Portland had done little to authentically engage frontline communities. In lieu of an actual public education campaign about the cleanup process, the city's survey contained three pages of background text—far too much to expect the average person to read prior to answering questions, yet far too little to actually prepare the average person to engage in such a complex issue. In addition to the poorly worded jobs question, the survey contained other misleading and confusing lines. Questions in the online version of the survey were not numbered, contained typos, and included undefined words that were likely incomprehensible to many Portlanders, such as "aggregated" and "sediment." According to one local organization leader, the Vietnamese translation was wholly unintelligible.

Despite the lull in PHCC's activities through summer and fall 2015, the coalition's flame had not fully extinguished. With several coalition member groups taking note of the impending comment period, PHCC members met in December, and again in January, to revitalize planning for outreach to impacted communities and to strategize about how to engage with the city. The City of Portland's tokenizing treatment of impacted communities, exemplified by the poorly designed survey, precipitated a clear shift for the coalition. The survey unequivocally symbolized a cleanup planning process that benefited polluters while ignoring the perspectives of those most impacted. PHCC leaders and members felt that Portland residents—and particularly those from frontline communities—deserved far more than what amounted to a poorly designed public opinion poll. The coalition had interacted in good faith with the city since 2012. PHCC members presumed that city officials would engage residents in a meaningful way in due time, in return. The survey, however, emerged as proof that this would not happen prior to the public comment period. But for the coalition to continue to engage residents, essentially doing for free what the city was legally obligated to do on its own or via a contract with a group such as PHCC, it would need resources.[2]

Taking a Stand: "We Want a Clean River instead of a Cheap Cleanup"

PHCC began to convene in full force around the matter of the survey in February and March 2016. The coalition launched a "name-blame-shame" campaign against the city. This tactic was designed to expose egregious behavior and push perpetrators to make amends. Coalition members consulted the City of Portland's Title VI Civil Rights policy, "designed to remove barriers and conditions that prevent underserved groups from accessing programs and services" (City of Portland, 2013), to gauge possible recourse. I had learned about the policy while attending a city-sponsored housing forum earlier that year and shared it with PHCC members. From PHCC's perspective, the city was *erecting* barriers for underrepresented groups rather than taking them down. Other passages from Portland's Title VI policy bolstered PHCC's position: "Historically excluded individuals and groups [should be] included authentically in processes, activities, and decision-making. Impacts, including costs and benefits, [should be] identified and distributed fairly" (City of Portland, 2013). Despite communicating with officials for years about the need for outreach to underrepresented groups, the City of Portland had done virtually nothing to "authentically" include "historically excluded individuals and groups" in decision-making related to the Superfund cleanup.

At an event hosted by PHCC member organization Líderes Verdes in March 2016, the first concrete steps of PHCC's campaign against the city took shape. Líderes Verdes members organized a dinner at the Sugar Shack to introduce community members, many of whom had recently emigrated from the Yucatán and elsewhere in Mexico, to the Superfund cleanup. A handful of neighborhood-based community organizations had recently purchased the former strip club and had begun turning it into a hub of activity for nearby residents. The chipped black-and-white tiled walls and stained red carpet had yet to be replaced, but the setting worked perfectly for PHCC's purposes that evening. Right 2 Survive members also attended the event in solidarity, as did a handful of people not affiliated with any particular organization, but who had heard about the event via PHCC's email announcement.

That night, everyone munched on *panuchos,* a mini tostada-like dish from the Yucatan Peninsula, while watching the film that PHCC had produced the previous year. The film featured the voices of over a dozen PHCC members, including several Líderes Verdes participants. Children shrieked as they ran and played in the next room. After the film, Líderes Verdes participants, who had learned how to give public testimony at a PHCC meeting the previous month, shared their testimonies as examples for others in attendance. The first speaker stood at the microphone:

> The sand, the water, and the fish are contaminated with industrial pollutants, which increases the possibilities of cancer and problems in development. I am really concerned about the state of the contaminants and toxins in the water. My family is directly exposed to that and the possibilities of getting sick from eating the fish. Or even if the kids are just playing in the sand or accidentally swallow some of the water. As a mother and a resident of this area near the Willamette River, I would like a cleaner environment for our children and for the coming generations also. So I would like to request from the EPA . . . the highest level of cleaning for the Willamette River because we have a right to enjoy the river, and we have a right to enjoy that river free of contaminants that directly affect our health.

Another Líderes Verdes member followed, sharing her own testimony:

> I'm concerned about the people who are unaware about the contamination in the river, and that they are concerning fish. My family likes very much to go fishing, and now that I understand that the river is polluted, I'm very scared to take them to the river. I will beg of the EPA to take into account our worries. It is not just people who eat the fish, it is other animals and birds.

The idea was that these two brave speakers would inspire others in attendance to summon their own stories that evening and to submit them to the EPA via written comment card or video. Líderes Verdes members facilitated conversations in small groups, passing out comment cards and moving off to the side to film one another using cell phone cameras.

During the discussion and testimony writing time, Steve Goldstein, a long-time PHCC supporter, wandered over. Steve had been involved with PHCC from time to time over the last few years, although somewhat less so in 2015 on account of his wife's health challenges. Given Steve's five decades working as a white community organizer with poor Black and white communities in Louisiana, North Carolina, and other places in the South, both during and following the civil rights movement era, as well as having trained at the Highlander Folk School off and on from 1969 to 1973, he brought an invaluable perspective to the coalition.[3] Steve was now serving as a volunteer with the Sierra Club, helping the organization follow through on commitments to bolster EJ movements; his main responsibility in this role was to support PHCC.

Steve asked how things were going. I summarized the survey situation and casually mentioned shared concerns about the city's serious violation of its Title VI responsibilities. "Not that the city doesn't violate people's civil rights all the time—just look at Fair Housing law violations," I lamented. Steve ignored my pessimism, declaring: "This is the way to quintuple the funding! I love it when someone lets their bare ass hang out. To me it's like Christmas." I looked at him quizzically. Steve went on, explaining his thinking: "What's needed is to shame them [the City of Portland] for their shameful conduct that's created an opening for people to demand that they do something significant instead of pretend. . . . As a community organizing tactic, how do we flame that embarrassment to provide resources for education, and to collect testimony?" Steve broke it down for me, humbling—yet validating—PHCC's work: "Look, we have this pitiful effort, which is magnificent in its self-sufficiency and its grassroots-ness. But it's not likely to produce a significant amount of testimony [to force changes]. This is a chance. . . . Is somebody willing to spearhead this and go to *Willamette Week* and go on TV, and write a letter to the *Oregonian*? And—preferably [with] an organization behind them—just have some fun, kick some ass?" I pondered Steve's question.

At that moment, Cassie and a few Right 2 Survive members also came over. Others in the room continued to chat among themselves at small tables, practicing their testimonies. We filled in a few more people on the conversation. This was an important moment, in more than one respect. Steve quickly convinced us to think seriously about ramping up action, although we agreed that a final decision about next steps needed to come from coalition members more broadly. We decided to convene an emergency meeting the next day.

As we compared calendars, an attendee of the Líderes Verdes event who had not previously participated in other Superfund-related activities stood up to share his testimony: "I am here to say that any child going to the river now experiences the river as dangerous to their health. This must be rectified for life's sake. The life of humans, the birds, the fish, the plants. Without clean water, and clean fish, we are not going to be healthy people. There are no boundaries between the river and its banks, the river and the air. The birds do not know to not eat the fish or die in a safe place so as not to pollute where they lay down." This newly engaged participant emphasized the necessity for action—"This must be rectified for life's sake"—and summarized the way that many PHCC members had come to understand the high stakes of the cleanup. It was becoming startlingly clear that, without more drastic measures, public agencies would do little to take PHCC constituents seriously. Several of us agreed to meet the next day. I shoved Kai's blanket into my backpack, grabbed a few *panuchos* for the road, hugged a half-dozen PHCC members who had by now become friends, and went out into the cold, dark night. Kai fell asleep against my chest before we got to the Killingsworth Street bus stop, half a block away.

The next day, a handful of us got together to plan our next steps. The day after, an even bigger group—over a dozen people, including representatives from Right 2 Survive, Líderes Verdes, GWPDX, the Portland Harbor Community Advisory Group, Sierra Club, and Columbia Riverkeeper—met again, at Floyd's Coffee Shop in Old Town. Just a hundred steps or so from the Willamette River and two blocks away from Right 2 Survive's self-run houseless rest area, Floyd's became unofficial headquarters for PHCC's organizing that spring.

There was a buzz of excitement at the meeting. Participants took turns laying out the situation as we understood it: on the eve of the public comment period, the city had yet to conduct any public outreach beyond the meager survey. And through its contractor, Oregon Kitchen Table, city officials were now offering $7,500 to PHCC in exchange for helping to disseminate the survey. Steve summed up the possibilities of the moment for those of us crowded around the table at Floyd's:

> We're at that point where everyone is busy, we're at a point of poverty in time, energy, and resources, yet it's crunch time. EPA says we'd be fine with eating eight ounces of fish a month, and yet people are not fishing for sport. They're fishing for supper. It's a big deal, but the people that have to pay for it want to do it on the cheap. . . . It's up to us to step up—we want a clean river instead of a cheap cleanup. Does anyone have any ideas of where to find the time, energy, people to keep things moving forward?

Someone answered Steve's question: "Call the city out on their bullshit and get them to finally do the right thing and support us!" After much discussion, the group came up with a plan. Despite serious flaws with the city's survey, coalition members would distribute it in exchange for $7,500 from BES, routed through Oregon Kitchen Table. PHCC members justified accepting funds for what was widely deemed a totally inadequate survey by committing to using it as a political education tool. PHCC members would sponsor more meetings and events to help impacted communities prepare for the comment period, like the Líderes Verdes event. Attendees would receive a link to the city's survey in the process—and would also learn about the egregiousness of the city's (in)actions. Additionally, at these events coalition members and leaders would help people develop testimony in preparation for the EPA's public comment period.

The $7,500 only scratched the surface of the resources needed to fully mobilize sufficient numbers during the comment period, however. We had heard that a few thousand people had turned out to testify about the Duwamish River Superfund Site in Seattle; we knew we would need at least that many, but likely more. Short on money and time, but realizing this was a political moment upon which the coalition could capitalize, PHCC decided to take our most conflict-oriented measures to date in engagements with the City of Portland.

On April 7, 2016, the coalition sent a letter to city commissioners and the director of the Bureau of Environmental Services. The opening paragraph communicated the coalition's main issue with the city: "Despite a legal and ethical mandate, the City of Portland has failed to conduct meaningful public engagement with underrepresented groups around the Superfund Site cleanup/redevelopment. Without directly engaging those most impacted, it is unlikely that these groups will benefit from cleanup/redevelopment." The letter went on to explain how Northwest Indigenous peoples "have inhabited lands along the Willamette River since time immemorial. . . . Native people were able to sustain their villages and trade with other tribes in large part due to the salmon, lamprey/eel, and other species that traveled in abundance through the river." It also articulated the historical relationship of Black residents to the harbor, as well as immigrants and refugees and houseless people of various backgrounds—PHCC's main constituents. The letter concluded with a series of demands, including funds for outreach to underrepresented groups.

The day after sending the letter, about forty PHCC members and supporters representing Indigenous, Black, immigrant, refugee, houseless, tenants' rights, labor, and environmental groups gathered on the front steps of City Hall for a rally and press conference. Attendees held a variety of signs depicting PHCC's demands. One featured a colorful drawing of a salmon, its eye crossed out with a bold black X. Following the rally, twenty PHCC delegates crowded into Commissioner Fish's meeting room and took turns addressing city officials. Steve summarized the spectacle and the group's impact: "We spoke twenty different languages, babies and children climbed on the tables, and some people hadn't showered since last Christmas. We scared them." The critical mass, bolstered by local news articles empathetic to the coalition's cause (e.g., VanderHart, 2016), made an impact. Within a week, the city's Bureau of Environmental Services released over $60,000 in grant funds for community organizations planning to conduct Superfund-related outreach to underrepresented groups.

While this represented a clear short-term victory for PHCC, the city's grant-making process was far from ideal. Instead of allowing PHCC to receive the entire amount in one lump sum, individual coalition member groups could apply for a maximum of $5,000 each. City staff said this would make it possible to disburse the money immediately rather than waiting for bureaucratic channels to funnel it through to the coalition, a process that could take months. While better than nothing, this approach forced PHCC to scramble to find fiscal sponsors for some groups, open separate bank accounts, and take other time-consuming steps to ensure that the coalition's collective spirit held steady. Some of the money ended up going to groups that PHCC felt were not actually working with underrepresented groups. Nevertheless, the funds bolstered PHCC's capacity to support impacted communities through the EPA's public comment period.

It is important to reflect for a moment on the key roles played by several people during this time. Steve's experience organizing in other contexts, in particular, is key to explaining PHCC's shift in tactics, from passive engagement to direct action. He helped coalition members recognize a political opportunity to publicly hold the city accountable, which in turn helped the coalition garner resources to further organize and mobilize people during the crucial public comment period. Cassie was another key person in this process. She had maintained connections with PHCC members even after she left GWPDX, and had followed the cleanup process from a distance. This allowed her to plug back in and help lead organizing and mobilization efforts. Edward, who took over for Cassie at GWPDX, had helped keep communications going at a time when few other PHCC members were engaged. Ibrahim, from Right 2 Survive, had encouraged Cassie and others to reconvene in December and January and helped a half-dozen people living unhoused fully engage in the coalition's work. I had time and experience that allowed me to help write the coalition's letter to the city, and I had also developed and maintained relationships with Right 2 Survive members that supported people plugging back into the coalition at this key moment. The relationships that Cassie and local American Indian Movement leaders had developed over the years, as well as people affiliated with other Indigenous-led groups, made it easy for other people to pick back up, even after a hiatus. Members of Líderes Verdes, including Velia, Mañuela, Lucía, Ana, and Don Pedro, were prepared to plug back in at a moment's notice. All told, more than a dozen of us had convened to plan the rally at City Hall, including alerting the media, making signs, and speaking to the crowd. Long familiar with flooding City Hall with its members, Right 2 Survive leaders mobilized over a dozen people to attend the rally. Other PHCC members played important roles by attending planning meetings, weighing in on key decisions, and bringing their friends and neighbors to the rally. A few empathetic local reporters helped amplify PHCC's demands on the radio and in newspapers. And leaders from local environmental organizations turned out, working in collaboration with PHCC. In short, it was a collective effort, with various people working in ways that suited their strengths, bringing all the pieces together at the right time.

The campaign resulted in critical resources for PHCC, allowing the coalition to hire three part-time organizers for the public comment period. And yet, as we will see, victory was somewhat fleeting. On June 8, 2016, the EPA released its *Proposed Plan*—which advised doing almost nothing to ensure the safe consumption of fish in the future. And by September 2016, when Commissioner Fish and Mayor Hales signed and submitted the City of Portland's official public comment letter to the EPA, it was clear where city leaders stood in relation to the *Proposed Plan* and therefore in relation to EJ communities: the city unequivocally championed the EPA's weak *Proposed Plan*, stating, "Overall, we are supportive of moving forward with EPA's proposal" (City of Portland, 2016:3). Somewhat unexpectedly for PHCC, the city's letter also referenced some of the coalition's broader concerns, around workforce development and the EPA's own inadequate public engagement process. PHCC representatives worried, however, that unless the EPA mandated a more thorough cleanup, this gesture would have little effect on actual outcomes.

Classic Growth Machine Influence

Throughout engagements with the city from 2012 through 2016, PHCC members operated on the implicit assumption that sustainability postpolitics were at play in city officials' refusal to meaningfully engage residents in the cleanup planning process. After all, people had become accustomed to viewing bike lanes as the proverbial bulldozers of the sustainability era, and to seeing green development as sustainability's urban renewal engine. Portland's residents of color, and especially Black folks, had been shut out of so much of Portland's planning by this time—and planning had become synonymous with sustainable development—that it almost went without saying that sustainability boosters were somehow responsible for keeping marginalized groups locked out.

Yet, over time it became clear that traditional polluters held just as much if not more sway over the cleanup planning and harbor redevelopment process. At the same time as Portlanders became accustomed to jumping off the docks into the cool river on hot summer afternoons, in county courtrooms polluters quietly scared city officials away from taking meaningful steps to ensure the river became safe for fish consumption—including doing public outreach. But why? To understand the city's motives, it is necessary to briefly revisit the last hundred years of river-focused contamination, cleanup, and activism.

As I recount in detail in chapter 2, environmentalists working as early as the 1920s eventually succeeded in establishing the Oregon State Sanitary Authority, in 1938, which mandated that pulp and paper industries stop dumping waste into the Willamette. Between 1947 and 1952, state-level officials also required the City of Portland to stop dumping sewage in the river, resulting in the city spending millions on a wastewater treatment plant and other infrastructure improvements. Then, in 2011, the city finished construction of the Big Pipe, a $1.4 billion initiative that has substantially decreased urban sewage overflow into the Willamette. These advancements came in large part due to advocates working on behalf of the river, as well as from tightening environmental regulations at the federal level.

Over time, Portland's water and sewer rates grew to among the steepest of all large cities in the United States, rising 71 percent between 2005 and 2015; construction of the Big Pipe, a crucial advance that helps limits sewer overflow into the river, accounted for much of the increase (Schmidt, 2015). As mentioned earlier in discussing the "ratepayer scandal," in response to the Big Pipe and other expenditures, lobbyist Kent Craford and attorney John DiLorenzo had led lawsuits against the city and BES, alleging illegal spending. These two were also behind a 2013 ballot measure campaign to reduce utility charges. Representing entities that include Portland Harbor PRPs such as Siltronic Corporation, Vigor Industrial, and Harsch Investment—companies that do little to promote themselves as "green"—Craford noted that water and sewer rates "affect everyone," and that it is through the courts that he is "speaking up for both residential customers and big industrial users" alike (Theen, 2014). In addition to opposing federally mandated infrastructure improvements such as the Big Pipe, Craford and DiLorenzo put forth a narrative around wasteful spending on several other relatively small "questionable projects," including construction of two buildings, one a house that demonstrated water-conservation technology, innovative public restrooms, and decorative park fountains. They also included Superfund-related expenditures in this list of dubious expenses. Despite putting relatively little money toward public outreach in the first decade and a half of the cleanup planning process, BES devoted over $50 million of ratepayer revenue (and another $8 million from the city's general fund) toward harbor-related expenses, including background studies, between 2001 and 2015 (Schmidt, 2015).

In December 2016 and January 2017, a Multnomah County Circuit Court judge ruled that most of the city's expenditures in question had been justified—including Superfund spending (Floum, 2017). But, in the interim, the lawsuits appear to have had a chilling effect on the city's advocacy for a fully remediated harbor, and precluding the city from dedicating resources for outreach to people who are most impacted by pollution and least likely to benefit from status quo redevelopment: expenditures for outreach fall into the grey area repeatedly targeted by corporations as illegal uses of ratepayer revenue.

Another substantive area of concern for city officials, however, was around the Comprehensive Environmental Response, Compensation and Liability Act's "Joint and Several Liability" clause. According to the EPA, "Joint and Several Liability" means that "any one potentially responsible party (PRP) may be held liable for the entire cleanup of the site" (Environmental Protection Agency, 2017a). In other words, the EPA can hand the entire cleanup bill to a single PRP, leaving it up to that entity to then wrangle money from other PRPs—but with no legal mechanism to ensure that they pay up. The clause is particularly susceptible to being invoked when "the harm caused by multiple parties cannot be separated" (EPA, 2017a), as is the case in the Portland Harbor. One Portland Harbor Community Advisory Group member reported that city officials disclosed concerns that if the EPA decided to invoke this clause, the City of Portland would be a particularly vulnerable target; whereas companies come and go, declare bankruptcy, and take other complicated turns, municipalities are constant. The more rigorous the cleanup plan put forth by the EPA, the higher the city's potential bill if the clause were invoked. City officials feared that bringing more attention to the Superfund site would generate residents' support for a more robust cleanup—and that ratepayers (or taxpayers, depending on the court's decision) would then be liable for the entire bill. Given that the EPA's estimated cleanup cost spread went as high as $9 billion, the most extreme outcome would have had significant consequences for the City of Portland and its residents. Paradoxically, however, if officials spoke too loudly about concern over the Joint and Several Liability clause, the city also faced the possibility of setting a precedent for its liability. Following release of the EPA's Record of Decision, it remained possible that the EPA could still invoke Joint and Several Liability and assign the entire bill to the city. But at that point, the ceiling of the city's obligation would be lower, closer to $1–2 billion rather than the original $9 billion.

This is the backdrop behind public officials' decision against conducting a robust public outreach process. Through the entire planning process from 2012 through 2015, PHCC by and large assumed that the city was blocking frontline communities out of the planning process for the same reasons as in other environmental projects: bike lanes, for instance, were technical solutions to an ecological problem, and all would benefit—so get out of the way. Yet, through the entire public comment period, in large part *because* of the lack of meaningful dialogue between public agencies and impacted communities, PHCC leaders and members were mostly in the dark about the forces at play in shutting residents out of the cleanup planning process.[4] Coalition members, myself included, were aware that ratepayer lawsuits were under way, but we did not quite understand the implications of the Joint and Several Liability clause and in general the city's concern about high cleanup costs and appeasing big business interests in this context. Instead, the coalition operated under the contradictory assumption that city leaders were operating like a polluter—and at the same time refusing to institute a robust engagement process as an extension of generalized apolitical sustainability discourse. Black residents were not meaningfully engaged when the city decided to put a bike lane through the heart of Albina; why would they be included in other environmental projects, including harbor cleanup? In a 2017 conversation, Cassie recalls:

> Officials kept saying we have this dual role that's complicated and we have to wait for this or that. They were always having these excuses about why they weren't able to start public involvement. . . . Every single person living in city boundaries that we would talk to and orient about the issue, people would say they never knew [about harbor pollution]. And they would feel personally responsible for not knowing, and we would say, 'No, it's by design that the city intentionally kept information from the public about Superfund, because they were concerned about their own liability.' They didn't want to be liable for cleanup. That's the bottom line, whether you're a public agency or the worst industry, you want to minimize your liability. . . . It's literally a conflict of interests. We view it that way. They [city officials] would argue it's not. But they are putting their liability first over the health and well-being of community folk.

But at the time, it was not apparent that polluters were playing such a central role in swaying the city. Moreover, PHCC made the mistake of lumping together green development and natural resource protection: the city has been by and large open to green development given the capacity to generate money without taking lots of land, whereas the natural resource track tends to take money and land from the powerful. Had PHCC better understood this dynamic as well as the larger picture of the city's potential liability earlier on, it is possible that the coalition might have worked more efficiently during the planning process. Instead, postpolitical sustainability discourse muddied the picture for PHCC, masking the durability of a status quo urban growth regime.

Conclusion

Despite the nonpoint source toxins that remain buried in the river's sand and sediment, Portland's early sustainability advocates helped land the city on the map as a leader in the environmental movement, starting in the 1970s. Portland's boosters have since leveraged the city's reputation as a sustainability steward by explicitly encouraging green-themed growth. Susan Anderson, director of Planning and Sustainability for the City of Portland from 2009 to 2018, bluntly explains the city's motivations: "We're not doing [sustainability] just to be altruistic . . . there's money to be made" (quoted in Minow Smith, 2012). But now, in the midst of a Superfund cleanup, and despite an ongoing reputation as an urban green paradise, it appears that the City of Portland has somewhat retracted its enthusiasm for tying together environmental stewardship and economic growth, at least in the Portland Harbor. Bob Sallinger, of Portland Audubon, explains, "What we saw in Superfund was very similar and consistent to what we saw on other issues related to Portland Harbor. Just because the city likes green buildings and bike lanes does not mean that it likes protecting and restoring river habitat. They have very different implications in terms of how they affect powerful business interests. We have made significant progress on the river over the years, but it has taken tremendous and sustained grassroots pressure to overcome powerful and entrenched business interests." The counterpoint to Anderson's statement, in other words, is that when there is money to be *lost* by doing sustainability, environmental stewardship—even of the sort that might promote economic growth in the long run—is prone to taking a back seat.

No matter how committed to a green growth agenda a municipality may appear, then, it is far from a foregone conclusion that sustainability is a totalizing force. What we see in the Portland Harbor Superfund Site is largely the work of a *status quo*, rather than green, growth machine. Based on the tendency for racial capitalism to internalize its own contradictions, this should not come as a surprise. But the underlying mechanisms by which Portland Harbor-related growth regime actors exert their influence are important to elucidate, if for no other reason than to better understand the obstacles that grassroots groups such as PHCC face. This is not a case of the City of Portland pandering to business elites hoping to use public subsidies to offset costs of building so-called eco-villages; rather, the city has capitulated under pressure from corporations that polluted the river throughout the twentieth century and that continue to make fortunes through decisively nongreen (or even superficially green) means.[5]

Officials have continually invoked depoliticized sustainability discourse in public communications about the Superfund site throughout the planning process. A rising green tide will lift all boats, and the sooner the cleanup begins, the better for all stakeholders involved, they say. In particular, local leaders have celebrated a newly acquired ability to safely swim in the Willamette thanks to large-scale infrastructure projects, which distracted the vast majority of Portlanders from harbor pollution's EJ implications.

PHCC's engagements with the City of Portland, as well as a series of news articles about an ongoing legal battle between the city and water and sewer ratepayers, reveal much about the environmental politics of so-called green cities. Lawsuits filed by polluters against the city ultimately, in part, diminished the city's willingness to conduct a public involvement process around the harbor cleanup. In other words, the city actively foreclosed spaces for people to influence the harbor cleanup, while publicly asserting how all will benefit from a cleaned-up harbor. But rather than green growth-oriented actors influencing the city to take this stance, as we might expect, it was *classic growth machine actors*, who make no pretense to being green, implicitly pushing the city to depoliticize the planning process.

The pervasiveness of a classic growth machine, in many ways, demystifies and de-fetishizes the idea of a paradigmatic green city. EJ groups must not only be wary of greenwashing, but also of municipal leaders deploying sustainability discourse that in essence portrays classic polluters as greenwashers. But it was only in retrospect that PHCC leaders realized the role that the lawsuits brought by polluters may have played in influencing the city's public engagement process, as well as the way in which larger land use planning system constraints shaped things, the ways in which the city pandered to business (rather than mainstream environmental) interests, and the reticence of labor and other groups to take on industry. While government agencies were the main entities with which PHCC was interacting, polluting corporations heavily mediated this process. Despite sustainability's neutralized discourse, perpetuated by green growth actors, it is therefore imperative that scholars and organizers not overlook the classic growth machine politics that continue to drive uneven development processes—even in paradigmatic sustainable cities, such as Portland.

Wayside Aster
Eucephalus vialis
Threatened

CHAPTER **6**

Remaking the City, Remaking Ourselves

Houseless-Led Community Organizing

One morning in September 2014, Roy, Loretta, and I took a walk along the Willamette River in North Portland. We started at Cathedral Park, under the towering green Gothic-style St. John's Bridge, and headed upriver. The sun shone brightly against the water. As we made our way along the rocky shoreline, over old dock pilings and around fallen trees, we passed a dozen or so makeshift shelters nestled into the riverbank. Some people had set up ripstop nylon tents complete with poles and rain covers. Others had lashed driftwood and branches together, weaving blue and brown tarps and scraps of particle board into lean-tos. We passed laundry lines with socks and jeans gently swaying as they dried, and at one camp we noticed planks of wood for shelves stocked with a few tins of beans and tuna alongside a can opener. Boulders and logs for sitting flanked fire pits at nearly every campsite. Above, a canopy of black cottonwoods, willows, big leaf maples, and Oregon ash trees provided shade. Crows screeched in the trees, and blackberry vines scratched at our ankles. We nodded hello to those we encountered who did not seem eager to chat, and we squatted on rocks for longer conversations with those who welcomed us. At each camp, we left a pamphlet we had made earlier that summer, called "Staying Safe and Healthy on the Rivers."

As we approached the bluff overlooking Willamette Cove that morning, a half mile or so into our walk, Roy suddenly stopped. "Holy shit!" he whispered. Loretta and I froze. Local newspapers occasionally reported dead bodies found floating in the river. Had we stumbled upon one? "I've been here before!" Roy exclaimed, returning to normal volume. Loretta and I looked at each other, confused. "Roy, didn't you say this was your first time up here?" Loretta asked, recalling our conversation on the bus that morning. "Yeah, but back in 1982, I dreamt I built a marina in this cove!" Roy went on, "It was a place for houseless boaters to come and fuel up, buy supplies. Dump their trash. It was a whole business I was runnin'!" Loretta and I looked over Roy's shoulder. Three faded thirty-foot long boats, tied together with rope, bobbed in the water about twenty-five steps from the shore. A recent fire smoldered a few feet from the high-tide line. It was easy to envision just what Roy described. Excitedly, we scrambled down the hillside to the Cove's rocky shore below.

Roy and Loretta were integral members of the houseless-led activist group Right 2 Survive (R2S) and residents at Right 2 Dream Too (R2DToo), the autonomously run houseless "rest area" founded by R2S. Both had spent considerable time sleeping near the river a bit further south in previous years, prior to moving into R2DToo. Established on a piece of land in the heart of downtown Portland, R2DToo provided space for up to a hundred houseless people to rest each day and night. Through this direct action, R2DToo had also become a hub for activism around a host of intersecting issues—including the harbor cleanup.

A half-dozen R2S members, give or take, attended nearly every PHCC function from 2012 through 2016. Roy, Loretta, and others played a central part in the coalition's work and pushed PHCC to deeply consider the needs of the city's most vulnerable residents. Key contributions included the collective production of "Staying Safe and Healthy on the Rivers," the pamphlet we passed out on our river walks. Highlighting ways to mitigate river-related hazards for houseless people, the guide included topics such as how to avoid getting toxic soil in tents, people's rights in encounters with the police, ways to safely use river water, and fish advisory information. R2S also mobilized hundreds of unhoused community members to testify to the inadequacy of the EPA's *Proposed Plan* in summer 2016. Furthermore, R2S members went on to play a central role in PHCC's efforts to secure community control over remediation and development of land along the river, including at the Cove, the site of Roy's dream three decades prior.

Roy, Loretta, and I, along with other PHCC members, would return to the Cove and other stretches of riverbank several more times over the next few years. Our main goals were to check in with people and pass out the river safety pamphlet we had created, in an effort to keep those living along the river apprised of the cleanup planning process and hear about on-the-ground shifts. We also hoped to recruit new people to join R2S and PHCC. An inlet north of downtown Portland and the harbor's main shipyard area, the Cove sits in the heart of the Portland Harbor Superfund Site. It is one of the most contaminated sites in the entire harbor, on account of past activities such as wooden barrel manufacturing. It is also one of the more accessible places for those seeking refuge from the near-constant "sweeps"—evictions or forced removals—that Portland's houseless community members experience in inner-core neighborhoods. Roy's dream of running a marina by and for houseless people reflected the mutual aid model of R2S's self-run rest area and depicted a vision for community-controlled solutions in the harbor. His dream would come to function as a sort of beacon, inspiring PHCC members to dream about alternative futures for the harbor more broadly that served ordinary people and wildlife rather than the pocketbooks of industrial and real estate tycoons.

Radical Incrementalism in Portland

Ultimately, R2S came to heavily influence PHCC's overarching approach to systemic change. Rest area members modeled how to build a new world, collectively. By demonstrating how to attend to immediate survival needs as a means of simultaneously building consciousness and forcing systemic change, R2S swayed other PHCC members to adopt a similar mindset. More broadly, R2S prompted the coalition as a whole to indirectly embrace tenets of radical incrementalism—including strategic engagement *and* disengagement with government agencies.

South African critical urban scholar Edgar Pieterse (2008) offers a crucial starting point for thinking through the organizing work of R2S and in turn PHCC, taking into account the linkages between the direct action efforts of R2S's rest area, capacity building, politicization, and systemic change. Pieterse suggests that the concept of radical incrementalism opens space for a necessarily generous reading of how change often happens, particularly when grassroots groups push for infrastructure and other improvements in informal settlements of Pieterse's hometown, Cape Town, South Africa. Radical incrementalism entails ordinary residents engaging the state on a project-by-project basis in pursuit of incremental change, with aims of more radical transformation over the long term. In many ways, radical incrementalism echoes the concept of "non-reformist reforms," put forth by French political theorist André Gorz (1967) in the late 1960s and more recently popularized by Ruth Wilson Gilmore (2007) and applied in the context of the Skid Row neighborhood of Los Angeles (Dozier, 2019). A non-reformist reform is a shift that makes it easier, rather than more difficult, to dismantle systems that ultimately need to be abolished; it is potentially transformative rather than solely transactional. Pieterse is particularly attuned to the *process* by which such change occurs and in turn to the *agents* of change working to bring about transformation. Key to a radical incrementalist framework is that, in the process of engaging in collective day-to-day struggles, *politicization* and *learning* transpire such that those involved build power to force more fundamental shifts.

Under this model, groups such as R2S and PHCC are implicitly attempting to "build something new in the shell of the old," as the anarchist adage goes, and in so doing transform the shell itself. For R2S, building something new has literally entailed building a self-governed place for hundreds of houseless community members to rest, doubling as a hub of political education, action, and dreams of more just futures. As we will see here and in the next chapter, a radical incrementalist framework also helps account for the sometimes contradictory ways in which such groups as R2S and PHCC strategically engage and *dis*engage with government agencies. Such groups are attempting to balance pushes for regulatory improvements with hands-on projects focused on day-to-day survival, and indeed the two strategies are interlinked.

In the sections that follow, I first lay out a brief history of modern-day U.S. homelessness, situating it within the prison industrial complex and an ongoing housing crisis. I then illustrate the origins of R2S and connect the organization to a broader houseless-led movement called Sleep Not Sweeps, Housekeys Not Handcuffs—and to green city environmental justice. Next, I recount steps that R2S members took during the summer of 2014 to create the river safety pamphlet, which became a key popular education tool for engaging houseless people and others in PHCC's work. I end with discussions about the contributions R2S has made to PHCC, including visions for community-controlled land, and related implications for organizing for more just, green cities.

Geographies of Carceral Homelessness and Resistance

An estimated 3.5 million people in the United States now experience homelessness each year. Today's crisis is a direct result of ongoing cuts to federal funds for affordable housing and mental health programs that began in the early 1980s, as well as a housing system that increasingly privileges profits over the human need for shelter (Mitchell, 2020; Western Regional Advocacy Project [WRAP], 2010). Disproportionate rates of homelessness for Black and Indigenous people stem from ongoing impacts of settler colonialism, slavery, and racial capitalism (Gilmore, 2007; Goetz, 2013; Olivet et al., 2018). People living on the streets contend with a host of issues, including lack of access to food and hygiene facilities, police violence, illness and disease, and exposure to the elements (National Law Center on Homelessness & Poverty [NLCHP], 2017; WRAP, 2010).

Anti-houseless policing involving recurrent fines, citations, "move along" orders, and seizure of belongings ensures a state of ever-present instability for unhoused people. While taking a dramatically different form of control than confined incarceration, such constant mobility is nevertheless comparably punitive (Beckett and Herbert, 2010; Herring, 2019; Herring et al., 2019). Such policing that keeps people on the move occurs in commercial and residential spaces, in the name of public safety and livability (Mitchell, 2020). It also occurs in "pristine" green spaces, in the name of environmental sustainability (Goodling, 2020; Mokos, 2017), even as urban green spaces remain places of relative material and spiritual refuge for some people living unhoused (Speer and Goldfischer, 2019). Deshonay Dozier (2019) and Forrest Stuart (2016) illustrate how entire neighborhoods with dense houseless populations, such as L.A.'s Skid Row, become extensions of the carceral system. Nevertheless, despite the constant sweeps, many houseless people prefer the streets over shelters, given the destabilizing, often jail-like conditions of shelters and the lack of any realistic pathway to stable housing via the shelter system (Herring, 2019; Speer, 2018).

It an effort to combat the sweeps and ensure some form of stability, a growing number of unhoused community members in cities across North America have joined together to construct cooperative spaces for conducting daily life over the last two decades. There are more self-organized houseless communities—tent cities, rest areas, tiny house villages, encampments—today than at any time since the Great Depression (Herring, 2014; Herring and Lutz, 2015). Although gauging an accurate number of such communities is impossible due to their transience and the necessity for many to remain hidden from public view to avoid eviction, a review of online media sources found a 1,342 percent increase in the number of unique encampments reported in the media between 2007 and 2017, with two-thirds of growth coming *after* the 2007–2012 recession (NLCHP, 2017).[1]

Yet, contrary to media claims that such communities emerged directly out of the recent recession, scholars argue that they are actually rooted in more long-standing urban penal and welfare policies, and that self-governed houseless communities developed as both "protest and containment" to simultaneously serve the preferences of houseless people and the needs of the neoliberal state (Herring and Lutz, 2015). "Containment" refers to cost-effective spatial control by local governments over what they consider to be a dissident population. Such spatial regulation is starkly visible in the growing number of governments, nonprofits, and religious organizations that have taken the helm of tent cities and tiny house villages—creating what Speer (2018) calls a proliferation of "tent wards" that entail a complex melding of containment *and* care. While providing the bare necessities of a roof and a cot, such outsider-run villages also often require strict adherence to dehumanizing rules and regulations. Tent wards thus constitute an extension of what Teresa Gowan (2002) describes as a carceral system predicated on a mutually reinforced cycle of incarceration and homelessness.

On the whole, however, those communities that resist the tent ward conversion, and that remain stable and self-organized, provide a safe place for unsheltered people to rest (Heben, 2014; Herring and Lutz, 2015; Weissman, 2017). They offer a place for people to "escape the public gaze" (Sparks, 2010) and to "feel human" (Sparks, 2017:349), and they reduce crime in surrounding neighborhoods (Schmid, 2018). A handful, like R2DToo, also serve as hubs of mutual support and collective action around a host of intersecting issues, such as environmental and infrastructure concerns (Goodling, 2020, 2022); they implicitly challenge a "white spatial imaginary" (Lipsitz, 2007) by prioritizing the use value over the exchange value of land (Logan and Molotch, 2007; Speer, 2016, 2017). In short, houseless people are implicitly attempting to "erase their own erasure" (N. Smith, 1992) through communal living and resistance strategies, however contested these may be.

Self-organized communities are far from immune to harm from environmental hazards, police violence, and eviction. At the same time, such communities offer examples of how people are working together to mitigate harm and challenge evictions that occur purportedly in the name of public health, hygiene concerns, and EJ. In response to calls for the eviction of encampments over hygiene in Fresno, California, for instance, one community collectively demanded sanitation provisions (Speer, 2016). With concerns about a wide variety of social and EJ issues, from the housing system to water contamination, police violence to air pollution, a growing number of houseless-run communities are joining up with broader movements (Goodling, 2020)—particularly during and in the wake of the Covid-19 pandemic. Several are involved in or leading campaigns to stop the sweeps of houseless people with nowhere else to go, to gain access to hygiene services such as toilets and trash collection, and to push for more humane housing policies. In cities from L.A. to Portland, Denver to Philadelphia, groups led by people living unhoused are seeking day-to-day survival and fighting for systemic change. Relatively few groups report involvement in explicit EJ work, however. R2S therefore offers a key opportunity to examine the challenges and possibilities of cross-race, cross-class organizing around environmental planning in so-called green cities.

Establishing the Right 2 Survive in the Early Years: Dignity Village and Reclaim

Around 2000, Ibrahim Mubarakand several others formed Dignity Village, one of the country's first visible houseless-run communities established in part to protest the city's inadequate response to homelessness. A Dignity Village leader discusses the community's origins: "Basically, we started out under the Fremont Bridge. And it was just a group of protestors that got tired of getting kicked out of the doorways by the police and herded like cattle, told they couldn't stay places, and they just got fed up with it and said, 'We are the public and this is public land, why can't we stay here?' And the city of Portland agreed that people had a right to live somewhere and there was no solution to the housing problem" (Weissman and Dickson, 2012:12).

For a few years, Dignity Village moved from site to site around the inner-core downtown area. After several evictions, members and supporters finally pushed local officials to secure an acre of land where the community could stabilize. Under the designation of "emergency campground," for a dollar a year, residents settled on an asphalt tarmac adjacent to "a toxic acre of former composting facility far removed from downtown and nestled between the Columbia River Correctional Institute, a few open fields and the PDX [Portland] International and Air National Guard runways, about a half mile from the mighty Columbia river" (Weissman and Dickson 2012:12–13). With the move out of the inner-core downtown area, Dignity Village became less a site of protest and more a site of communal living, and it has remained a prominent model of an autonomously run community ever since.

By 2008, on the cusp of the Great Recession, Portland and so many U.S. cities seemed to burst with folks sleeping unhoused. People responded in urgently creative ways to crisis. Various grassroots groups dedicated to fighting homelessness and supporting people living unhoused sprang up closer to downtown Portland. HOMEpdx, for example, hosted meals on the waterfront between the Morrison and Hawthorne Bridges in response to an uptick of young people living on the streets. One night in late 2008, Ibrahim attended one of HOMEpdx's dinners. In a 2015 interview, Ibrahim recalls: "I was going to a feed, and I was walking across the Hawthorne Bridge, and it was HOMEpdx, that's the name of it. It was Ken Lloyd that founded the underground group HOMEpdx. . . . He said, 'Look at all these people, all the youth around here,' and he said, 'We need to do something.'" According to Ibrahim,

> We start talking, and [Ken] said what can he do, and I told him that I hadn't been doing activist work in a while, and he said what can he do to bring me out of retirement. I said, "Get me a cellphone." And he got me a cellphone. So, with that. . . . He went with me and he paid for it, and he said, "It's up to you to keep it going." He put like three months on it to give me time to make up money to keep it going, and with that, I went to KBOO [a local radio station] and I got Trilliam's phone number, and then I would get some of the anarchists' phone numbers, and I started—they said, "Well, just come to us. We do the work."

Cell phone in hand, Ibrahim used the last ten dollars in his pocket to make copies of a flyer inviting people to a meeting, and he began handing them out to houseless people around downtown Portland and the inner eastside, across the river from downtown. A dozen people showed up to the first meeting, and more and more began to get involved in the weeks to come. By early 2009, the group was holding regular meetings at the Red and Black Café, a local anarchist hub, as well as at Sisters of the Road, a nonprofit cafe across the river in Old Town that works to "create systemic change that will end poverty and homelessness by providing nourishing meals in a safe, dignified space" (Sisters of the Road, 2015). People also met at a house in the fast-gentrifying, historically Black Albina area, off Mississippi Avenue. According to Ibrahim, the goal of the group was to build on the groundwork laid by Dignity Village and "figure how to stop the criminalization of houseless people and stop people from getting pushed out."

One day in 2009, an activist from Florida with Haitian roots named Max Rameau arrived at Sisters of the Road. Max had helped found the multistate organization Take Back the Land and later wrote a book about the experience (Rameau, 2006). He also later organized with Pan-African Community Action in Washington, D.C., pushing for community control over police. Max's 2009 visit to Portland would have a profound effect on Ibrahim and many others. This was Max's second trip to Portland, actually. The first was in the early 2000s, when he came to town to learn about Dignity Village in preparation for creating Umoja, the Black-led autonomous village he cofounded in Miami in 2006—and that burned to the ground six months later.[2]

During his 2009 visit, Max talked with attendees about tactics his group had been using in Florida, including squatting in empty bank-owned houses.

In reciprocal fashion, Max inspired Ibrahim and the rest of the group to form a local chapter of an organization called "Reclaim," which also had chapters in Minnesota, Florida, Chicago, New Jersey, and Madison, Wisconsin. Ibrahim explains: "So, we start scouting out houses, liberating the houses and putting people in there with the guidelines of Take Back the Land from Max Rameau. Due to the housing crisis with the mass evictions, during which the banks put more and more people out on the street, there were many empty houses. It was feasible to reclaim houses under the radar. The goal was to get people back into housing."

Reclaim's method was relatively straightforward. Members would look up real estate listings, locate nearby pre-foreclosed houses owned by banks, and scout them out. If there appeared to be little "mobilization," or movement in or out of the house for several weeks, Reclaim members would break in the back, change the locks at night, move people in with a U-Haul ("on a Saturday around one o'clock . . . looks like normal people moving in," recalled Ibrahim), and request utilities be turned on in the new residents' names. Receiving mail was key: once someone received mail at an address, they learned, the city had to actually take them to eviction court in order to oust them.

At the same time as Reclaim was getting going, a sister group—Right 2 Survive—also formed. "In a sense, we had the 'R' in 'Reclaim,'" Ibrahim explains, "so we were saying, 'Hey, everybody have a right to survive.' We took 'everybody have' and put [the] 'Right 2 Survive.' That's how we got the name, R2S, Right 2 Survive." In all, Reclaim and R2S "liberated," as Ibrahim and others phrase it, seven Portland-area bank-owned, pre-foreclosed houses. Eventually, the two groups parted ways, in part because of a disagreement about the necessity of screening people for the houses. Reclaim wanted to put people in the reclaimed houses who had just been evicted, whereas R2S wanted to prioritize people who had already been on the street for some time. Additionally, around this time authorities began investigating the groups' activities, which also prompted some people to leave. Nevertheless, this key chapter in houseless activism laid important groundwork for much more to come.

May Day Protest and Pitch-A-Tent 2010

Following the breakup, R2S continued to evolve. Leaders went to the U.S. Social Forum in Detroit in June 2010, and Ibrahim began a radio show at KBOO radio station, highlighting issues facing Portland's houseless community. On the Freedom Bus to Detroit, Ibrahim met Mic Crenshaw, a Portland-based hip-hop artist with roots in Chicago and Minneapolis. During the ride, Mic and his wife, Janna, wrote a theme song for the R2S radio show, "Somebody Help Me." The first verse asserted the role of the state in the immiseration of millions of people, at the same time as it celebrated the capacity of ordinary people to rise up:

> I let the music raise funds for community centers / start a high school that is soon to be finished / Thinking about starting a community garden / Trillions on the war when the poor people are starving. / Music is a tool in the hands of the artist / Do the right thing and it makes you a target / When the pigs murder the innocent and walk scott free. / We gotta occupy the property and block the streets / I man the intersection between love and liberation, indoctrination and occupation. / I demand a response to this emergency, so the government is conscious of its urgency / So much work to do, so few jobs to find / The financial sector loots and robs you blind.

The chorus further avowed faith in ordinary people coming together to transform the world: "Somebody help me; this is not healthy. I am not wealthy, but I do have the power to break the chains." Later lines again asserted a skepticism that the state would do the right thing—"I believe in the government with the faith of an atheist"—and asserted the need for *action* centered on the control of land: "Exploited by greed and racial prejudice / The president will bomb ya, Iraq to Pakistan / I'm marching in Detroit to *take back the land* . . . So how do we stop this obnoxious nonsense? A meeting? A forum? A concert? A conference? / I understand the need to talk and process / But we need ACTION, not thoughts and concepts."

By March 2020, the radio show was still going, and Mic and Janna's song portended the approach that R2S would take in the decade to come. Ibrahim and R2S members continued to network and organize, particularly around the (il)legalities of existing in public space, with which Ibrahim had plenty of recent firsthand experience. In a 2015 interview, he explains:

> [We were] just talking to see what we can come up with that help educate people on their rights because I had defeated the trespass [charge], when they tried to get me for trespassing and took me to court. I said, "What property was I trespassing on?" I asked the DA, and he said, "You was on the sidewalk." I said, "Isn't the sidewalk public property?" He said, "Yeah." I said, "Last I checked, public don't go with no social status, and because I'm houseless don't mean I'm not the public." And the judge started laughing and dismissed the case, and I started letting people know how I defeated the trespassing charge.

Ibrahim felt somewhat lucky this time around. As a Black, Muslim man experiencing homelessness, he knew the odds were stacked against him when encountering the police and court system. So many others were dealing with similar charges in Portland, including citations for sleeping and fines for panhandling.

Then a newcomer to the city, someone with nearly a decade of experience fighting sit-lie ordinances in Seattle, arrived on the scene just in time to help launch a major anti-criminalization campaign. In March 2009, Leo Rhodes moved south to Portland. Originally from Arizona and a member of the Pima tribe, Leo was instrumental in establishing Seattle's second wave of houseless-run communities, including an encampment called Nickelsville. He also helped start an indoor shelter for fellow urban Indigenous people called the Chief Seattle Club. Leo came to Portland hoping to rest, but instead he ended up getting involved with R2S, just as the group began working against the City of Portland's sit-lie ordinances and holding meetings with the Portland City Council about establishing more tent cities like Seattle's Nickelsville and Portland's Dignity Village.

R2S's first big action with Leo in the mix came in spring 2010, on May Day. R2S members had noticed that the school district had long abandoned Washington High School, on the corner of SE Stark and 12th, just across the river from downtown in the central eastside area. It was a block away from Saint Francis, a church that had operated a variety of services for houseless people for years, and people often slept in the school's doorways and on the surrounding grounds and sidewalks. On May Day, R2S and other groups staged an action in the field adjacent to the school—part rally, part protest, and part street fair. Representatives from an organization called Flush attended, for instance, teaching people how to make a composting toilet. Members of In Other Words, a local feminist bookstore and community center, were also in attendance, as were representatives from a number of local anarchist and other leftist groups. At some point, people got inside the school in a symbolic effort to establish a permanent place for unhoused people to live. Ibrahim remembers the energy: "I mean, people just came out the woodwork. So, we had that whole field. We had food, we had composting toilets, we had tents, we had clothing, we had information."

Energized by the May Day action, R2S members began focusing on an ordinance that allowed people to put tents on sidewalks the night before the annual June Rose Festival Parade, long a Portland tradition. Parade-goers would spend the Friday before the Saturday parade scoping out prime spots along the route throughout downtown Portland and across the river in the

Lloyd Center area. After setting up lawn chairs and tents, coolers and boom boxes, campers would settle in for the night. Saturday morning, these go-getters had front-row seats to the marching bands and flower-covered floats.

R2S recognized the hypocrisy in allowing housed Portlanders to camp on sidewalks for leisure the night before a parade, but not for survival the rest of the year. The group decided to launch a parade sleep-out of its own, and an annual event called "Pitch-A-Tent" was born. Leo explains that they intended the action to "show the city that [houseless people and non-houseless people] can sleep side by side." The group invited dozens of people to set up tents along two and a half blocks of downtown, with the main action happening on the corner of SW 4th and Washington. R2S recruited members of Cop Watch and the local chapter of the National Lawyers Guild to help with lookout. Some of Leo's comrades from Seattle came down as well. The Radical Cheerleaders also attended, leading participants in chants and setting a festive tone.

To no one's surprise, the owner of a nearby business called the police the night before the parade. The police came and said, "'Y'all have to move'" Ibrahim recalls. "I said, 'We not gonna move unless you make them move,' because it was housed people putting tents up too." Ibrahim gestured down the street to another group assembling their tents and folding chairs along the parade route. When several more police officers arrived to clear (houseless) people away, R2S members showed them the ordinance that allowed people to set up tents for the parade. Ibrahim remembers interacting with the police:

> They tried to stop us from doing that, and we showed them the ordinance [allowing tents for the parade]. And that's when we realized the police really don't know what's going on in this city because they didn't know about the ordinance, they just—some business people called them and said homeless people were putting tents up on the sidewalk. And we said, "Well," and we showed them the ordinance, "We can do this." It didn't say housed people or Black people or Native American or white people could do that. It just said it's an ordinance to put up a tent.

The police brought the assistant DA in, and she confirmed that camping was allowed—but threw her card on the ground in front of the tents. "You don't throw me nothing and tell me to pick it up," Ibrahim asserted. "So, it was still there, and then the police came back and said, 'You keep your people in order.' I said, 'You keep *your* people in order,' and I kept pointing at the housed people, you know. It was always, whatever you say is gonna go right back to you because this is a public event." In all, more than a hundred people slept out that night as part of R2S's first annual Pitch-A-Tent event. "There was nothing but homeless people all over, just wall to wall," Leo recalls. "You could barely walk."[3]

Twenty-four hours later, however, after the parade ended and people were packing up to leave, a sadness settled over the group. Several attendees reported it was the best rest they had gotten in a long time, surrounded by like-minded people that whole night. "People asked, 'Now where do we go?'" recalls Lisa Fay, who had joined R2S earlier that year and later became the chair of the board. This question—where do we go?—would become a rallying cry of sorts in cities across the United States in the decade to come and was even adopted as the name of a houseless-led organization in Berkeley, California.

Fighting for the Right 2 Dream, Too

Inspired by the restful sleep and good energy of Pitch-A-Tent, R2S members continued networking, learning, and base building—and soon built a self-run "rest area" in the heart of downtown Portland. Right 2 Dream Too (R2DToo) served as a place for unsheltered people to rest—to survive—using a mutual aid model of providing support for those in need, at the same time as the site became a hub for politicization and collective action. The opportunity to build the rest area came from an unexpected source. In summer 2011, a local paper published an interview with a man named Michael Wright, who said he wanted to give land to the founders of Dignity Village to start another houseless-run community. Wright had an infamous past, owing to a murder conviction for which he had served two years several years prior and for his role in a sophisticated cocaine ring that landed him in prison for part of the 1980s and much of the 1990s (Theen, 2013a). In 2009, Wright was one of four co-owners of Cindy's Bookstore. The group had fined City Commissioner Randy Leonard, the City of Portland, Portland General Electric, and others nearly $1 million, arguing that Leonard selectively enforced ordinances against the adult bookstore (Saker, 2009). Wright and fellow plaintiffs asserted that Commissioner Leonard intended to drive Cindy's out of business in order to acquire and develop the property, situated on a prominent corner in the heart of downtown Portland on SW 4th and Burnside, adjacent to an ornate entrance to Chinatown. When the lawsuit and an appeal were ultimately unsuccessful, city officials ordered the building that housed Cindy's and an adjacent structure be torn down.

Wright and his crew demolished the buildings, and in an attempt to generate money on the now-empty land, they applied for a permit to operate a food cart pod similar to others in downtown Portland. When that failed, Wright publicly proposed the idea of opening an encampment for unhoused people on the land. Later that summer, Wright met with R2S leaders and attended R2S meetings to learn about the group and their vision. Leo remembers the impression that R2S leaders made on one of Wright's co-owners: "He was like, 'I thought you guys were just some yahoo homeless people. . . . But I'm really impressed! You guys really know what you are doing.'" Wright and his collaborators agreed to lease the lot on 4th and Burnside to R2S for one dollar per year.

On October 11, 2011, ten people set up tents on the gravel lot where Cindy's had once stood. "We got permission from the landowner to set this up so we can have houseless people come and get a decent rest," Ibrahim explained in an interview with the *Oregonian* the day R2DToo opened (Hottle, 2011). "As I was walking, I kept seeing the houseless people and I know people get moved and don't get to sleep." That first night, Leo remembers, one person slept for nearly twenty-four hours, took a short walk, and came back and slept another half-day. Getting more people more sleep was at the heart of the direct action—as was creating a community where learning and social change work took precedence. R2S sent out a press release immediately prior to setting up tents, announcing the group's intensions:

> On World Homeless Day, Right 2 Dream Too is proud to announce the 1:00 PM opening of our new space at W. Burnside & NW 4th Avenue in Portland.
>
> *Portland, OR—Right 2 Dream Too (R2DToo) is today establishing a membership space at the corner of West Burnside and NW 4th Avenue, in Portland, OR. The purposes of the space are as follows:*
>
> *To awaken social and political groups to the importance of safe and undisturbed sleep.*
>
> *To create a safe, secure place for members to be.*
>
> *To create places where members can sleep safely and undisturbed.*
>
> *To engage in other educational activities as the Board of Directors shall determine.*
>
> *R2DToo is a newly founded Oregon nonprofit organization supported by members of Right 2 Survive, a group of houseless and formerly houseless individuals dedicated to defending the human, civil and constitutional rights of people experiencing homelessness.*
>
> *R2DToo's facility will provide refuge for Portland's unhoused community who cannot access the insufficient stock of affordable housing and shelter space to rest or sleep undisturbed. Currently, because of city ordinances that pro-*

hibit camping on public property and restrict people's rights simply to sit or lie on sidewalks, Portland's unhoused population is frequently under tremendous stress and unable to get the proper amount of rest. This is one of the principle contributing factors to the tremendous health disparities and high morbidity rates of people experiencing homelessness in our community.

R2DToo's new space will also provide a safe, welcoming place for people who daily and nightly face the threat of violence on our city streets. All members agree to abide by a code of conduct that respects the rights of fellow members and our neighbors to share our public spaces civilly and equitably. Our space will be guided by and adhere to principles of nonviolence. Plans include the possibility of providing limited storage space for members to address the need for unhoused individuals to have a secure place for storing belongings.

R2DToo hopes to offer educational programs and other forms of mutual support and aid as resources become available. It is R2DToo's intention to take input and direction from its members in designing programs, trainings, events and activities. R2DToo believes that people experiencing homelessness are the experts at surviving on the streets and are capable of providing the essential peer support that is currently lacking in efforts to address the homeless crisis in our city and our country.

Ibrahim Mubarak, co-founder of Right 2 Survive, Dignity Village and Board Member of R2DToo, says "This is a direct result of the government's failure to admit that we have a housing problem in this country—not only has the government failed to admit it, it has failed to act on it." The housing crisis that has come to national attention since 2008 has deeper roots in the refusal of the Federal government to recognize housing as a human right. As long as this remains the case, homelessness will not end and we must explore alternative, cost-effective pathways for those who lack housing or who current programs, for a variety of reasons, do not serve. R2DToo hopes its space and the programs it develops will serve as a model for addressing the unmet needs of thousands of Portlanders and will inspire others in possession of empty lots or buildings to consider creating similar spaces. (Copy of press release shared with author)

Tent donations came pouring in, and within a few weeks, approximately ninety people began resting on the land each night. Over the next few months, residents and supporters brought in porta-potties, set up trash service, developed an evolving set of rules, established a membership and governance structure, created a system of rotating security and chore shifts, and much more.

In an interview with the *Oregonian*, Wright praised the fledgling community: "I learned that [unhoused residents] can self-discipline, they can
self-help, they can be a very responsible group of people . . . They've done
an awful lot of good with very few resources" (quoted in Theen, 2013b). In
fact, the rest area cost less than $1,500 a month to operate, with in-kind do-
nations coming from dozens of supporters. Trash service was the most expensive line item. Wright's assessment of R2DToo members' competence
contrasted sharply with that of city officials. Occupy Portland had started
just a few days prior to R2DToo, across the street from City Hall. Whereas
city officials had thus far tolerated Occupy's occupation of the municipal
park and had even stopped enforcing various city codes at the Occupy site,
the city viewed R2DToo as an imminent threat to the status quo and wasted
no time in asking nearby businesses to help log R2DToo's code violations.
The city also fined Wright and his co-owners $1,346 a month for allowing
what the Bureau of Development Services deemed an illegal campsite (Harbarger, 2017). Wright and his co-owners nevertheless allowed R2DToo to
remain.

A week after its founding, over 150 Occupy protestors marched over to
R2DToo to vocalize enthusiasm for the encampment, shouting "We support
the right to dream!" One person carried a sign that said, "Right 2: Survive,
Shower, Sleep, Speak, Sit, Lie, Shelters." Ibrahim analyzed the paradox of the
city's simultaneous sanction of Occupy and condemnation of R2DToo in an
interview with the *Portland Mercury*:

> I don't want to pit [Occupy] against us, we are in solidarity with them, we re-
> spect them. I think the city is trying to pit us against them. The city looks at
> them as privileged, white, middle class making a statement, but they see us as
> not any of that. It shows where their reasoning is at—how can the city allow
> people who have somewhere to stay sleep in the park, but when people who
> have nowhere to go try to build a community, the city tries to kick us out?
> That place is costing the city money, we're not costing anybody. We're voters,
> too, we just don't have the money. We're outcasts. We're nobody. (Quoted in
> Mirk, 2011)

City officials did not give up, and in December 2012, attorney Mark
Kramer filed a lawsuit on behalf of Wright and R2DToo against an "unsym-
pathetic city" (Koffman, 2012). At a rally in front of City Hall, attended by
approximately a hundred people including many R2DToo residents, Kramer
explained, "Right 2 Dream Too is not a Boy Scout Camp or a KOA, it's a temporary shelter, there because the city cannot meet people's housing needs."

Local newspapers reported that rally-goers held signs with slogans such as "Camping for survival is not recreation" and "Housekeys not Handcuffs." The lawsuit asked the courts to waive all fines and designate the site not as a recreational park but rather as transitional housing accommodation. Oregon law allowed for two such sites within the city limits at the time, and Dignity Village was sanctioned under the law as the first. When R2DToo members—self-identified "Dreamers"—entered City Hall to present the lawsuit to city commissioners, security guards blocked their advancement beyond the lobby and called police for backup. In the midst of the commotion, Ibrahim was able to get through the blockade, climb the stairs to the third floor, and deliver the lawsuit to the mayor's office.

In the meantime, nearby business owners and developers increased pressure on the city to continue fining Wright and to permanently evict the rest area community. Chief among them was prominent developer David Gold, who intended to turn the rundown hotel across the street from R2DToo's site into a swanky youth hostel and restaurant. The Portland Development Commission had agreed to loan Gold nearly $2.65 million for the project, and Gold complained that no restaurant tenant would lease the space across the street from a homeless encampment (Koffman, 2012).

In the end, the city settled the lawsuit and waived the $20,957 in fines that had accrued to Wright and R2DToo. Throughout 2013, City Commissioner Amanda Fritz earnestly searched for a new site for R2DToo. It at first appeared that her fellow city council members were in agreement that a city-owned lot under the Broadway Bridge in the Pearl District, not far from R2DToo's Chinatown site, would suffice. But Mayor Charlie Hales ultimately objected to the relocation, citing the opposition of developer mogul Homer Williams, who owned a nearby hotel. Williams offered to purchase the lot from the city for $1 million; $200,000 would go to the city as compensation for the land, and $800,000 would be allocated to R2DToo, to help the community relocate elsewhere. Following a lengthy back-and-forth drama between city council members and the rest area community, mediated by wealthy real estate developers and business leaders attempting to block any move that might jeopardize their projects, it took more than four more years for city officials to finally find a new site for R2DToo (Harbarger, 2017). In spring 2017, after five and a half years on the corner of Northwest 4th and West Burnside under the Chinatown gates, R2DToo members and supporters moved across the Willamette River to a less prominent, less convenient, but also quieter site, between the Memorial Coliseum and the train tracks running along the river near the entrance to the Steel Bridge.

Right 2 Survive Joins the EJ Movement

One of the most vital aspects of R2DToo's model in its early years was that to become a member, residents committed to putting in several hours a week keeping the rest area running—and to connecting with other groups that were also fighting for a more just, green city. In this way, the group's approach explicitly linked survival with politicization and, in turn, the dismantling of oppressive structures. Approximately twenty-five permanent members of R2DToo slept in private tents surrounding the perimeter of the gravel lot. Up to one hundred nonmembers slept in large communal tents in the interior of the site on any given day or night, in twelve-hour shifts. Members who lived in the perimeter tents full-time were responsible for working security shifts, which meant greeting people as they arrived, making sure those seeking shelter had blankets and other necessities, and walking the surrounding blocks to check in on houseless neighbors and keep an eye on the neighborhood. R2DToo members also gave near-daily tours of the rest area, which helped build outside support for the unique model. Some days, up to fifty or more individuals, students, politicians, service providers, and others came through to witness R2DToo's unique approach.

Another key activity for members was participating in meetings, actions, and events. The "must attend" list included R2DToo governance meetings every Sunday, R2S membership meetings every other Thursday, neighborhood association and other government-convened meetings that were relevant to the rest area and the Old Town/Chinatown neighborhood, and meetings and other events convened by outside groups that might be willing to work in solidarity with R2S and R2DToo. Over time, R2S's model of interacting with dozens of social and EJ groups wove a loose and growing web of houseless activists and advocates throughout the city, working on a number of interlinked issues. R2S members began to forge alliances in likely and unlikely places alike, which helped build empathy for a much-maligned population and generated a groundswell of support for R2DToo and houseless people more broadly.

One of the groups that connected with R2S and R2DToo soon after the rest area's founding was PHCC. Jeri Jimenez, who had helped initiate the formation of PHCC, knew Ibrahim from previous years of activism. Jeri invited Ibrahim to attend PHCC's first convening at the Talking Drum Bookstore, in early 2012. In a 2015 interview, Ibrahim recalls that it was somewhat unique that Cassie Cohen, and PHCC more generally, included houseless people as peers from day one:

I've interacted and witnessed coalitions that invite Right 2 Survive and then don't really know what they are getting themselves into and then change their minds. . . . What I love about Cassie was, she was open, and she never showed no fear. Her concern was, "Was I comfortable, or was Right 2 Survive comfortable?" And then my concern was, "Are you comfortable?" because we are secure within ourselves. And she opened up the doorway, she said, "Do what you need to do, let me know, and we will follow your first step."

In a 2015 interview, Lisa Fay, another R2S leader, summarizes the connections between homelessness and the harbor cleanup that prompted the group to join PHCC:

There were many houseless people that lived along the river, and that were being impacted with every aspect of their daily life along the river, health issues, environmental issues. They were worried about their health. They knew that there were toxins in the river. They knew they couldn't drink, or cook from the river. They knew that they shouldn't—although in many cases they didn't have a choice—clean their clothes from the river. They used the river to bathe and were concerned that that was an extra health risk being brought in through their pores.

Lead, dioxins, arsenic, and other toxins in the soil, too, posed a significant concern for those living along the river bank, and PCBs contaminated fish and shellfish, which many houseless Portlanders relied on for sustenance. R2S was also worried that as the cleanup unfolded, houseless people would be the first to be displaced—and permanently excluded from the harbor if the city allowed planned green space and condos that catered to wealthier residents to replace the old industrial infrastructure and existing green spaces. An R2S member summarizes how this confluence of concerns drove R2S to work with PHCC:

[Houseless people] were worried about the soil contaminants on the surface on the shores and in the vegetation. Some had pets that had gotten sick from running through the vegetation. So, a lot of people were aware there were hazards; they just didn't know the extent of the hazards until we would do outreach, and we would walk and talk with people, and find out about their situations. We knew that there were groups out there that were involved [in the cleanup], but we just hadn't made any strong connections with anybody to see where our group could fit in [prior to joining PHCC].

Ibrahim recalls that R2S was able to take on a core leadership role within

PHCC, a coalition of majority-housed people, in part because the group had been practicing democratic governance internally: "Because [PHCC was] creating an organization that I guess wasn't used to organizing different people, and [R2S was] used to it, [R2S] took the lead and started facilitating [meetings], started doing things, modeling how to do things."

For R2S members, participating in PHCC was an extension of the work they were already doing, focused on fighting for a Homeless Bill of Rights that asserted the "right to rest" in the absence of stable housing for all. One R2S member, a middle-aged white man named Mike Summers, recalls that Ibrahim encouraged him to attend a PHCC meeting just a few weeks after arriving at R2DToo: "We knew what we were expected to do. . . . Ib said, 'I need you guys to go tonight and see if this is something you'd be interested in.'" Mike and his partner, Trish, attended nearly every PHCC meeting and event from 2013 through 2016 and beyond. They both took on important leadership roles, including teaching fellow unhoused people to give written and oral testimony, writing newsletter articles, and strategizing how to move through Portland's political landscape. Another R2S member echoes Mike: "I was just like, 'Well, okay, let's just see what it is all about, and if I don't necessarily like it I don't have to go to another meeting.' But almost a year later, I'm still going." Loretta reflects on her first PHCC meeting, a few months prior to our outing to the Cove when Roy first recalled his dream: "I was skeptical about it, and a little bit scared because I didn't know what was going to happen. But when I went to the first PHCC meeting and we started talking about [the harbor] . . . once I started getting more involved, I realized this was going to answer a lot of my questions . . . and I appreciated it."

Creating Popular Education Materials

Right away, R2S members began spending more time along the river, talking with people at riverside encampments and learning about the ecology of the harbor. Several people with R2S, for instance, interviewed houseless people near Cathedral Park and ultimately made a five-minute-long film documenting pollution and discussing its impacts on houseless people and their pets. Ibrahim explains one motive for producing the mini-documentary: "The industrial capitalists are blaming the houseless communities for the toxicity in the rivers. And so we wanted to prove a point. They've been doing this for hundreds of years, dumping lead, waste, and stuff into the river." Lisa describes the film's impacts: "We were opening people's eyes to what the houseless people were going through, how they were suffering, how they were drinking the water, bathing, eating toxic fish."

Importantly, the short film served not only as an internal rallying point and political education tool for R2S and PHCC, but it also opened the eyes of public agency staff to a wider array of human impacts beyond those associated with fish consumption. Ibrahim reflects on the film's influence on government officials' thinking about the Cove, in particular, at a R2S meeting in June 2016:

> Because of the film Right 2 Survive folks made [that] we already shared months ago with the EPA, and with the city, and with the state, it scared them enough and made them aware enough that they started [thinking about] doing early cleanup on the Willamette Cove beach area that was so toxic for families and for houseless folks that were staying there. This is an early win that all of us can actually claim as a victory because of the work of the video and getting our issues out that otherwise the agency wouldn't have cared about or known about or seen.

R2S members—many of whom were also R2DToo members—also brought to PHCC the experience of establishing, living in, running, and fighting for a self-governed community. Over time, housed PHCC members adapted a generous reading of the causes of homelessness and the joint implications of the homelessness crisis and harbor pollution. In particular, R2S's model of pursuing a means of survival, while simultaneously creating a spectacle intended to force changes to how public space is governed, to the police and criminal justice system, and to the entire housing system, would come to influence PHCC, as we shall see in chapter 7.

In summer of 2014, R2S members decided to get more systematic about outreach to people living along the river by creating a pamphlet, "Staying Safe and Healthy on the Rivers." This pamphlet would become emblematic of R2S's radical incrementalist approach, given its simultaneous emphasis on survival and political education toward systemic change. For years, every other week, R2S members and supporters conducted outreach throughout downtown Portland and along the waterfront. In summer 2014, Roy, Loretta, other R2S members, and I had begun regularly walking along the river north of downtown, near Cathedral Park, where this chapter begins. In addition to our passing out socks, granola bars, and other supplies, these walks allowed us to check in with people and circulate a bimonthly newsletter with information about R2S's campaigns, poetry of R2DToo members, and updates on city and national policies. The idea was that a pamphlet that specifically addressed the hazards of life along the river would supplement R2S's newsletter and inform people of hazards. It would also help people live a bit more safely, provide political education about who had polluted the harbor and who was responsible for its cleanup, and open conversation to potentially recruit new members to R2S and PHCC.

Fueled by countless cups of black coffee and self-rolled cigarettes, R2S members and I met at R2DToo throughout summer 2014 to put together the pamphlet. The creation process was one of true collaboration: a core group of six of us met nearly every week that summer, and at least a dozen other R2S members and residents who were around on any given day also joined us from time to time. Gathering in the southwest corner of R2DToo, we sat on buckets, rusty folding chairs, and wooden benches set up in a semi-circle. Tacked to the plywood wall flanking us was the now-ubiquitous Western Regional Advocacy Project poster, an alliance of houseless-led groups in the western United States, of which R2S was a core member, demanding "House Keys, Not Handcuffs!"

Over the course of our work together, we discussed which categories of information to include in the pamphlet. We also debated the tone it would take ("It shouldn't look like a government form you gotta sign!" one person declared) and had numerous conversations on what to call it. Throughout this dialogue process, all involved made crucial contributions. One person, for example, shared their extensive experience as an angler. Another had become an expert on statutes dictating the rights of houseless people in engagements with law enforcement agents, and someone else knew where to find all the important county and state health department phone numbers. One person set up a meeting with someone at the Oregon Health Authority, to see if they had suggestions on the fish advisory information we included. Nearly all involved drew on their direct expertise at surviving unhoused. My role was to take meeting notes and help with the pamphlet layout, once we had the content set. We all learned from each other and contributed something different to the project.

The trifold leaflet evolved to contain information about which fish are safer to eat than others, what to do if police violate one's rights while living outdoors, how to mitigate health problems from exposure to toxins in water and soil, and news about the Superfund cleanup timeline. "Staying Safe and Healthy on the Rivers" thus communicated in a succinct way some of the cumulative and interconnected ways that houseless people are impacted by pollution in the harbor, alongside the way in which other threats to people's health and safety, such as police violence, compound environmental hazard challenges.

Following its original creation that summer, we periodically updated the pamphlet over the next few years. With each iteration, "Staying Safe" fueled additional political education within and beyond R2S and PHCC. Several public agency staff commented that the guide helped them understand more about what is at stake for houseless people, for instance. And it contributed directly to the decision of Oregon State's Department of Environmental Quality to pursue early remediation of the Cove. In spring 2016, the pamphlet proved a vital part of R2S's and PHCC's work in yet another way. When it became clear that submitting testimony in support of a cleaned-up river would be one of the clearest ways to influence a more robust remediation plan, R2S members utilized "Staying Safe and Healthy on the Rivers" to initiate conversations with over one hundred houseless people who ultimately testified to the EPA in support of PHCC.

Incremental Steps toward Radical Shifts

In the early 1980s, around the time that the Reagan administration was cutting federal funding for affordable housing and visible homelessness was becoming widespread in the United States for the first time since the Great Depression, Roy was dreaming about how unhoused people might live peacefully along urban waterways without fear of police violence and with regular access to food, toilets, and places to dispose of trash. Roy had experienced homelessness off and on himself throughout his adult life, interspersed with periods of employment working on docks in the Puget Sound and warehouses along Portland's rivers. In *A People's View of the Portland Harbor*, the twenty-two-minute film that my students helped PHCC create in 2015, Roy articulates the challenges of living on the Willamette's banks after being laid off from his job: "We lived on the river for quite a while, and it had its many challenges. The river goes up and down with the weather. We had the rain to battle with, the snow, the police, the parks, our stuff being stolen from us." Later in *A People's View*, Roy discusses the direct impacts that depending on the harbor for shelter and sustenance have had on his body: "We [found] out about a year or so ago that the river's completely contaminated. A lot of pesticides, leads, mercuries. . . . I've fished out of these rivers. I've eaten out of these rivers. . . . Once we found out the river was contaminated . . . we found it more complicated. . . . I just recently beat cancer. I don't know that [the cancer] wasn't because of [living along the river]. . . . There are a lot of cancer-causing agents that are in these rivers."

A year after filming, however, lung cancer caught up with Roy. He died on May 16, 2016. Our last conversation was a few weeks before he passed. Roy pounded his shaking fist on the table at Floyd's Coffee, saying, "Damn it! If I wasn't fighting for my life, I'd be fighting for the river" (Goodling, 2016).

Roy had spent countless hours working to improve the conditions he and fellow houseless people faced living along the river and tucked beneath building eaves and under freeway overpasses, through a combination of mutual aid, popular education, direct action, and policy advocacy. The marina Roy envisioned in his dream mirrors the kind of mutual aid that houseless people have provided for one another at R2DToo. What is so notable about R2DToo is that not only has the rest area provided a safe place for hundreds, if not thousands, of people to sleep over the years, but it has also served as an alternative model to the top-down social service model that has become so prevalent over the last four decades (Brown, 2022). At R2DToo, houseless people formed a community to govern itself, at the same time as the group joined with others to fight for new, more just systems.

The existence of the community likewise transformed the way in which both elected officials and ordinary residents thought about housing, home, homelessness, and public space. In an interview with the *Oregonian* in December 2012, more than a year after R2DToo's founding, Michael Wright, the landowner who leased the corner of SW 4th and Burnside to R2S, portended the impact R2DToo would come to have: "The city listens to people with power and money; they need to listen to people like this who have come together to do something good." In the time that R2DToo was located in Old Town / Chinatown, hundreds of people's lives stabilized such that they gained and maintained employment, pursued art and music, completed school programs, gave birth to and raised children, and renewed relationships with family members. This all took place in a very public way, on display on SW Burnside and 4th Avenue.

Little by little, the rest area indeed helped force Portland residents and local government officials to come to terms with the reality that ending homelessness would require a massive influx of funding for a social safety net and affordable housing, and much more robust anti-displacement and anti-eviction measures, particularly with the rise in housing market speculation and gentrification from the 1990s onward. Although public agencies at all scales have been far from prepared to deliver a holistic social safety net, let alone actual social housing, the City of Portland substantially adjusted its stance on self-run encampments: by 2018, city officials sanctioned four communities, including R2DToo, and begrudgingly tolerated a handful more. In an interview, former R2S and R2DToo member Brad Gibson describes R2DToo's model and its impact: "The location of the [R2DToo] tent site, this site of protest, was central and conspicuous. It housed worst-off poor people in tents within minutes of access to central missions, churches, welfare offices and other supports . . . R2D2 was also highly visible to the mainstream" (Weissman and Dickson, 2012:99). The combination of R2DToo's prominent location and its open-door policy for all to see the ways in which a self-governed community was taking care of its own needs, combined with an aggressive commitment to showing up at City Hall and leveraging media coverage, enabled R2S to help force the city's shift. R2DToo would go on to serve as a model for other cities. Representatives from over a dozen U.S. cities either visited R2DToo or paid the way for R2DToo leaders to come visit their sites to help develop similar rest areas. While few immediately adapted the explicit activist edge that defined R2DToo at its founding, they nevertheless contributed to shifting the conversation about homelessness, its management, and root causes and solutions across the country.

R2S also became a member of—and helped connect PHCC to—a local coalition called Anti-Displacement PDX (ADPDX), which was an alliance of local community organizations and service providers focused on instituting a variety of anti-displacement provisions in the City of Portland's Comprehensive Plan (Bates, 2019). Recognizing the important ways that local land use laws would shape the possibilities for PHCC's constituents to access land for community-controlled housing, food production, restoration, and more, and wanting to stem the tide of racialized displacement, R2S and PHCC decided to join ADPDX. Representatives from R2S, including Mike, Trish, Roy, and Brad, played particularly key bridging roles between ADPDX and PHCC, including giving updates at meetings to keep the two coalitions abreast of each other's work.

In addition to connecting up with PHCC and ADPDX, R2S became a core member of the Western Regional Advocacy Project (WRAP), a then-regional alliance of houseless-led and accountable organizations with a mission to "expose and eliminate the root causes of civil and human rights abuses of people experiencing poverty and homelessness in our communities." One of WRAP's core goals—combining outreach and organizing, direct action, public education, legal action, and policy change work—has been to "unite local social justice organizations into a movement," focused on decriminalizing poverty, restoring federal affordable housing funding, and ensuring that policies at all levels of government are "grounded in the common truths of poor and homeless people." Starting just after the founding of R2DToo, WRAP member groups, including R2S, led a campaign to institute a Homeless Bill of Rights in its three member states, seeking to end laws and practices that criminalize basic survival in public space. R2S members campaigned around the state of Oregon for the Right to Rest Act and also led an "in your face" campaign at the local level. A minimum of a dozen R2S members attended every single Portland City Council meeting for months in 2014 to testify about the city's mistreatment of houseless people. While the Right to Rest Act has yet to pass, WRAP members continue to push for it and build support around more humane treatment of unhoused people, having run the legislation nine times in three states as of 2021.

Conclusion

A week after R2DToo's founding, a local public radio station posed two questions on its website: "Should [R2S's] encampment be considered a form of political expression or a necessity for the city?" From a radical incrementalist perspective, the answer is *both*. Nearly any time of day that I dropped in to R2DToo, conversation vacillated between managing the day-to-day operations of the rest area, coordinating the Homeless Bill of Rights campaign and Right to Rest Act, recruiting new people to testify at City Hall and orchestrating related direct actions, and organizing R2S members and newcomers to participate in activist efforts around the city concerning a whole host of interrelated issues. Indeed, the R2S model has entailed attempting to build a new society in the shell of the old. Radical incrementalism entails ordinary residents engaging the state on a project-by-project basis in pursuit of incremental change, with aims of systemic transformation over the long term. Not only does this model of change promise the possibility of a redistribution of material resources, but it also alters who is "in the know" of city-building processes. In the process of engaging in collective day-to-day struggles, politicization and learning has transpired such that those involved are building power to force more fundamental shifts in the city's treatment of unhoused people. In building bottom-up capacity through collective survival and politicization efforts, grassroots groups such as R2S gain power to force more radical change over time.

As we will see in the next chapter, Roy's dream and the work of R2S have influenced PHCC's broader collective work in profound ways. Most basically,

getting to know Roy and other R2S members and witnessing their commitments to PHCC have helped housed coalition members develop empathy for
people living on the margins of the city. R2S members also influenced PHCC
to strategically take a more direct action approach, eschewing the tokenizing
participatory process of public agencies. Furthermore, R2S's community-controlled model and Roy's dream of a self-organized marina have inspired coalition members to dream big dreams of their own. Since 2014, for instance,
PHCC has tried various ways to bring the Cove under PHCC's purview, to
serve as a pilot site for community-controlled remediation and development.
In summer 2022, after years of pushing by the Yakama Nation, PHCC, R2S,
the Audubon Society, and nearby residents, public agencies finally agreed to
fund a full cleanup of Willamette Cove. Cleanup will involve hauling away
contaminated dirt rather than simply placing a cap over toxins. While far
short of full remediation of the entire ten-mile stretch of river designated as
a Superfund site, frontline groups consider the Cove to be a tremendous victory. Roy would be so pleased, particularly given the central role that R2S and
fellow unhoused people played in securing massive shifts for land, river, and
people.

Kincaid's Lupine
Lupinus sulphureus
Threatened

CHAPTER 7

(Dis)Engagements with the Sustainability State

For decades now, the environmental justice (EJ) movement has largely called upon the state, in particular the Environmental Protection Agency (EPA) and state-level regulatory agencies, to regulate the kinds of polluters that have contaminated the Portland Harbor. But this strategy has proven less effective than hoped thus far, particularly at the federal level, given the EPA's meager track record of responding to complaints filed by EJ communities. As of January 2014, out of 298 Title VI complaints filed against the EPA for perceived discrimination, all but *two* have been dismissed (Pulido et al., 2016; see also Engelman-Lado, 2017; Harrison, 2019). At the local scale, EJ scholar Melissa Checker (2020) likewise asserts that development, sustainable or otherwise, has often moved forward regardless of the seemingly endless number of meetings, hearings, and committees attended by EJ activists and others concerned about racial justice. "Rather than channeling democratic action," Checker writes, "participatory politics drained activists' time and energy and siphoned it away from their long-term goals" (23). Pulido and her colleagues (2016) have long engaged with organizers on the front lines of the EJ movement; they characterize the lack of structural changes resulting in discernable outcomes, regardless of tireless work by EJ activists, as "EJ failure." Some EJ scholars and activists urge that the EJ movement therefore ought to disentangle itself from the state-led participatory programs and pursue other, more autonomous and direct action channels toward change (e.g., Pellow, 2018; Pulido, 2017; Pulido et al., 2016). Others call for a renewed commitment to holding the state accountable and lament that some EJ activists are pursuing a neoliberal path toward improvements that prioritize small-scale projects such as community gardens *without* pushing for stricter state regulations (Harrison, 2019).

These important analyses offer a springboard to examine and articulate the hybrid approach that has transpired in Portland. At the same time as PHCC explored initiatives that would create a new way of doing things, the coalition also attempted to transform the system itself. This path neither wholeheartedly engaged state agencies nor wholly disengaged from the state. In fact, during a crucial time in the Superfund cleanup planning process, PHCC at times simultaneously engaged with the state *selectively* and *confrontationally*. Moreover, PHCC's work has by and large bypassed the more neoliberal-minded path that Harrison cautions against, even as the coalition has made moves to acquire control over particular parcels of land for community-controlled remediation and use. Rather, PHCC has sought to engage ordinary people in day-to-day life-sustaining activities while acknowledging the limits of engaging with regulatory agencies—all the while simultaneously holding strong to a belief that public agencies must be impelled to act.

The houseless-led group Right 2 Survive (R2S) influenced PHCC's approach in many ways, as we saw in chapter 6, implicitly following a framework of change proposed by South African critical urban scholar Edgar Pieterse (2008). Pieterse argues that neither the pole of "Marxist revolution" nor that of managerial mainstream "good governance" is sufficient to enact transformative politics in African cities. "Radical incrementalism" instead opens space for a more generous reading of how change often happens. As I show here, a dialectical framework that embraces tensions and multi-scalar complexity is likewise necessary in the U.S. green city context. The case of PHCC helps clarify that a radically incremental approach in the context of a U.S. green city entails engagements with the state that occur cooperatively and collaboratively, as well as confrontationally and antagonistically. The mechanisms of social change pursued in this context likewise entail both regulatory and policy shifts, as well as nonregulatory (i.e., direct action, mutual aid) means. The temporal scale of remedy emphasizes immediate survival at the same time as more longer-term, systemic shifts remain a central priority. Substantive areas of focus involve not only hazard remediation but also development of amenities and access to basic services for marginalized communities. Finally, the locus of expertise is squarely democratic while recognizing that there may be some roles for technocratic experts to play, but only if their priorities are aligned with those on the front lines.

In other words, PHCC has operated in a dialectic, tension-filled space in response to the promises and perils of the sustainable city paradigm. Not only does this model of change promise the possibility of a redistribution of material resources, but it also alters who is "in the know" of city-building processes. In shifting the hierarchies of knowledge through new ways of doing things, grassroots groups gain power to force more radical change over time. In attending to fundamental structural shifts that occur in incremental fashion (as opposed to via monumental, sudden revolution), this framework is attuned to the *process* of change, opening space to account for the sometimes-contradictory ways in which groups such as R2S and PHCC strategically engage and disengage with government agencies in an effort to gain the means of survival in the short term and more large-scale systemic shifts over the long term.

I argue that PHCC's particular radically incremental approach in part stems from the contradictions of the sustainability context in which many EJ groups are now working. The sustainability paradigm promises improved environmental conditions for all, including fresh air and clean water. Green city boosters also promise equitable access to improvements in the built environment, including public transit, decent housing, walkable and bikeable neighborhoods, parks, living-wage green jobs, and more. Yet, these are the same amenities that are part and parcel of eco-gentrification and displacement, and that have largely accrued for white, wealthier residents. Crucially, environmental cleanup is by and large under the purview of regulatory agencies such as the EPA, whereas built environment improvements mainly come under the control of local agencies. Given this multi-scalar governance structure, it is an incredibly complex task for frontline communities to bring about an improved urban environment in the sustainability era—and to actually have access to environmental improvements rather than be displaced by rising housing costs tied to urban greening. At the same time as PHCC seeks to bolster environmental regulations and fully remediate the harbor, the coalition also seeks access to environmental amenities and fundamental provisions such as housing and decent-paying jobs that are promised to all sustainable city residents. Ultimately PHCC aims to help dismantle oppressive systems and ensure more just conditions for all. The case of PHCC therefore offers an opportunity to understand the logic behind pursuing a bi-pronged strategy and to begin to analyze the utility of this hybrid approach.

With a mission to "raise the voices of those most impacted" by pollution in the Portland Harbor, PHCC members spent nearly four years, from early 2012 through mid-2016, engaging fellow community members around the harbor cleanup and its myriad social and EJ issues. PHCC's work revolved around building a collective understanding of the pollution in the harbor and its effects on various groups over the last two centuries, as well as developing an understanding of the cleanup planning process itself and how remediation is entangled with concerns about housing, labor, public land access, gentrification, and more. The coalition hosted dozens of popular education-style workshops and events, and some of these activities were designed to help prepare people to testify during the EPA's public comment period. The comment period was the official channel for "the public" to influence the Superfund cleanup plan. In the years leading up to it, PHCC representatives also made a consistent effort to participate in EPA programs aimed at involving ordinary people, as well as to engage with local agencies. Activities included meeting with EPA, state Department of Environmental Quality (DEQ), and City of Portland officials; communicating with EPA staff via email and phone; and engaging with staff from these and other agencies at coalition meetings and other events. PHCC members hoped that communications with the city, DEQ, and EPA would sway the planning process to better account for the needs and perspectives of impacted communities on myriad issues.

As this chapter illustrates, early interactions between PHCC and government agency representatives were, on the whole, personable—"Portland nice," as one PHCC member described them. PHCC had selectively and strategically engaged with the EPA from the time of the coalition's founding, for instance. But after struggling to "play their games" for over four years, as another longtime coalition member put it, PHCC members grew weary of what seemed like a series of false promises by public agencies that never came to fruition. The coalition shifted to take a more confrontational approach at the city scale, to fully disengage from the EPA at the national scale, and to remain cautiously involved with the EPA at the regional scale.

Multi-Scalar (Dis)Engagements with the EPA

Whereas the City of Portland conducted little public outreach with the exception of a poorly designed survey in the lead-up to the comment period, the EPA held several information sessions, and officials attended a handful of PHCC-organized events. But these interactions amounted to tokenizing treatment, serving to further depoliticize the decision-making process. PHCC leaders felt that prior to the release of the Proposed Cleanup Plan, EPA staff members were simply "going through the motions" rather than substantively engaging with the coalition throughout the cleanup planning process. In a 2017 conversation, Cassie Cohen summarizes:

> The bottom line is that EPA designated one EPA staff at less than half time, to be the sole person responsible in the Portland area for conducting outreach since around 2012. . . . The coalition found that over time, up through 2016, the EPA had very inconsistent follow-through on communication, was not helpful in collaborating or jointly planning public involvement strategies with the coalition—although this was our request—and conducted isolated outreach to

different stakeholders without providing transparency about the plans nor opportunities for collaboration. Several times we requested that EPA staff let the coalition know if they approach new underserved groups or if new groups expressed interest in the Portland Harbor so that we could better coordinate with more populations. This never happened. We even requested early on to see a draft of their community involvement plan and to use the draft as a way to jointly plan our ongoing outreach efforts with EPA, and this never happened.

Three vignettes help illustrate the tokenizing nature of PHCC's experiences engaging with the EPA. The first demonstrates how the EPA ignored PHCC's early requests for assistance conducting an Environmental Justice Analysis—a formal analysis of the ways in which communities with EJ concerns are impacted by a given circumstance—and instead engaged PHCC leaders' precious time and energy in conversations about a web-based tool that would have had little utility for the coalition. The second illustrates the EPA's propensity to adhere to a public involvement checklist rather than meaningfully engaging frontline communities. The third focuses on the EPA's pattern of inadequately making information available to the public, particularly during the EPA's public comment period. When taken together, these vignettes reveal how the federal agency's outreach, like that of the City of Portland, had little positive impact on the inclusion of marginalized groups in the planning process—and why the coalition decided to strategically *disengage* at the federal level while maintaining engagements with EPA officials at the regional level.

Wasting time with Web-Based Tools

Starting in 2013, PHCC communicated with EPA officials regarding concerns about whether the planning process would be accessible to impacted communities. Coalition leaders sent EPA officials an email in September 2013, for instance, outlining several ways that PHCC hoped the EPA would support frontline groups. The memo requested that the EPA require a formal "EJ Analysis," a systematic assessment of EJ-related risks and impacts. As far as coalition leaders knew, there was no legal mandate to conduct such an analysis in Superfund processes. But PHCC representatives had been in touch with Duwamish River Cleanup Coalition leaders, in Seattle, and heard that the EJ Analysis conducted there had been integral to grassroots successes in pushing for a stricter cleanup, community benefits agreements, and other positive outcomes for frontline communities.

Instead of pursuing an EJ Analysis, in mid-2014, EPA officials agreed to meet with PHCC leaders to update the coalition on the status of a web-based tool that the EPA had designed to help communities with EJ concerns. While not quite the same as an EJ Analysis, the tool featured environmental and demographic data that would supposedly allow for patterns of impact to emerge and to correlate health outcomes with land uses. EPA officials stressed that the technology would allow users to compare trends happening in multiple places.

But PHCC representatives quickly realized that there were major shortcomings with the tool. How would a snapshot of present-day contamination and demographics help the coalition's advocacy, given PHCC members' complex historical ties to the harbor? Indigenous and Black communities, in particular, had been displaced over the course of more than a century and did not live in neatly organized zip codes near the river. Immigrants and refugees who fished in the harbor were dealing with cumulative impacts of toxins in their home countries and Portland alike, even as most lived far from the harbor. The EPA's tool would not reflect such complexities, coalition representatives stressed. Moreover, many people travel hundreds of miles to fish, canoe, and pray in the Portland Harbor. The mapping tool could not account for such a wide-ranging radius, nor would it capture impacts to unhoused people living along the river today.

In addition, even though EPA officials were encouraging PHCC to use the tool, it was not actually recognized by the EPA as appropriate for use in Superfund site decision-making processes. At first, officials emphasized that the tool could help the coalition focus attention and prioritize where to put its energy. In Portland, for example, there are high breast cancer rates along the Interstate 5 corridor; the tool could therefore help PHCC address this health disparity in a "scientific" way, officials explained in a meeting with PHCC representatives. PHCC members asked, "But what about the Portland Harbor? That's what the coalition is concerned about." The tool was not designed for high-profile Superfund sites, officials admitted. One PHCC representative summarized what the rest of us were thinking: "So it could be a valuable tool for EJ communities in some contexts . . . but not for PHCC." We left the meeting shaking our heads.

In the end, despite several more requests, the EPA never pursued an EJ Analysis for the harbor. This omission left PHCC to piece together its own data and narrative in an attempt to demonstrate disparate impacts during the public comment period.

Checking Boxes

The EJ Analysis conversation was an early indicator of the way relations between PHCC and the EPA's Region 10 office would unfold. In addition to help with an EJ Analysis, in a September 2013 email PHCC asked for assistance from the EPA in other areas. The list included provisions for outreach to underrepresented groups so that people from frontline communities could participate in the cleanup planning process. PHCC requested support in hosting information sessions for culturally specific groups; a conversation with EPA officials about how the federal agency might recognize and support urban Indigenous groups, in addition to federally recognized tribes; inclusion of PHCC in congressional-level meetings and other important convenings; regular updates from other important meetings, even if PHCC representatives could not attend; support developing multilingual outreach materials on Portland Harbor; and a commitment to public hearings with full two-way interpretation services in support of non-English speakers. And, more generally, PHCC sought support to ensure that impacted communities would benefit from outcomes of the cleanup. The coalition requested that EPA staff work with PHCC to help translate existing PHCC priorities and values into choices and recommendations on cleanup alternatives, and that the EPA help the coalition understand Superfund job training possibilities.

By spring 2015, however, despite dozens of emails and meetings with EPA staff over the previous few years, PHCC leaders and members held out little hope that the federal agency would actually support the coalition in these areas. In April 2015, nearly a dozen PHCC members convened for a conference call with EPA's Region 10 and National Environmental Justice Office officials, outlining concerns about EJ implications in the EPA's Superfund cleanup planning process.

During the call, national EPA officials thanked PHCC for its work on behalf of impacted communities. But instead of responding directly to PHCC's concerns, officials enumerated a list of all the public involvement activities conducted by the agency over the previous several years. PHCC representatives requested a written response a few weeks later, anticipating a more direct address of PHCC's concerns. Again, however, PHCC received an inventory of the EPA's public involvement activities. It appeared that EPA officials, even in the national EJ office, were far more concerned with ticking boxes on a checklist than engaging substantively with vulnerable communities.

In contrast to PHCC's assessment of the EPA, which highlighted a lack of meaningful engagement with communities, EPA officials described things another way. As another 2016 email to PHCC leaders explained:

> Over the past years, informational outreach, community based computer resource tools, as well as grant funds supporting community outreach have been provided to communities. EPA has been in the community offering in-

formation and answering questions about risks, cleanup technologies, job programs, Portland Harbor background and next steps. In addition to regular EPA outreach, the PHCC was invited to attend quarterly briefings with the EPA, Regional Administrator to hear project updates and to express concerns. In recent months, EPA organized a series of community-wide information sessions, a webinar and conducted in-person sessions with various community organizations in order to prepare people to comment on the Proposed Plan. Translation assistance was provided for the information sessions hosted by EPA. Along with the series of information sessions offered by EPA, the Agency also participated in community forums hosted by community groups. (Copy of EPA email shared with author)

The EPA's email went on to directly address Cassie Cohen, implicitly chastising her for questioning the agency's intentions:

Cassie, with your previous role as the convener of the PHCC and Director of Groundwork Portland, you are aware that EPA has been actively engaged with the PHCC since its inception. The Agency has provided training, participated in discussions, provided translated materials and demographic maps to the members. The EPA EJ coordinator also has also been actively involved with PHCC and its members over the years and offered training workshops on EPA based mapping tools to support community engagement. The EJ coordinator also participated in numerous meetings to better understand and offer solutions to requests from the PHCC.

While the EPA did hold several public information sessions, from PHCC's perspective, the agency did not appropriately partner with local organizations, nor did it effectively advertise the events; the proof lies in the poor attendance by impacted community members at EPA-sponsored meetings and hearings. One public comment period hearing, for example, took place at a local social service agency catering to immigrants and refugees. Leaders at the center, however, reported that almost none of their clients attended. They said that the EPA only requested to reserve the space, making few moves to actually partner with the organization in the planning process to ensure that the event appealed to service recipients.

Although the EPA may have conducted a long list of outreach activities, these had little bearing on the actual capacities of impacted communities to meaningfully participate in or sway the planning process. In a 2017 conversation, Cassie offered a blunt conclusion: "These are examples of what EPA refers to as a successful outreach to diverse populations, but we refer to as failed outreach." There is a wide gap in inviting people to meetings and really welcoming people, engaging with them, ensuring that the content and format of the event meets people where they are at culturally and in terms of the information they are seeking. While the EPA may well have met the letter of the law in terms of public participation, engagements from 2012 through 2016 did not meet the spirit of true inclusivity.

"We Have Offered Numerous Informational Sessions (and a Webinar!)"

Examining activities during the EPA's public comment period reveals a third way in which the EPA dismissed the concerns of those who have suffered the most from harbor pollution. The most obvious way, to PHCC, that the EPA ignored the needs of frontline communities during the public comment period was the agency's refusal to grant more than a 30-day extension to the mandatory 60-day window during which time the public could comment on the Proposed Cleanup Plan. In early July, after the Portland Audubon and other groups requested additional time, the agency extended the comment period to 90 days. Then, on July 19, 2016, PHCC leaders emailed a request to the EPA for an additional extension, for a total of 120 days. PHCC's letter cited one main reason for the additional 30-day request: "As of July 7th [30 days into the comment period], the EPA did not yet have project materials translated into Spanish. . . . One of our organizers visited the EPA Portland office, and the only translated material available was a Spanish glossary of terms. This is inadequate for Spanish speakers to be fully informed. . . . Providing all residents equal access to public participation is required under federal Title VI Civil Rights laws." PHCC leaders also worried that many coalition members were out of town, particularly Indigenous and Latinx members, visiting extended family during the summer months. An additional extension would provide more opportunity for members of these communities to mobilize their friends and neighbors to submit comments.

Ten days later, EPA officials responded with an email, denying PHCC's request for an extension. In the same manner that the EPA had responded to PHCC's EJ concerns a few months' prior, the email summarized all of the ways that the EPA had conducted outreach to date. The accounting began, "As you are aware, over the past 6 months, we have offered numerous Informational Sessions (and a webinar!) at different locations in the greater Portland area prior to the release of the *Proposed Plan*, specifically designed to foster robust discussion and information sharing" (copy of email shared with author). The email went on to enumerate the four Portland Harbor *Pro-*

posed Plan meetings that the EPA had organized, describe the translation services that were offered at these meetings, and list the various publications in which the EPA summarized the *Proposed Plan* and provided information about upcoming meetings. To address PHCC's concern about translated materials being unavailable, the email stated, "On July 6th a member from the PHCC requested and picked up Fact Sheets and a Glossary of Terms translated into Spanish, Russian, Vietnamese and Chinese from the Portland EPA Office. While a Spanish Fact Sheet was unavailable at the time (it was being revised to include updated information) everyone may now access both the Fact Sheet and the Glossary of Terms in English, Spanish, Russian, Vietnamese and Chinese." But the Fact Sheets included only a tiny slice of the information contained in the 151-page *Proposed Plan*, and coalition leaders questioned the utility of translated glossaries when the *Proposed Plan* itself was only available in English.

The EPA's email also described the various opportunities available for public comment and explained: "We have worked hard to make each public meeting as accommodating as possible for all communities. After early initial discussions with area groups and individuals, we specifically planned meetings to span work hours and evening hours, offering various locations and formats that allowed for oral comments in a public forum as well as in private for those more comfortable in that setting." The email ended with an acknowledgment of the sparse attendance at Public Comment meetings:

> While there were many opportunities for diverse communities to engage during the comment period, and despite repeated, focused efforts to publicize and communicate with organizations like yours and the PHCC about those opportunities, we hoped there would have been broader turnout to our Public Comment meetings. At this time, the EPA does not plan on scheduling additional public meetings. We encourage you and everyone wishing to comment on the Proposed Plan to submit your comments either in writing or by e-mail by the September 6, 2016 public comment deadline. Community input is a very important part of the cleanup planning process and we value public comments on the Proposed Plan. All forms of comment (written, e-mailed and spoken) are treated equally and will receive a written response when the Record of Decision is signed.

Accepting that time was running short and that the EPA was unlikely to grant any more extensions, PHCC leaders began to mobilize people to attend the EPA's fourth and final hearing, scheduled for Wednesday, July 20, 2016. PHCC leaders had publicized the first three hearings via email and social media but had not explicitly organized people to attend them. For one thing, some of the City of Portland funds that had enabled PHCC to hire three part-time community organizers were not available until after the public comment period had already begun. Second, PHCC's organizers focused much of their energy on planning culturally specific events to collect testimony, held separately from the EPA's officially sanctioned hearings. PHCC leaders knew that the EPA would (or at least should) treat all forms of testimony equally, and knew that community members were more likely to attend a street party or cookout in the park than a government-sponsored event.

What the EPA did not acknowledge, however, was that this short public comment period took place in the context of the PRPs being given *fifteen years* to plan and negotiate, during which time many of them stalled, missed deadlines, produced inaccurate reports, and attempted to deceive the public. The PRPs in essence were allowed to delay the behind-the-scenes process for years, but when it came time for the *public* process, local, state, and federal agencies insisted they stick to a very tight, short timeline.

Moreover, the EPA continued its tokenizing treatment during the public comment period in another way: presenters rarely delivered content during information sessions and hearings in a way that PHCC's constituents could actually understand and use. On the evening of the fourth and final hearing, for example, PHCC organizers mobilized a strong showing. A half-dozen Líderes Verdes members attended, as well as a few dozen representatives from East European Coalition, Groundwork Portland's youth Green Team, Right 2 Survive, and local Indigenous and Black-led organizations that had recently become involved with the coalition. Our crew sat in the back of the room, huddled together on conference room chairs upholstered in mustard yellow fabric. The air-conditioned space contrasted starkly with the intense summer heat outside, and the fluorescent lights flattened the windowless room, compounding the monotone presentations and resulting in a disorienting experience for attendees.

The first presenter spent twenty minutes of the two-hour session summarizing the *Proposed Plan*. The slides included histograms, diagrams, and flow charts that were entirely illegible to the average person in attendance. One slide alone included undefined terms such as "bathymetric survey," "deposition rates," and "anthropogenic factors." A PHCC member who had been learning about the cleanup for over two years, developing plenty of background understanding compared to the average Portlander, whispered to me, "I have no idea what she's talking about." I, too, after spending nearly five years in the National Science Foundation's flagship interdisciplinary graduate education program at Portland State University, designed to help emerging social scientists learn to engage in biophysical science conversations and vice versa, felt confused and disengaged.

My seatmates and I squinted to make sense of the rows and columns on a slide depicting eight alternative cleanup scenarios. For each situation, the table listed associated dredge volumes, dredge areas, dredge/cap areas, cap areas, in situ areas, acres of Enhanced Natural Recovery, acres of Monitored Natural Recovery, construction time frames, and costs.

As we exchanged confused looks, a coalition member's phone vibrated against her knee. She whispered, "Oh god," and held her phone up for me to see an image of a Black man lying on his back in the middle of a road, both hands raised straight up. The news headline read: "Cop Shoots Caretaker of Autistic Man Playing in the Street with Toy Truck" (Rabin, 2016). We skimmed further and sat in disbelief. The man was unarmed, the article reported. When the shooting victim asked the Miami police officer why he shot him, the officer responded by saying, "I don't know." Later, we would learn the name of the man shot by police: Charles Kinsey.

I sank into my chair, cheeks flushed. Here we were, watching a dog and pony show, listening to EPA officials utter acronym after acronym after acronym about a cleanup plan that we feared would ultimately be inadequate to lift fish advisories, let alone allow frontline communities to access other benefits of the cleanup, such as jobs and affordable housing near the river. At least three people pointed out in their oral testimony following the official presentation that they would be long gone by the time remediation was complete. I thought about those who, like the man bleeding in a Miami street, might not make it to next week without abolition of the police and prison system. Or through the winter without a serious revamping of housing and health-care systems. I had recently read Pulido et al.'s (2016) scholarly critique of the EPA, which cited the federal agency's abysmal record addressing environmental justice communities, which I had shared with PHCC members—so we all knew that the possibility of a formal complaint being taken seriously by the EPA was virtually nil. I wondered, was it worth it for people to turn out to this public hearing potentially to fruitlessly testify about the harbor cleanup, while so many struggled to survive just one more day at the hands of police? But I also knew that these issues were interlinked: the police protected (white people's) property, and the fate of not only a beloved stretch of land and river but also housing accessibility, jobs, police treatment of houseless people; so much more was at stake in the harbor cleanup.

Strategizing to Avoid EJ Failure

Ultimately, despite the egregious actions on the part of the EPA described here, PHCC members decided against filing a formal Title VI complaint and instead focused on mobilizing as many people as possible to call for a much more thorough cleanup during the comment period. By the end of the summer, over five thousand people had submitted comments on the *Proposed Plan*; the vast majority called for more robust remediation measures. In addition to PHCC, others, including the Yakama Nation, the Oregon chapter of the Sierra Club, Willamette Riverkeeper, Columbia Riverkeeper, Portland Audubon, and the Portland Harbor Community Advisory Group, had solicited comments from their membership bases. Additionally, local housing activist and independent bookstore owner Chloe Eudaly was running for city commissioner at the time, largely on a tenant's rights platform but also with an outspoken river cleanup agenda. Her campaign staff worked with PHCC members to produce a short, animated film taking polluters to task and encouraging people to speak out during the comment period.

PHCC submitted an enumeration of its own to the EPA in its official comment—but of a much different character than the EPA's lists detailing lukewarm public involvement activities. In contrast to the EPA's accounting, PHCC's public comment letter highlighted a sharply divergent interpretation of the treatment of impacted communities throughout the months, years, and centuries leading up to the comment period. Elaborating on the letter PHCC submitted to the city just a few months' prior, the coalition's testimony letter of summer 2016 opened with a historical narrative about its core members:

> We are the Portland Harbor Community Coalition (PHCC), an alliance of over a dozen member organizations and supporting groups. We represent those most impacted by contamination in the Portland Harbor Superfund site: Native people, Blacks/African Americans, immigrants and refugees, people experiencing houselessness/homelessness, and working-class Portlanders of all races and ethnicities. The ways that our people have been impacted by Portland harbor pollution are varied and complex, but must be understood by EPA in order to make an informed decision that fulfils its ethical and legal responsibilities. (Copy of letter shared with author)

Following the introduction, the letter went on to specify how frontline communities have suffered at the hands of polluters. The letter then took the EPA to task for its shoddy participation process:

When evaluating community acceptance, EPA must do more than invoke the concept of the community, or "the public." It must acknowledge that the community most affected by toxic contamination is the most important voice when judging the adequacy of a remedy, as it has suffered the most serious harm. This harm is not at all comparable to the financial cost that is properly borne by PRPs; this recognition was part of the original understanding of CERCLA, and is embodied in the very name "Superfund," which presumed polluters would pay in advance, and would pay the full cost of their pollution to maintain a healthy environment.

It is in this light that we must condemn the extremely short, highly inadequate, and improperly managed public process surrounding this Proposed Plan. After nearly 16 years of intense negotiations between the EPA and the PRPs, the public has been rushed through a very hasty process that has included failure by EPA to translate key documents, failure to maintain a functioning email account to receive public comments, poorly publicized hearings that convey information in an overly technical manner, and are therefore not accessible to average attendees (let alone those most impacted) . . . and refusal to grant reasonable extensions to the comment period. . . . All of the issues just listed have been informed by an unrealistic timeline for a ROD [Record of Decision]. Peter deFur, the technical Superfund Advisor retained by the Community Advisory Group, told the public that for the EPA to reach a ROD by the end of the year, they will have to work in record time once the comment period ends, and that, more likely than not, *the ROD has already been written.*

The ROD timeline and its technical requirements, combined with the procedural failures outlined above, creates serious doubt that what we have witnessed over the last few months was a meaningful public process. . . . We now believe that EPA's handling of this public comment period may violate Title VI of the Civil Rights Act.

The letter then implored the EPA to "uphold our constitutional rights, our civil rights, and our fundamental human right to a clean environment," as well as "to honor the federal government's treaties with Tribal nations," and enumerated the ways in which the *Proposed Plan* currently was likely to be in violation of legally protected rights and treaties.

The tokenizing treatment that PHCC experienced in interactions with the EPA is indicative of a depoliticized planning process devoid of opportunity for members of marginalized communities to meaningfully participate. Although PHCC did not engage in direct action or other tactics falling outside of the EPA's established channels as a result of interactions with the agency (as with the city), the coalition nevertheless also did not place faith in the

EPA's time-consuming formal complaint process. Instead, coalition members focused on garnering as much public support as possible for a more robust cleanup, in conjunction with placing pressure on the city to respond to the needs of its most vulnerable residents.

Conclusion

PHCC's (dis)engagements with public agencies stem from the contradictions of the sustainability context in which many EJ groups are now working. The sustainable city promises fresh air and clean water, public transit and bike-able neighborhoods to all. Yet, without explicit anti-displacement provisions, such amenities are part and parcel of eco-gentrification and displacement, and they have largely accrued for white, wealthier residents. Crucially, environmental cleanup is by and large under the purview of regulatory agencies such as the EPA, while built environment improvements largely come under the control of local agencies. Given this multi-scalar governance structure, it is an incredibly complex task for frontline communities to figure out how to bring about an improved urban environment in the sustainability era—and to actually have access to environmental improvements rather than be displaced by rising housing costs tied to urban greening.

As we saw in chapter 5, the City of Portland's public engagement process did little to include members of marginalized groups, let alone provide a pathway for PHCC's constituents to actually sway outcomes of the cleanup planning process or to have a say in the harbor's next chapter.

At the federal level, the online tool that EPA officials offered PHCC would have consumed the coalition's time and energy, while contributing little to advance the interests of frontline communities in the harbor cleanup. Then, when PHCC expressed discontent with the EPA's outreach process, officials repeatedly responded by accounting for all of the public engagement activities the agency had conducted, with no explanation for how these activities *meaningfully* engaged frontline communities or actually contributed to eliminating disparate outcomes. Overall, PHCC's experience with the EPA's public engagement process was that it was ineffective in providing underrepresented communities the information needed to adequately participate in and sway the decision-making process. And yet, after receiving over 5,300 public comments, the vast majority in favor of a stronger cleanup plan, the EPA's final Record of Decision released in January 2017 called for nearly double the amount of contaminated sediment to be removed from the river bottom (EPA, 2017b). Following remediation, it is expected that people will be able to safely consume approximately 25 percent more resident fish than the original *Pro-*

posed Plan would have allowed. Rose Longoria, Yakama Nation Fisheries Regional Superfund projects manager, summarizes the collaboration that this outcome required in a 2022 interview: "We worked really hard together, all of us—Audubon, Portland Harbor Community Coalition, Willamette Riverkeeper, the Portland Harbor Community Advisory Group—to engage the community. EPA received more comments from the public than almost any other Superfund site in the nation. The sheer number of public comments really meant something. I believe our collaboration was a significant factor in that final cleanup decision." While far from an ideal outcome, PHCC members and allies nevertheless considered the ROD an important step forward toward healthier fish and communities.

Recall that nearly all of the Title VI complaints filed against the EPA prior to January 2014 have been dismissed. In other words, EJ communities' reliance on the state to check the power of polluters actually *inhibits* achievement of more just results. The case of PHCC provides an actually existing example of a grassroots group that has attempted to find a more effective way forward, by engaging public agencies partially outside of established channels. And yet, PHCC has not pursued particularly intense direct action tactics employed by many groups fighting for social and environmental justice, such as marching in lanes of traffic, dangling off of bridges, staging hunger strikes, instituting boycotts and strikes, and other more drastic counterpower measures. In fact, at one summer 2016 meeting, coalition members discussed how to best sway the EPA to extend the public comment period another 120 days, and one participant suggested staging a "die-in" on the Burnside Bridge, as Black Lives Matter activists had recently done following the murder of Philando Castile, an unarmed Black man, by Minneapolis-St. Paul police. Other PHCC members, some of whom had been active with Portland's racial justice groups and others working for police abolition, disagreed with this tactic. The impact of harbor pollution on people has indeed been horrible, and the exploitation of land for profit is sickening, impacting communities' lives and livelihoods in disruptive and unjust ways for generations, they agreed. But cleaning up the harbor generally and extending the public comment period specifically were not quite on par with the urgency of addressing the state-sanctioned murder of Black people on a near-daily basis. Nor could everyone afford to risk arrest and bodily harm for this particular cause. And more simply, the resources (i.e., time, funds, bodies) needed to mobilize this sort of action were in short supply. Coalition members instead decided to rely on the mounting number of people signing onto the coalition's collective public comment letter, as well as submitting their own public comments to sway the EPA from *within* established channels, even as the coalition decided not to file a Title VI grievance against the EPA—a clear move to conserve resources.

PHCC is a grassroots organization that has been open to taking a more confrontational approach rather than simply engaging through bureaucratic channels, and indeed it has employed a combination of tactics in its work. PHCC members came to understand the limits of engaging with regulatory agencies while simultaneously arguing that public agencies must be impelled to act. In the case of PHCC then, we see an example of how change has unfolded in *radically incremental* ways. PHCC has engaged with government agencies around one particular project and has sought the redistribution of public resources. PHCC has forced the City of Portland and EPA to consider a wider range of issues and has helped hundreds of frontline community members—many with little to no prior knowledge of the Superfund site process—learn about all aspects of the harbor, policy processes at multiple scales, and each other in order to bring about a more just world. The coalition emerged out of critiques of the cleanup planning process and is rooted in community organizing and building the power of frontline communities. Through a combination of direct action and more participatory means, the coalition garnered funds to continue organizing and deepen members' engagement and critical analysis. In formal and informal communications with local and federal agencies, coalition members articulated grievances that public agencies had previously ignored. In large part, this required PHCC members to cut through the depoliticized, science and technology-heavy discourse that permeates sustainability discussion, illuminating the reality that sustainable development often further exacerbates rather than alleviates racialized poverty and oppression.

PHCC members ultimately forced officials to begin to acknowledge the power relations that produce and perpetuate disparities, resulting in policy changes and, notably, public commitments from city and EPA officials to be more responsive to impacted communities going forward. PHCC will no doubt face challenges during the implementation phase of these policy shifts, but what is clear is that ordinary people banded together to demand resources and policy shifts, and in so doing they gained power to sway future decision-making processes at the interconnected city and federal scales.

Wapato
Sagittaria latifolia

Conclusion

As I write the conclusion to this book, in late July 2020, people are out in the streets in U.S. cities on a scale unseen since at least the 1960s, and possibly ever. There is an unprecedented pandemic—and revolution, hopefully—underway. Last night I donned a bike helmet and snowboard goggles and headed downtown with our neighbor, a fellow white mama who has protested three or more times a week since the uprisings began, in the dark. I felt scared to potentially face powerful tear gas and rubber bullets, but I reminded myself: Black mothers have been showing up, over and over, for more than four hundred years. Following the murder of George Floyd by officer Derek Chauvin in Minneapolis, Minnesota, on May 25, 2020, the Black Lives Matter movement galvanized hundreds of thousands of people to demand an end to white supremacy, an end to racism, an end to policing as we know it today. "Racism is the Pandemic" is one popular slogan, hand-lettered on cardboard signs. And, over and over, "Black Lives Matter." With an estimated forty thousand people turning out one warm June night in Portland, and over sixty thousand people submitting testimony to the city in support of cutting $50 million from the police budget, the city emerged early on as an epicenter of the uprisings. And for sixty nights and counting, Portlanders have shown up. The Portland Police Bureau (ROD) has responded in full force, deploying so-called less lethal munitions against people exercising their first amendment rights. Weapons have included tear gas, rubber bullets, pepper balls, flash bangs, sonic weapons, baton beatings, and more. ROD officers have explicitly targeted medics, legal observers, and journalists and have purposefully destroyed medical supplies. Nightly, they have declared riots in response to little beyond chanting and singing, in order to justify the use of such force. They have "kettled" protestors, trapping them in areas with no escape route, only to attack when people fail to follow unfollowable dispersal orders.

On June 26, 2020, President Donald Trump signed an executive order to protect "Federal monuments, memorials, statues, or property." A week later on July 4, following a day-time Indigenous-led march for Black Lives through downtown Portland, at least 114 federal troops from various U.S. Department of Homeland Security agencies attacked protestors in the dark. The assault was led by the Border Patrol Tactical Unit (BORTAC), authorized to carry out "high-risk missions" both domestically and abroad while carrying deadly weapons such as grenade launchers, high-powered gas guns, sniper rifles, and assault rifles. Coordinating with Portland police officers and Multnomah County Sheriff's deputies to attack Black Lives Matter supporters, for more than four straight weeks BORTAC agents used massive amounts of tear gas and pepper balls in an attempt to disperse crowds. They indiscriminately shot nonviolent protestors in the face with rubber bullets and struck people with batons. My friend's housemate, a journalist, was shot fifteen times one night. Unidentified Border Patrol agents wearing camouflage have also kidnapped people off the streets, grabbing them and shoving them into unmarked vans. Trump asserts that deploying troops to Portland is part of his plan to "take over cities" where crime is allegedly surging.

City of Portland mayor and police commissioner, Ted Wheeler, condemned the federal occupation—yet continued to authorize the Portland Police Bureau to use the exact same tactics as federal troops, resulting in injuries to thousands of people exercising their first amendment rights. In fact, during the first week of August, after federal troops retreated from being visibly present on the streets (while remaining in the city and supporting the local and Oregon State Police behind the scenes despite media claims to the contrary), police began using the most violent tactics yet: bull-rushing protestors while wearing full riot gear, slashing tires of vehicles, deploying massive amounts of tear gas in residential neighborhoods, and refusing to charge a presumed white supremacist who weaponized his pickup truck, blowing through a fence and barricades and narrowly missing dozens of protesters. I am shocked and relieved that police and vigilantes have yet to murder anyone out on the streets of Portland this summer, given the viciousness with which they have responded to chants of "Black Lives Matter."

As my neighbor and I walked across the Hawthorne Bridge over the Willamette River toward the protest that late July evening—a bridge on which PHCC had staged a march for a cleaned-up harbor six years earlier—downtown Portland looked eerily quiet. Few other pedestrians were out, despite the warm summer air; most residents slept at home, quarantining from both a deadly pandemic and the nightly street violence. Finally, we began to hear a faint drum beat. As within a volcano cauldron, with lava bubbling and pre-paring to explode, the actions focused on federal troops have mostly stayed in-side a few blocks contained by skyscrapers downtown. From just a few hun-dred steps away, we began to glimpse hints of what was happening within: smoke drifted down the street, cop SUVs circled surrounding blocks, helicop-ters chopped overhead, bikers blocked intersections in a courageous attempt to keep fellow protestors as safe as possible. To really see the action, however, required entering the park blocks right in front of the Justice Center and Fed-eral Courthouse.

As we approached the courthouse, the sounds began to grow louder. "Black Lives Matter! Black Lives Matter!" Then, "No Justice, No Peace! No Justice, No Peace!" I felt tear gas and pepper spray in my throat, even though none had been deployed yet that night: it was stuck in the trees from the previous several nights. Banned by the Geneva Convention in times of war, it was also stuck in peoples' bodies and the Willamette River. Dozens and dozens of sto-ries have come to light of protesters experiencing extremely concerning symp-toms as a result of the tear gas and other chemical weapons, including heavy periods multiple times a month or for several weeks at a time, fist-sized blood clots, and debilitating cramps. The toxic sludge also threatens the Willamette, and several groups have filed a lawsuit against public agencies in response. The city has deployed crews attempting to clean out the storm drains before rains wash it all into the river; no doubt some has already leached into the wa-terway (R. Ellis, 2020; Samayoa, 2020).

In the dark that night, a helicopter of unknown origin circled overhead. I viscerally felt the words of a blogger I had read earlier that day, who described the choppers as "flaying your skin from the inside out." People wore black ban-danas and gas masks, swim goggles and bike helmets. Our fellow protestors wielded homemade wooden shields with stenciled fists raised high, umbrel-las to block people's faces from security cameras and tear gas canisters thrown from the "murder holes" in the federal building above, and, taking a page out of Hong Kong's own recent uprising, leaf blowers to redirect tear gas and other toxic substances back toward the feds. People also carried hockey sticks, to swipe gas canisters away from the crowd. George Clinton filled the air, blasted from tinny speakers in a bike basket. One person walked through the crowd, anointing us with burning sage. Others passed out homemade tear gas wipes and cans of yerba maté, ear plugs and bottled water. A few people shook the heavy fence the feds had erected around the courthouse. "No good cops in a racist system!" people chanted, rhythmically. A small trash fire burned on the sidewalk. The massive stone edifice behind the fire looked like a freeway underpass rather than a stately courthouse in the reflected light of the flames. A drone swooped low overhead, and several people attempted to hit it with plastic water bottles. The air was simultaneously festive and serious. People knew what to expect and had grown semi-impervious to the munitions in the moment—but also knew that the unforeseen could happen at any time. Throughout the night, drummers kept the energy high.

Over the rhythms, a robo-voice suddenly blared: "This is the first warning. Disperse immediately or you will be subject to arrest, citation, or the use of impact weapons or tear gas." All around us people bristled, becoming more alert. As we tightened our respirators and gas masks and huddled closer together, the crowd drowned out the warning with howls and more chanting. Green lasers swirled against the stone facade in an attempt to block the view of snipers posted high above. "Stay together! Stay tight! We do this every night!" A few minutes later, smoke billowed into the crowd, and federal agents streamed out of the blockaded building. Coughing and choking, people stood their ground, arms locked. A street medic calmly guided someone away as they gasped and gagged on tear gas that stung the air and lungs, even through respirators. The crowd retreated a dozen steps, then moved forward again, arms still linked. More canisters skidded, more sparks flew in chaotic directions. Legal observers and reporters jockeyed for position against the fence to witness and document. Someone put a bright orange traffic cone over a smoking cylinder, and their partner immediately poured water through the cone's hole; the smoke dissipated, the canister neutralized.

The action happened not only after dark. Earlier that afternoon, Kai, now four years old, and I had both felt hot tear gas and pepper ball residue in our throats when we went down to check in with people living at the park across the street from the federal building. Dozens of unhoused people have long made their home in the park blocks—now ground zero of the federal occupation. We brought Abolish the Police posters and Know Your Rights pamphlets, focused on the rights of unhoused community members when police and city contractors come to sweep—forcibly remove or evict—them. We also brought a case of donated Dr. Bronner's soap to go with the handwashing stations that comrades had made from garbage cans and spigots earlier that week. Such efforts played the tiniest of roles in support of Riot Ribs, a crew of largely Black, unhoused people and supporters grilling ribs, hotdogs, and veggie dogs 24/7 since July 4th in the park, stopping only momentarily when the feds shot pepper balls into all the grills, slashed cases of water, and contaminated trays and trays of food with tear gas. Yet, each time within twenty-four hours of the destruction the crew set back up with dozens of donated coolers and barbeques and crates of water and so many other supplies. That afternoon, Kai and I watched cooks expertly paste shiny red sauce on long racks of ribs, free to anyone who needed some sustenance. Next to the food tables was an overflowing hygiene station, as well as an art table and huge spread of sack lunches for people getting released from jail at the Justice Center a block away. Piles and piles of well-organized donated supplies, everything from tampons to ketchup, musical instruments to shaving kits, socks to bike helmets, beckoned people to come and get what they needed.

Movements for a More Just City, and World

What does the summer 2020 uprising, in a time of pandemic, have to do with PHCC and the coalition's efforts to reshape one so-called sustainable city? Nothing, and everything. In the epigraph to a paper in *English Language Notes*, EJ activist-researchers Lindsey Dillon and Julie Sze (2016) quote a line from Frantz Fanon's 1952 book, *Black Skin, White Masks*, commonly depicted on Black Lives Matter signs: "When we revolt it's not for a particular culture. We revolt simply because, for many reasons, we can no longer breathe." In invoking Fanon's words, Black Lives Matter activists affirm that the *breath* is a political space, "a metaphor for police violence in the United States" (Dillon and Sze, 2018). Dillon and Sze draw on the differential ways in which asthma, for instance, affects Black people living in San Francisco, paralleled by the anti-Black death of Eric Garner at the hands of the NYPD. "I can't breathe" were Garner's last words as NYPD officer Daniel Pantaleo put him in a chokehold after attempting to arrest him for the "crime" of illegally selling cigarettes, suffocating Garner to death. More recently, George Floyd also uttered the words "I can't breathe" over and over as Officer Derek Chauvin kneeled on his neck for eight minutes and forty-six seconds, galvanizing the summer 2020 uprising. Environmental racism and police brutality, Dillon and Sze assert, "constrict breath" for the same population. And they are interconnected, given that police are charged with protecting property in less polluted places, pushing Black and Indigenous communities and other people of color into hazardous spaces.

In turn, today hundreds of thousands of people are risking their own breath coming out in the streets—and in the case of unhoused residents, remaining in the streets. Not only is a fully unchecked deadly respiratory pandemic underway, with no signs that the state will take meaningful action to halt its spread, but police are indiscriminately deploying chemical weapons such as tear gas, pepper spray, mace, and smoke bombs, inducing coughing, gagging, and vomiting, and potentially inflicting long-term damage to people's lungs. Most affected are those protesting and living outdoors, as well as families living in nearby homes. At least one Portland-based mutual aid group has been distributing gas masks and respirators to households with children living near police precincts and other protest sites. Those who have suffered from years of environmental racism and the effects of a highly racist and classist health-care system differentially along lines of race, gender, ability, age, and other axes of difference no doubt are the most susceptible to such cumulative harms. Critical EJ scholar David Pellow (2018:19) explains, crucially, "While the *experiences* of these various groups are qualitatively distinct (they are not equivalent), the *logic* of domination and othering as practiced by more powerful groups against them provides a thread of intersectionality through each of their oppressions."

While much work remains to undo systems of white supremacy and to bring an end to the white supremacist logics that infuse even justice-seeking coalitions such as PHCC, such grassroots groups have for years been laying groundwork to dismantle racist, colonial, patriarchal, heteronormative structures. PHCC members and supporters, past and present, have turned out to protests all during summer 2020 and played myriad other roles in attempting to force an end to white supremacy and settler colonialism: leading, participating in, and donating to Black- and Indigenous-led organizations; amplifying struggles in news outlets and on social media; pushing the city to abolish, or at minimum substantially defund, the police in policy discussions; demanding that the feds leave our city alone; getting water to nearby tribes who are so harshly impacted by the Covid-19 pandemic. The current "movement moment" was made possible by the foundation laid by countless grassroots and homemade efforts over decades and centuries, including PHCC members.

Regardless of short-term outcomes in the Portland Harbor, so many people who have crossed paths in harbor-related work have played small and large parts in erecting the base upon which today's movements stand, through relationship building, politicization, working through internal conflicts, strategizing, speaking truth to power, getting shut down, trying again. People experience a sense of belonging, of something larger than themselves, through such work. We begin to see how our own lives are entwined with others' when we learn each other's histories—and we also see how different groups benefit from the oppressions of others. People become politicized when they come together to analyze how public agencies dismiss their concerns and tokenize their experiences. They learn some of the pros and cons of different strategies and tactics. All this experience enables ordinary people to contribute to larger "movement moments" like the one unfolding in the streets today.

A main premise of *Green City Rising* is that the sustainable city-building paradigm forecloses opportunities for grassroots groups to meaningfully shape urban greening processes, and at the same time it presents possibilities for progress toward a more just, green future, in part because of the ways in which frontline groups such as PHCC have pushed new narratives of the past and future. To bring about truly transformative change, it is necessary to tell and hear a different story about urban sustainability and city building more broadly. This narrative must center the perspectives of historically and presently uprooted communities and their bold visions for an antiracist and decolonial world.

Fights for EJ in so-called green cities, where sustainability initiatives too often reify existing racialized disparities upheld by racist police forces, are full of contradictions. My goal in writing this book is to highlight struggles for EJ in an era of mainstream urban greening, underscoring the perspectives of those who have carried the burdens of toxic industry for generations and who are now leading the way toward a more *just* sustainability. Diverse grassroots groups are attempting to reconcile the racist, colonial past and present as these groups redefine what an environmental movement can be, and who it can serve. They are exploiting cracks in the "green growth machine" for more humane processes and outcomes. As I attempt to show here, the paradoxes of green development are particularly stark in Portland, making it an important place to tell a contemporary story of EJ organizing.

The contradictions that PHCC has encountered in attempting to push the harbor toward a more just future informs a theory of change that helps explain what is happening in cities across the United States in this era of mainstream environmental concern. Like so many groups, at the same time as PHCC seeks to bolster environmental regulations and fully remediate the harbor, the coalition also seeks access to environmental amenities and fundamental provisions such as housing and decent-paying jobs that are promised to all sustainable city residents. Yet, environmental cleanup is by and large under the purview of regulatory agencies such as the EPA, whereas built environment improvements largely come under the control of local agencies. Given this multi-scalar web of governance, it is an incredibly complex task for frontline communities to figure out how to bring about an improved urban environment in the sustainability era—and to actually have access to environmental improvements rather than be displaced by rising housing costs tied to urban greening.

PHCC has attempted to navigate this complex maze by implicitly taking a "radical incrementalist" approach, adapted to the U.S. sustainable city context. This path has entailed selectively engaging *and* disengaging with the EPA and local public agencies, sometimes cautiously and cooperatively and other times confrontationally, and it has meant pursuing regulatory as well as non-regulatory mechanisms of change. In so doing, PHCC members have simultaneously prioritized short-term survival *and* kept an eye toward the horizon of long-term systemic change, focusing on exterminating hazards alongside building access to a healthy, sustainable environment for all. While far from perfect, the process by which the coalition has pursued change has endeavored to be democratic, centering the voices of those most affected while embracing the support of those who have benefited from the harbor's contamination and cleanup. PHCC's particular radically incremental approach stems from the scalar contradictions of the sustainability context in which many EJ groups are now working; the case of PHCC therefore offers an opportunity to understand the logic and utility of a hybrid approach to change, one that groups in cities across the country have similarly embraced.

Green City Rising tells the story of a beloved river and its people as they attempt to come together across lines of race and class to undo our society's commitment to the interconnected domination of land and people. Through the nightly chants of "Stolen lands, stolen people" and the dialogue occurring in the streets and in organizing meetings, this broader theme envelopes the summer 2020 uprising as well. How can a city that purports to be livable and sustainable for all actually live up to its promise? How can those in power be impelled to cede control? How might a transition to a new world transpire, and is it happening now? What might that new world, a new way of doing things, look like? To me and so many others, a new world does not look like getting gassed by an occupying police force, worrying about your child's safety at the hands of police as they walk to school, nor getting shut out of decades or centuries of government decision-making processes. A new world worth fighting for looks like this: grilling for anyone who is hungry in the park blocks while people chat on benches nearby. Indigenous people having full control over ancestral lands. A world free of racialized police violence, instituted to bolster (white people's) property rights. An end to ableism, homophobia, xenophobia, transphobia, misogyny. People caring for one another, sharing what they have, taking what they need. Stable homes, balanced ecosystems. Clean air and water, healthy fish and birds. Ceremonies on the banks of urban rivers, cookouts in the sand.

NOTES

1. Superfund sites exist throughout the United States. They include former manufacturing facilities, landfills, mines, and processing plants. In 1980, in large part in response to advocacy focused on toxic waste, Congress established the Comprehensive Environmental Response, Compensation and Liability Act (CERCLA). Informally referred to as "Superfund," CERCLA enables the Environmental Protection Agency (EPA) to oversee and enforce cleanup of contaminated sites.

2. Portland Audubon, a long-time PHCC ally, responded to Wheeler's tone-deaf statement in a 2016 social media post: "Perhaps the soon to be Mayor of Portland is not aware that just a few miles downstream from his first 'Swim with the Mayor' event, people are in fact being directly exposed to 'mud' with toxic levels of dioxin, lead, arsenic and other contaminants. Perhaps he is also not aware that just a few miles downstream of his 'Swim with the Mayor' event, people, many of whom depend on the river for food to survive, are eating toxic fish loaded with PCBs that have been contaminated by that toxic mud that he swims above. We hope that in future 'Swim with the Mayor' Events, Ted Wheeler will provide a more accurate picture of the state of our river and become an advocate for cleaning-up the more than 2,000 contaminated acres of polluted river bottom in Portland rather than somebody who simply swims above it" (copy of social media post shared with author).

3. Crucially, such crises stem not only from overproduction but also from collective action. "Racial capitalism," historian Robin D. G. Kelley explains, "experiences periodic crises that are not only the result of business cycles or relative overproduction, etc., but also generated by struggle, insurgencies especially around the legitimacy of the racial regime, which is always unstable and must constantly change and adapt" (quoted in Retish, 2020). See also Kelley's forthcoming book, *Black Bodies Swinging: An American Postmortem.*

4. Literary scholar Jodi Melamed (2015) draws on Cedric Robinson's (1983) seminal *Black Marxism: The Making of a Black Radical Tradition* to assert the centrality of racism to capitalism. Creating and maintaining severely unequal social relations between groups—such as those who own the means of production and workers, creditors and debtors, property owners and the dispossessed—require, in Melamed's words, "loss, disposability, and the unequal differentiation of human value" (77). It is racism that "enshrines the inequalities that capitalism requires" (77); racism, in other words, makes capitalism possible.

5. While defining "environmental justice (EJ) communities" remains a contested, context-dependent undertaking, grassroots groups operating under this umbrella commonly adopt a broad definition, giving the term its "rhetorical power" while refraining from limiting the kinds of issues encompassed under the term (Holifield, 2001). Many groups also now operate under the mantle of "climate justice."

6. For more on shifting frames within the EJ movement, see Carter, 2016; McCreary and Milligan, 2018; Pearsall and Pierce, 2017; Schlosberg, 2004; G. Walker, 2012; S. Walker, 2009.

7. See also Carter, 2016; Ottinger, 2013; Perkins, 2015.

8. Echoing Ruth Wilson Gilmore (2007), Deshonay Dozier (2019) offers a parallel conceptualization to radical incrementalism, drawing on Clyde Woods's "Blues development" concept to articulate how the largely Black houseless population in Los Angeles's Skid Row engages in a contradictory push and pull of grassroots planning to ultimately produce what French social theorist André Gorz (1967) calls "non-reformist reforms." In examining the politics of property on Skid Row, Dozier defines "non-reformist reforms" as those that institute "transformative policies and practices that abolish carcerality" (183). While particular acts of resistance may not eliminate homelessness on the whole, she argues, asserting a right to property nevertheless has produced "limited gains at reducing carceral strategies" (183)—something to celebrate at the same time as grassroots groups continue the fight for full abolition.

9. For more on radical incrementalism in Cape Town organizing, see Ernstson et al. (2014) and Lawhon et al. (2014).

10. Writing about gentrification, community organizer Matt Hern (2016:19) stresses: "The domination of land enables and ennobles the domination of people, but the reverse is equally true. Undoing our commitments to one means undoing the other."

CHAPTER 1. "LITTLE BUGS IN THE MUD"

1. In 2001, EJAG joined a lawsuit led by the United Steelworkers of America against Oregon Steel Mills (now part of Evraz, a Russian-owned Portland Harbor PRP) (Strom, 2003). EJAG was concerned about work conditions at Oregon Steel, as well as air pollution emitted by the company's steel smelting operations that impacted communities of color (especially Black residents) living in North Portland. In 2003, Oregon Steel settled the lawsuit by agreeing to pay for air quality monitoring—a win for EJAG, according to Jeri.

2. Bob Sallinger, from Portland Audubon, notes in a 2021–2022 email exchange the relentlessness with which polluters attempted to evade accountability and intimidate regulators, not only via the lawsuit but also through a ballot measure: "I helped lead the fight against the ballot measure that was brought by the PWUC to remove the Bureau of Environmental Services from the City of Portland control. We called it out for what it was—a bunch of Superfund polluters trying to intimidate, weaken, and destroy the city's environmental programs. Notably although the public overwhelmingly rejected that ballot measure, I think it did have a real impact. I am very convinced that the city's incredibly weak position on the Superfund [Record of Decision] was in large part driven by the intimidation of the PWUC. Politicians did not want to go through

more battles like this so they took weak stances. We had some huge confrontations with City Hall post ballot measure over the fact that after we went to war to protect the city's environmental programs (and won), they then stood down on Superfund and other environmental issues."

3. For historical context, PHCC was far from the first cross-race, cross-class coalition to form around the intersection of environmental and social justice issues. Notably, in the mid-1990s, Urban League of Portland, Oregon Ecumenical Ministries, 1000 Friends of Oregon, Portland Audubon, housing advocates, and others convened the Coalition for a Livable Future (CLF), which lasted until 2013. CLF helped lay groundwork for the intersectional organizing that would unfold later, in the 2010s and beyond. Moreover, PHCC emerged out of and onto a scene in which local environmental organizations had been engaged in negotiating various river-related conflicts such as the Willamette Greenway Plan, the River Plan, Airport Futures, West Hayden Island land use, and others, all of which were precursors to Superfund. "It took a huge amount of effort to lay the groundwork for the fight we are now having," explains Portland Audubon's Bob Sallinger.

CHAPTER 2. A PEOPLES' HISTORY OF THE PORTLAND HARBOR

1. Historians continue to debate this detail (see Kentta and Lewis, 2010).

CHAPTER 4. *PRODUCING* A PEOPLES' HISTORY OF THE PORTLAND HARBOR

1. At this particular meeting, interpretation took place via *consecutive interpretation*: one person speaks and pauses while an interpreter repeats what is said in another language. Consecutive interpretation allows people to fully witness everything being said and requires no extra equipment or electricity, but it takes twice as long since everything must be said twice, and it can interrupt the flow of conversation. Whenever possible, PHCC borrowed equipment from another local organization, enabling *simultaneous translation*. Simultaneous translation involves people wearing headsets that allow them to hear an interpreter repeating the words spoken in one language in another language in real time.

2. Curriculum from the course went on to win the Association of Collegiate Planning Schools / Lincoln Institute of Land Policy's Curriculum Innovation Award in 2020.

CHAPTER 5. GREEN-WASHED GREENWASHING

1. Portland's unique commission form of government entails the mayor appointing responsibility for city bureaus to city council members; it also means that each time a new mayor takes office, responsibilities for the bureaus may be shuffled.

2. It is important to note that cities are not typically responsible for outreach on Superfund. Rather, it is the purview of the oversight agency, the EPA. The City of Portland was in an unusual situation for Superfund processes: it was not only a PRP and a regulator, but it was also charged with a public accountability and engagement role.

Community groups such as PHCC, not surprisingly, often had a difficult time navigating and understanding the decision-making structure.

3. Myles Horton and others founded the Highlander Folk School in Tennessee in 1932. The school provided organizer training for the labor movement in Appalachia. It also played a crucial role in the civil rights movement, including providing training to Rose Parks, members of the Student Nonviolent Coordinating Committee, Martin Luther King Jr., John Lewis, and many other key movement figures, and continues to influence grassroots movements led by poor communities (now renamed the Highlander Research and Education Center).

4. It is important to note that had the City of Portland taken a more "collaborative planning" approach (Innes and Booher, 2010), it would have offered no guarantee of more just outcomes given "deep differences" (Watson, 2006) in rationalities between decision-makers and community members. PHCC, however, might have had more information with which to work had the city followed more of a communicative process.

5. One notable exception is Zidell Corporation. Just upriver from the Portland Harbor Superfund Site, in the South Waterfront area, a dozen glass-encased condominium towers stretch toward the sky. The priciest units overlook the Willamette River. On warm summer afternoons, condoowners, shoppers, and tourists sit on barstools in ground-level bistros, sipping martinis and slurping oysters while bright red and yellow kayak flotillas glide by. Occasionally, a tugboat pushing a barge mounded with gravel lumbers past, reminding residents and tourists of the Willamette's legacy as a *working* river (Abbott, 1983; Hillegas-Elting, 2018; W. Lang, 2010). In fact, the condos and bars of today sit atop and adjacent to land that once hosted a second-hand machinery sales business and later the largest post–World War II shipbreaking operation in the United States, run by Zidell Machinery & Supply Co.

As in the hotspots dotted throughout the Superfund site just north of the Zidell empire, the lucrative shipbreaking industry in the harbor came with a steep cost to the river and nearby land. In the mid-1990s, Zidell agreed to address pollution along a half mile of riverfront land, spending $20 million over twenty years. And yet, court rulings ensured that Zidell "recouped a large portion of their expenses from insurance companies" as well as from the federal government, which provided the ships. Moreover, in classic rent-gap form, the subsidized remediation has opened thirty acres for new development. Plans for Zidell Yards have included 1.5 million square feet of office space, 2.2 million square feet of residential housing, and substantial areas devoted to retail and open recreational space (Profita, 2016). Further, environmentalists contend that Zidell was held to a low standard in its remediation efforts.

While Zidell voluntarily undertook environmental remediation ahead of an imminent EPA mandate to do so, in many ways the Zidell tale prefigures what parts of the ten-mile-long Superfund shoreline might look like in decades to come, absent robust anti-displacement and other social equity-oriented provisions. It also serves as a site of comparison that helps illuminate the dynamics at play in the Portland Harbor Superfund Site, which starts just a half-mile downstream. At the end of the day, it is many of the same growth machine actors at work, whether the development in question is gray, green, or greenwashed.

CHAPTER 6. REMAKING THE CITY, REMAKING OURSELVES

1. An unprecedented new wave of houseless communities had also began to surface prior to the time of publication, given all manner of crises precipitated by the Covid-19 pandemic.

2. Max would again come to Portland, this time in spring 2019, on an invitation from R2S to speak with Black-led groups and diverse houseless-led groups about community control over land and policing.

3. R2S's Pitch-a-Tent wasn't the first ever PAT-type event, however. As early as 2000 people were pointing out hypocrisy of allowing camping for Rose Parade and Blazer games but not survival (Milne, 2000).

REFERENCES

Abbott, C. (1983). *Portland: Planning, Politics and Growth in a Twentieth-Century City.* Lincoln: University of Nebraska Press.

Acker, L. (2016a, August 10). "Ted Wheeler to Swim the Willamette Again." *OregonLive.* https://www.oregonlive.com/portland/index.ssf/2016/08/ted_wheeler_to_swim _the_willam.html (last accessed August 7, 2020)

Acker, L. (2016b, August 18). "We Swam across the Willamette with Ted Wheeler and It Wasn't Even Gross at All." *OregonLive.* https://www.oregonlive.com/trending/ 2016/08/we_swam_across_the_willamette.html (last accessed August 7, 2020)

Agyeman, J. (2013). *Introducing Just Sustainabilities: Policy, Planning, and Practice.* New York: Zed Books.

Anguelovski, I. (2016). "From Toxic Sites to Parks and (Green) Lulus? New Challenges of Inequity, Privilege, Gentrification, and Exclusion for Urban Environmental Justice." *Journal of Planning Literature,* 31(1), 23–36.

Ansley, F. (1989). "Stirring the Ashes: Race, Class, and the Future of Civil Rights Scholarship." *Cornell Law Review,* 74(6), 994–1077.

Arnstein, S. (1969). "A Ladder of Citizen Participation." *Journal of the American Institute of Planners,* 35(4), 216–224.

Aurand, M. (2015). "The Floating Men: Portland and the Hobo Menace, 1890–1915." M.A. thesis, Portland State University.

Banzhaf, H., and E. McCormick (2012). "Moving beyond Cleanup." In H. Banzhaf (ed.), *The Political Economy of Environmental Justice.* Stanford: Stanford University Press, pp. 23–51.

Barber, K. (2019). "We Were at Our Journey's End": Settler Sovereignty Formation in Oregon." *Oregon Historical Quarterly,* 120(4), 382–413.

Bates, L. (2019). "Growth without Displacement: A Test for Equity Planning in Portland." In N. Krumholz and K. Wertheim Hexter (eds.), *Advancing Equity Planning Now.* Ithaca: Cornell University Press, pp. 21–43.

Bates, L., A. Curry-Stevens, and Coalition of Communities of Color (2014). "The African American Community in Multnomah County: An Unsettling Profile." http:// pdxscholar.library.pdx.edu/cgi/viewcontent.cgi?article=1135&context=socwork_fac (last accessed August 7, 2020)

Beauregard, R. (2006). *When America Became Suburban.* Minneapolis: University of Minnesota Press.

Beckett, K., and S. Herbert (2010). *Banished: The New Social Control in Urban America.* Oxford: Oxford University Press.

Bergman, M. (2008). "'We Should Lose Much by Their Absence': The Centrality of Chinookans and Kalapuyans to Life in Frontier Oregon." *Oregon Historical Quarterly*, 109(1), 34–59.

Blalock, B. (2012). *Portland's Lost Waterfront: Tall Ships, Steam Mills, and Sailors' Boardinghouses*. Charleston, S.C.: History Press.

Bogle, K. (1992). "Collections: Oral History Interview: Kathryn Hall Bogle on the African-American Experience in Wartime Portland." Interview by Rick Harmon, Oregon Historical Society. *Oregon Historical Quarterly*, 93(4), 394–405.

Boyd, R. (1999). *The Coming of the Spirit of Pestilence: Introduced Infectious Diseases and Population Decline among Northwest Coast Indians, 1774–1874*. Seattle: University of Washington Press.

Boyd, R. (2013). "Lower Chinookan Disease and Demography." In R. Boyd, K. Ames, and T. Johnson (eds.), *Chinookan Peoples of the Lower Columbia*. Seattle: University of Washington Press, pp. 229–249.

Boyd, R., and Y. Hajda (1987). "Seasonal Population Movement along the Lower Columbia River: The Social and Ecological Context." *American Ethnologist*, 14(2), 309–326.

Brenner, N., and N. Theodore (2002). "Cities and the Geographies of Actually Existing Neoliberalism." *Antipode*, 34(3), 349–379.

Brooks, K., G. Bosker, and T. Gelber (2012). *The Mighty Gastropolis Portland: A Journey through the Center of America's New Food Revolution*. San Francisco: Chronicle Books.

Brown, L. (2022). "Sheltering the Housing Crisis: The Contradictions of Shelters in the Neoliberal City." PhD diss., University of British Columbia.

Brulle, R., and D. Pellow (2006). "Environmental Justice: Human Health and Environmental Inequalities." *Annual Review of Public Health*, 27(1), 103–124.

Bruno, T. (2021). "Environmental Injustice and Black Sense of Place in the Social and Biophysical Afterlife of Slavery." PhD diss., University of Oregon.

Bullard, R. (2000). *Dumping in Dixie: Race, Class, and Environmental Quality*. Boulder: Westview.

Bullard, R., P. Mohai, R. Saha, and B. Wright (2008). "Toxic Wastes and Race at Twenty: Why Race Still Matters After All of These Years." *Environmental Law*, 38(2), 371–411.

Bunce, S., and G. Desfor (2007). "Introduction to 'Political Ecologies of Urban Waterfront Transformations.'" *Cities*, 24(4), 251–258.

Carter, E. (2016). "Environmental Justice 2.0: New Latino Environmentalism in Los Angeles." *Local Environment*, 21(1), 3–23.

Checker, M. (2011). "Wiped Out by the 'Greenwave': Environmental Gentrification and the Paradoxical Politics of Urban Sustainability." *City & Society*, 23(2), 201–229.

Checker, M. (2020). *The Sustainability Myth: Environmental Gentrification and the Politics of Justice*. New York: New York University Press.

Cho, S., K. Crenshaw, and M. Leslie (2013). "Toward a Field of Intersectionality Studies: Theory, Applications, and Praxis." *Signs: Journal of Women in Culture and Society*, 38(4), 785–810.

Choudry, A. (2015). *Learning Activism: The Intellectual Life of Contemporary Social Movements*. Toronto: University of Toronto Press.

City of Portland (2012). *The Portland Plan: Prosperous, Educated, Healthy, Equitable*.

City of Portland (2013, June). "City of Portland Civil Rights Title VI Plan." Office of Management and Finance, Bureau of Internal Business Services. http://www .portlandoregon.gov/oehr/article/523687 (last accessed August 7, 2020)

City of Portland (2016, September 6). Letter from Nick Fish, commissioner, and Charlie Hales, mayor, to Kristine Koch, U.S. Environmental Protection Agency. https://www .portlandoregon.gov/bes/article/588692 (last accessed August 7, 2022)

Cole, L., and S. Foster (2001). *From the Ground Up: Environmental Racism and the Rise of the Environmental Justice Movement*. New York: New York University Press.

Coleman, K. (2019). "'We'll All Start Even': White Egalitarianism and the Oregon Donation Land Claim." *Oregon Historical Quarterly*, 120(4), 414–437.

Columbia River Inter-Tribal Fish Commission CRITFC (1994). *A Fish Consumption Survey of the Umatilla, Nez Perce, Yakama and Warm Springs Tribes of the Columbia River Basin*. Technical Report No. 94-3. Portland: CRITFC.

Corburn, J. (2005). *Street Science: Community Knowledge and Environmental Health Justice*. Cambridge, Mass.: MIT Press.

Crenshaw, K. (1991). "Mapping the Margins: Intersectionality, Identity Politics, and Violence against Women of Color." *Stanford Law Review*, 43, 1241–1299.

Curran, W., and T. Hamilton (2012). "Just Green Enough: Contesting Environmental Gentrification in Greenpoint, Brooklyn." *Local Environment: The International Journal of Justice and Sustainability*, 17(9), 1027–1042.

Curran, W., and T. Hamilton (2018). *Just Green Enough: Urban Development and Environmental Gentrification*. New York: Routledge.

Curry-Stevens, A., A. Cross-Hemmer, and Coalition of Communities of Color (2010). "Communities of Color in Multnomah County: An Unsettling Profile." Portland: Coalition of Communities of Color.

Curry-Stevens, A., A. Cross-Hemmer, and Coalition of Communities of Color (2011). "The Native American Community in Multnomah County: An Unsettling Profile." https://pdxscholar.library.pdx.edu/cgi/viewcontent.cgi?article=1093&context =socwork_fac (last accessed August 7, 2020)

Davidson, M., and K. Iveson (2014). "Recovering the Politics of the City: From the 'Post-Political City' to a 'Method of Equality' for Critical Urban Geography." *Progress in Human Geography*, 39(5), 543–559.

Dillon, L. (2014). "Race, Waste, and Space: Brownfield Redevelopment and Environmental Justice at the Hunters Point Shipyard." *Antipode*, 46(5), 1205–1221.

Dillon, L., and J. Sze (2016). "Police Power and Particulate Matters: Environmental Justice and the Spatialities of In/securities in U.S. Cities." *English Language Notes*, 54(2), 13–23.

Dillon, L., and J. Sze (2018). "Equality in the Air We Breathe: Police Violence, Pollution, and the Politics of Sustainability." In J. Sze (ed.), *Sustainability: Approaches to Environmental Justice and Social Power*. New York: New York University Press, 246–270.

Dooling, S. (2009). "Ecological Gentrification: A Research Agenda Exploring Justice in the City." *International Journal of Urban and Regional Research*, 33(3), 621–639.

Dozier, D. (2019). "Contested Development: Homeless Property, Police Reform, and Resistance in Skid Row, L.A." *International Journal of Urban and Regional Research*, 43(1), 179–194.

Dubet, F. (1994). "The System, the Actor, and the Social Subject." *Thesis Eleven*, 38, 16–35.

Dubet, F. (2004). "Between a Defence of Society and a Politics of the Subject: The Specificity of Today's Social Movements." *Current Sociology*, 52(4), 693–716.

Ducre, K. (2018). "The Black Feminist Spatial Imagination and an Intersectional Environmental Justice." *Environmental Sociology*, 4(1), 22–35.

Duffy, L. (2014, May 7). "Portland Proves to Be 'America's Bike Capital' in U.S. Census." OPB News Blog. *Wallowa County Chieftain*, Enterprise, Ore. https://www .wallowa.com/news/portland-proves-to-be-americas-bike-capital-in-u-s-census /article_a44a952e-a5ff-523f-bd1c-1a2ef08e9d9d.html (last accessed August 9, 2023)

Dunbar-Ortiz, R. (2014). *An Indigenous Peoples' History of the United States.* Boston: Beacon.

Ellis, D. (2013). "Cultural Geography of the Lower Columbia." In R. Boyd, K. Ames, and T. Johnson (eds.), *Chinookan Peoples of the Lower Columbia.* Seattle: University of Washington Press, pp. 42–62.

Ellis, R. (2020, July 29). "'It's Like They're Testing It on Us': Portland Protesters Say Tear Gas Has Caused Irregularities with Their Periods." Oregon Public Broadcasting. www.opb.org/article/2020/07/29/tear-gas-period-menstrual-cycle-portland/ (last accessed August 7, 2020)

Engelman Lado, M. (2017). "Toward Civil Rights Enforcement in the Environmental Justice Context: Step One: Acknowledging the Problem." *Fordham Environmental Law Review*, 29, 46–94.

Environmental Protection Agency (EPA) (2016). "Superfund Community Advisory Groups." https://www.epa.gov/superfund/community-advisory-groups (last accessed February 8, 2017)

Environmental Protection Agency (EPA) (2017a). "Superfund Liability." https://www.epa .gov/enforcement/superfund-liability (last accessed August 7, 2020)

Environmental Protection Agency, Region 10 (EPA) (2017b). "Record of Decision: Portland Harbor Superfund Site, Portland, Oregon." https://yosemite.epa.gov/OA/EAB _WEB_Docket.nsf/Filings%20By%20Appeal%20Number/8E7D7BFBAF5BD41B-8525815B0074263A/$File/Portland%20Harbor%20ROD...12.pdf (last accessed August 7, 2020)

Ernstson, H., M. Lawhon, and J. Duminy (2014). "Conceptual Vectors of African Urbanism: 'Engaged Theory-Making' and 'Platforms of Engagement.'" *Regional Studies*, 48(9), 1563–1577.

Estes, N. (2020, July). "The Empire of All Maladies: Colonial Contagions and Indigenous Resistance." *The Baffler*, no. 52. https://thebaffler.com/salvos/the-empire-of-all-maladies-estes (last accessed August 11, 2020)

Finney, C. (2014). *Black Faces, White Spaces: Reimagining the Relationship of African Americans to the Great Outdoors.* Chapel Hill: University of North Carolina Press.

Floum, J. (2017, January 5). "Portland OK to Spend Millions of Utility Ratepayer Money on Superfund Cleanup." *OregonLive.* www.oregonlive.com/politics/index.ssf/2017/01 /portland_okay_to_spend_million.html (last accessed August 7, 2020)

Freire, P. (1970). *Pedagogy of the Oppressed.* London: Bloomsbury Academic.

Gibbs, L. (2011). *Love Canal and the Birth of the Environmental Health Movement.* Washington, D.C.: Island Press.

Gibson, K. (2004). "Urban Redevelopment in Portland: Making the City Livable for Everyone?" In C. Ozawa (ed.), *The Portland Edge*. Washington, D.C.: Island Press, pp. 61–83.

Gibson, K. (2007). "Bleeding Albina: A History of Community Disinvestment, 1940–2000." *Transforming Anthropology*, 15(1), 3–25.

Gibson, K., and C. Abbott (2002). "City Profile: Portland, Oregon." *Cities*, 19(6), 425–436.

Gilmore, R. (2007). *Golden Gulag: Prisons, Surplus, Crisis, and Opposition in Globalizing California*. Berkeley: University of California Press.

Goetz, E. (2013). *New Deal Ruins: Race, Economic Justice, & Public Housing Policy*. Ithaca: Cornell University Press.

Gongaware, T. (2010). "Collective Memory Anchors: Collective Identity and Continuity in Social Movements." *Sociological Focus*, 43(3), 214–239.

Goodling, E. (2016, June 2). "Roy Pascoe: 'If I Wasn't Fighting for My Life, I'd Be Fighting for the River.'" *Street Roots*. https://news.streetroots.org/2016/06/02/roy-pascoe-if-i-wasn-t-fighting-my-life-i-d-be-fighting-river (last accessed August 7, 2020)

Goodling, E. (2019). "Urban Political Ecology from Below: Producing a 'Peoples' History' of the Portland Harbor." *Antipode*, 53(3), 745–769.

Goodling, E. (2020). "Intersecting Hazards, Intersectional Identities: A Baseline Critical Environmental Justice Analysis of U.S. Homelessness." *Environment and Planning E: Nature and Space*, 3(3), 833–856.

Goodling, E. (2022). *House on Fire: Housing & Climate Crisis, Housing & Climate Resistance*. https://antipodeonline.org/wp-content/uploads/2022/09/House-On-Fire_Housing-Climate-Crisis-Housing-Climate-Resistance.pdf (last accessed August 2023)

Goodling, E., J. Green, and N. McClintock (2015). "Uneven Development of the Sustainable City: Shifting Capital in Portland, Oregon." *Urban Geography*, 36(4), 504–527.

Goodling, E., and D. Smith (2018, July 13). "Below the Surface: A People's History of Portland Harbor." *Street Roots*. https://www.streetroots.org/news/2018/07/13/below-surface-people-s-history-portland-harbor (last accessed August 7, 2020)

Gorz, A. (1967). "Reform and Revolution." In *Le socialisme difficile*. Paris: Seuil.

Gottlieb, R. (2001). *Environmentalism Unbound: Exploring New Pathways for Change*. Cambridge, Mass.: MIT Press.

Gould, K., and T. Lewis (2019). *Green Gentrification: Urban Sustainability and the Struggle for Environmental Justice*. New York: Routledge.

Gowan, T. (2002). "The Nexus: Homelessness and Incarceration in Two American Cities." *Ethnography*, 3(4), 500–534.

Greenberg, M. (2015). "'The Sustainability Edge': Competition, Crisis, and the Rise of Green Urban Branding." In C. Isenhour, G. McDonogh, and M. Checker (eds.), *Sustainability in the Global City: Myth and Practice*. New York: Cambridge University Press, pp. 105–130.

Gunder, M. (2006). "Sustainability: Planning's Saving Grace or Road to Perdition?" *Journal of Planning Education and Research*, 26(2), 208–221.

Hackworth, J. (2007). *The Neoliberal City: Governance, Ideology, and Development in American Urbanism*. Ithaca: Cornell University Press.

Hanlon, B. (2009). "A Typology of Inner-Ring Suburbs: Class, Race, and Ethnicity in U.S. Suburbia." *City & Community*, 8(3), 221–246.

Harbarger, M. (2017, April 6). "Right 2 Dream Too: A Timeline." *OregonLive*. https://

www.oregonlive.com/portland/2017/04/right_2_dream_too_highlights_f.html (last accessed August 7, 2020)

Harris, F. (2006). "It Takes a Tragedy to Arouse Them: Collective Memory and Collective Action during the Civil Rights Movement." *Social Movement Studies*, 5(1), 19–43.

Harrison, J. (2015). "Coopted Environmental Justice? Activists' Roles in Shaping EJ Policy Implementation." *Environmental Sociology*, 1(4), 241–255.

Harrison, J. (2016). "Bureaucrats' Tacit Understandings and Social Movement Policy Implementation: Unpacking the Deviation of Agency Environmental Justice Programs from EJ Movement Priorities." *Social Problems*, 63(4), 534–553.

Harrison, J. (2019). *From the Inside Out: The Fight for Environmental Justice within Government Agencies.* Cambridge, Mass.: MIT Press.

Harrison, J. (2022, online). "Environmental Justice and the State." *Environment and Planning E* (issue information forthcoming). https://doi.org/10.1177/25148486221138736 (last accessed August 7, 2020)

Harvey, D. (1989). *The Urban Experience.* Baltimore: Johns Hopkins University Press.

Heatherton, C. (2012). "The Color Line and the Class Struggle: The Mexican Revolution and Convergences of Radical Internationalism, 1910–1946." PhD diss., University of Southern California.

Heben, A. (2014). *Tent City Urbanism: From Self-Organized Camps to Tiny House Villages.* Eugene: Village Collaborative.

Hern, M. (2016). *What a City Is For: Remaking the Politics of Displacement.* Cambridge, Mass.: MIT Press.

Herring, C. (2014). "The New Logics of Homeless Seclusion: Homeless Encampments in America's West Coast Cities." *City & Community*, 13(4), 285–308.

Herring, C. (2019). "Between Street and Shelter: Seclusion, Exclusion, and the Neutralization of Poverty." In J. Flint and R. Powell (eds.), *Class, Ethnicity and State in the Polarized Metropolis.* Cham, Switzerland: Palgrave Macmillan, pp. 281–306.

Herring, C., and M. Lutz (2015). "The Roots and Implications of the USA's Homeless Tent Cities." *City*, 19(5), 689–701.

Herring, C., D. Yarbrough, and L. Alatorre (2019). "Pervasive Penalty: How the Criminalization of Poverty Perpetuates Homelessness." *Social Problems*, 67(1), 131–149.

Hillegas-Elting, J. (2018). *Speaking for the River: Confronting Pollution on the Willamette, 1920s–1970s.* Corvallis: Oregon State University Press.

Holifield, R. (2001). "Defining Environmental Justice and Environmental Racism." *Urban Geography*, 22(1), 78–90.

Horton, M., and P. Freire (1990). *We Make the Road by Walking: Conversations on Education and Social Change.* Philadelphia: Temple University Press.

Hottle, M. (2011, October 10). "Nonprofit Right 2 Dream Too Sets Up Homeless Camp in Old Town-Chinatown Neighborhood." *OregonLive*. https://www.oregonlive.com /portland/2011/10/nonprofit_right_2_dream_too_se.html (last accessed August 7, 2020)

Hunt, S., and R. Benford (2004). "Collective Identity, Solidarity, and Commitment." In D. Snow, S. Soule, and H. Kriesi (eds.), *The Blackwell Companion to Social Movements.* Malden, Mass.: Blackwell, pp. 433–457.

Innes, J., and D. Booher (2010). *Planning with Complexity: An Introduction to Collaborative Rationality for Public Policy.* New York: Routledge.

Johnson, G. (2008). "Constellations of Struggle: Luisa Moreno, Charlotta Bass, and the Legacy for Ethnic Studies." *Aztlan: A Journal of Chicano Studies*, 33(1), 155–172.

Jonas, A., and A. While (2007). "Greening the Entrepreneurial City?" In R. Krueger and D. Gibbs (eds.), *The Sustainable Development Paradox: Urban Political Economy in the United States and Europe*. New York: Guilford Press, pp. 123–159.

Katz, M., M. Creighton, D. Amsterdam, and M. Chowkwanyun (2010). "Immigration and the New Metropolitan Geography." *Journal of Urban Affairs*, 32(5), 523–547.

Kentta, R., and D. Lewis (2010). "Western Oregon Reservations: Two Perspectives on Place." *Oregon Historical Quarterly*, 111(4), 476.

Kilgore, D. (1999). "Understanding Learning in Social Movements: A Theory of Collective Learning." *International Journal of Lifelong Education*, 18(3), 191–202.

Kim, E. (2017). "Restoring a River to Reclaim a City? The Politics of Urban Sustainability and Environmental Justice in the Los Angeles River Watershed." PhD diss., University of California, Berkeley.

Kneebone, E., and E. Garr (2010, January 20). "The Suburbanization of Poverty: Trends in Metropolitan America, 2000 to 2008." Brookings Institute. https://www.brookings.edu/research/the-suburbanization-of-poverty-trends-in-metropolitan-america-2000-to-2008/ (last accessed August 7, 2020)

Knox, P., and R. Florida (2014). *Atlas of Cities*. Princeton: Princeton University Press.

Koffman, R. (2012, December 10). Right 2 Dream Too Homeless Campers Sue City of Portland to End Fines. *OregonLive*. https://www.oregonlive.com/portland/2012/12/right_2_dream_too_homeless_cam.html (last accessed August 7, 2020)

Krueger, R., and D. Gibbs (2007). *The Sustainable Development Paradox: Urban Political Economy in the United States and Europe*. New York: Guildford.

Lang, M. (2018). "'A Place under the Sun': African American Resistance to Housing Exclusion." *Oregon Historical Quarterly*, 119(3), 365–375.

Lang, W. (2010). "One City, Two Rivers: Columbia and Willamette Rivers in the Environmental History of Twentieth-Century Portland, Oregon." In C. Miller (ed.), *Cities and Nature in the American West*. Reno: University of Nevada Press, pp. 96–111.

Lang, W. (2013). "The Chinookan Encounter with Euro-Americans in the Lower Columbia River Valley." In R. Boyd, K. Ames, and T. Johnson (eds.), *Chinookan Peoples of the Lower Columbia*. Seattle: University of Washington Press, pp. 250–271.

La Paperson (2014). "A Ghetto Land Pedagogy: An Antidote for Settler Genvironmentalism." *Environmental Education Research*, 20(1), 115–130.

Lawhon, M., H. Ernstson, and J. Silver (2014). "Provincializing Urban Political Ecology: Towards a Situated UPE through African Urbanism. *Antipode*, 46(2), 497–516.

Lewis, D. (2009). "Termination of the Confederated Tribes of the Grand Ronde: History, Politics, Identity." PhD diss., University of Oregon.

Lewis, D. (2016). "The Grand Ronde Acreage History." *NDNhistory Research*. https://ndnhistoryresearch.com/2016/12/09/the-grand-ronde-acreage-history (last accessed August 7, 2020)

Lewis, D., and T. Connolly (2019). "White American Violence on Tribal Peoples on the Oregon Coast." *Oregon Historical Quarterly*, 120(4), 368–381.

Lewis, D., E. Thorsgard, and C. Williams (2013). "Honoring Our T*ilixam*: Chinookan People of Grand Ronde." In R. Boyd, K. Ames, and T. Johnson (eds.), *Chinookan Peoples of the Lower Columbia*. Seattle: University of Washington Press, pp. 307–325.

Lindner, J. (2019). "Liberty Ships and Jim Crow Shipyards: Racial Discrimination in Kaiser's Portland Shipyards, 1940–1945." *Oregon Historical Quarterly*, 120(4), 518–545.

Lipsitz, G. (1988). *A Life of Struggle: Ivory Perry and the Culture of Opposition*. Philadelphia: Temple University Press.

Lipsitz, G. (2007). "The Racialization of Space and the Spatialization of Race: Theorizing the Hidden Architecture of Landscape." *Landscape Journal*, 26(1), 10–23.

Logan, J., and H. Molotch (2007). *Urban Fortunes: The Political Economy of Place*. Berkeley: University of California Press.

Long, J. (2014). "Constructing the Narrative of the Sustainability Fix: Sustainability, Social Justice and Representation in Austin, TX." *Urban Studies*, 53(1), 149–172.

Low, S. (1992). "Symbolic Ties That Bind: Place Attachment in the Plaza." In I. Altman and S. Low (eds.), *Place Attachment*. New York: Plenum Press, pp. 165–184.

MacColl, K., and H. Stein (1988). *Merchants, Money, and Power: The Portland Establishment, 1843–1913*. Portland: Georgian Press.

MacLeod, G. (2011). "Urban Politics Reconsidered: Growth Machine to Post-Democratic City?" *Urban Studies*, 48(12), 2629–2660.

Manzo, L., and P. Devine-Wright (2014). *Place Attachment: Advances in Theory, Methods and Applications*. London: Routledge.

Marino, E. (2015). *Fierce Climate, Sacred Ground: An Ethnography of Climate Change in Shishmaref, Alaska*. Fairbanks: University of Alaska Press.

Massey, D., and N. Denton (1993). *American Apartheid: Segregation and the Making of the Underclass*. Cambridge, Mass.: Harvard University Press.

McCann, E. (2017). "Mobilities, Politics, and the Future: Critical geographies of Green Urbanism." *Environment and Planning A*, 49(8), 1816–1823.

McCarthy, J. (2013). "We Have Never Been 'Post-Political.'" *Capitalism Nature Socialism*, 24(1), 19–25.

McCreary, T., and R. Milligan (2018). "The Limits of Liberal Recognition: Racial Capitalism, Settler Colonialism, and Environmental Governance in Vancouver and Atlanta." *Antipode*, 53(3), 724–744.

McElderry, S. (2001). "Building a West Coast Ghetto: African-American Housing in Portland, 1910–1960. *Pacific Northwest Quarterly*, 92(3), 137–148.

McGurty, E. (2007). *Transforming Environmentalism: Warren County, PCBs, and the Origins of Environmental Justice*. New Brunswick: Rutgers University Press.

McKittrick, K. (2006). *Demonic Grounds: Black Women and the Cartographies of Struggle*. Minneapolis: University of Minnesota Press.

McKittrick, K. (2011). "On Plantations, Prisons, and a Black Sense of Place. *Social and Cultural Geography*, 12(8), 947–963.

McKittrick, K., and C. Woods (2007). *Black Geographies and the Politics of Place*. Boston: South End Press.

Melamed, J. (2015). "Racial Capitalism." *Critical Ethnic Studies*, 1(1), 76–85.

Mesh, A. (2012, March 27). "What the Muck?" *Willamette Week*. www.wweek.com/portland/article-18986-what-the-muck.html (last accessed August 7, 2020)

Metropolitan Group (2016). *Metropolitan Group*. http://www.metgroup.com/what-we-do/ (last accessed August 7, 2020; no longer a working link)

Milne, M. (2000). "Tent City: Activists Propose a New Kind of Encampment for the Homeless." *Portland Mercury*.

Minow Smith, D. (2012, November 2). "Breaking: Portland Sustainability Chief Admits 'Portlandia' Isn't Really a Parody." *Grist.* https://grist.org/cities/breaking-portland-sustainability-chief-admits-portlandia-isnt-really-a-parody/ (last accessed August 7, 2020)

Mirk, S. (2011, October 18). "Occupying Is Fine, Unless You're Actually Homeless." *Portland Mercury.* https://www.portlandmercury.com/BlogtownPDX/archives/2011/10/18/occupying-is-fine-unless-youre-actually-homeless (last accessed August 7, 2020)

Mitchell, D. (2020). *Mean Streets: Homelessness, Public Space, and the Limits of Capital.* Athens: University of Georgia Press.

Mokos, J. (2017). "Stigmatized Places as Therapeutic Landscapes: The Beneficial Dimensions of River-Bottom Homeless Encampments." *Medicine Anthropology Theory*, 4(1), 123.

Molotch, H. (1976). "The City as a Growth Machine: Toward a Political Economy of Place." *American Journal of Sociology*, 82(2), 309–332.

Morello-Frosch, R., M. Pastor, and J. Sadd (2001). "Environmental Justice and Southern California's 'Riskscape': The Distribution of Air Toxics Exposures and Health Risks among Diverse Communities." *Urban Affairs Review*, 36(4), 551–578.

National Law Center on Homelessness & Poverty (NLCHP) (2017). *Tent City, USA: The Growth of America's Homeless Encampments and How Communities Are Responding.* https://homelesslaw.org/wp-content/uploads/2018/10/Tent_City_USA_2017.pdf (last accessed May 9, 2023)

Nixon, R. (2011). *Slow Violence and the Environmentalism of the Poor.* Cambridge, Mass.: Harvard University Press.

Olivet, J., M. Dones, M. Richard, C. Wilkey, S. Yampolskaya, M. Beit-Arie, and L. Joseph (2018). *Supporting Partnerships for Anti-Racist Communities.* Needham, Mass.: Center for Social Innovation.

Oregon Department of Fish and Wildlife (2016). "Trustee Council Fact Sheet." Oregon Department of Fish and Wildlife. https://www.fws.gov/portlandharbor/sites/portland/files/resources/TrusteeCouncilFactSheet.pdf (last accessed August 7, 2020)

Oregon Sustainable Agriculture Land Trust (OSALT) (2016). "We Preserve Land for Future Generations of Oregonians." https://www.osalt.org (last accessed 7 August 2020; no longer a working link)

Ottinger, G. (2013). *Refining Expertise: How Responsible Engineers Subvert Environmental Justice Campaigns.* New York: New York University Press.

Pearsall, H., and J. Pierce (2017). "A Spoiled Well (of Data): Addressing the Procedural Injustice of Contemporary Environmental Justice Research through Collaborative Qualitative Data Gathering." *Local Environment*, 22(3), 388–392.

Pearson, R. (1996). "African Americans in Portland, Oregon, 1940–1950: Work and Living Conditions—a Social History." PhD diss., Washington State University.

Peck, J. (2005). "Struggling with the Creative Class." *International Journal of Urban and Regional Research*, 29(4), 740–770.

Peck, J., and A. Tickell (2002) "Neoliberalizing Space." *Antipode*, 34(3), 380–404.

Pellow, D. (2016). "Toward a Critical Environmental Justice Studies: Black Lives Matter as an Environmental Justice Challenge." *DuBois Review*, 13(2), 221–236.

Pellow, D. (2018). *What Is Critical Environmental Justice?* Cambridge: Polity Press.

Pellow, D., and R. Brulle (2005). *Power, Justice, and the Environment: A Critical Appraisal of the Environmental Justice Movement*. Cambridge, Mass.: MIT Press.

Perkins, T. (2015). "From Protest to Policy: The Political Evolution of California Environmental Justice Activism, 1980s–2010s." PhD diss., University of California, Santa Cruz.

Perkins, T. (2022). *Evolution of a Movement: Four Decades of California Environmental Justice Activism*. Oakland: University of California Press.

Pieterse, E. (2008). *City Futures: Confronting the Crisis of Urban Development*. Lansdowne, South Africa: University of Cape Town Press.

Polishuk, S. (2019). "'They Can't Come In through the Front Door Because You Guys Won't Let Them': An Oral History of the Struggle to Admit African Americans into ILWU Local 8." *Oregon Historical Quarterly*, 120(4), 546–563.

Polletta, F., and J. Jasper (2001). "Collective Identity and Social Movements." *Annual Review of Sociology*, 27, 283–305.

Portland African American Leadership Forum (PAALF) (2017). *The People's Plan*. https://www.portlandoregon.gov/oehr/article/713241 (last accessed August 7, 2020)

Portland Harbor Community Coalition (PHCC) (2015). *A People's View of the Portland Harbor* [film]. https://www.youtube.com/watch?v=uVCpyrNbNx8www .ourfutureriver.org (last accessed August 7, 2020)

Portney, K. (2005). "Civic Engagement and Sustainable Cities in the United States." *Public Administration Review*, 65(5), 579–591.

Profita, C. (2014). "A Guide to the Portland Harbor Superfund Site." Oregon Public Broadcasting. https://www.opb.org/news/blog/ecotrope/a-guide-to-the-portland -harbor-superfund-site/ (last accessed August 7, 2020; no longer a working link)

Profita, C. (2016, December 8). "Portland's Toxic Graveyard for World War II Ships." *Portland Tribune*. https://portlandtribune.com/pt/9-news/335347-214776-portlands -toxic-graveyard-for-world-war-ii-ships (last accessed 7 August 2020)

Pulido, L. (2017). "Conversations in Environmental Justice: An Interview with David Pellow." *Capitalism Nature Socialism*, 28(2), 43–53.

Pulido, L. (2018). "Geographies of Race and Ethnicity III: Settler Colonialism and Nonnative People of Color." *Progress in Human Geography*, 42(2), 309–318.

Pulido, L. (2024). "Wildfire Rumors and Denial in the Trump Era." In I. Allen, K. Ekberg, S. Holgerson, and A. Malm (eds.), *Political Ecologies of the Far Right*. Manchester: Manchester University Press.

Pulido, L., and J. De Lara (2018). "Reimagining 'Justice' in Environmental Justice: Radical Ecologies, Decolonial Thought, and the Black Radical Tradition." *Environment and Planning E: Nature and Space*, 1(1–2), 76–98.

Pulido, L., E. Kohl, and N. Cotton (2016). "State Regulation and Environmental Justice: The Need for Strategy Reassessment." *Capitalism Nature Socialism*, 27(2), 12–31.

Quastel, N. (2009). "Political Ecologies of Gentrification." *Urban Geography*, 30(7), 694–725.

Rabin, C. (2016, July 21). "Cop Shoots Caretaker of Autistic Man Playing in the Street with Toy Truck." *Miami Herald*. https://www.miamiherald.com/news/local/crime /article90905442.html (last accessed 7 August 2020)

Rameau, M. (2006). *Take Back the Land: Land, Gentrification, and the Umoja Village Shantytown*. Edinburgh: AK Press.

Redclift, M. (2005). "Sustainable Development (1987–2005): An Oxymoron Comes of Age." *Sustainable Development*, 13(4), 212–227.

Reese, A. (2018). "'We Will Not Perish; We're Going to Keep Flourishing': Race, Food Access, and Geographies of Self-Reliance." *Antipode*, 50(2), 407–424.

Retish, A. (2020, November 14). "'Black Radicals Not Only Anticipated the Rise of Fascism; They Resisted Before It Was Considered a Crisis': An Interview with Robin D. G. Kelley." *The Volunteer*. https://albavolunteer.org/2020/11/robin-d-g-kelley-on -fascism-then-and-now/ (last accessed November 14, 2020)

Robinson, C. (1983). *Black Marxism: The Making of the Black Radical Tradition*. Chapel Hill: University of North Carolina Press.

Rome, E., and J. Bell (2012). "Community Perspectives on the Future of the Portland Harbor and the Willamette River." Portland: Portland State University.

Rose, G. (1997). "Situating Knowledges: Positionality, Reflexivities, and Other Tactics." *Progress in Human Geography*, 21(3), 305–320.

Rose, J. (2016, April 23). "Homelessness: Portland's Great Depression Hoovervilles vs. 'Hales-villes.'" *OregonLive*. https://www.oregonlive.com/history/2016/04 /homelessness_portland_hoovervi.html (last accessed 7 August 2020)

Roy, A. (2009). "The 21st-Century Metropolis: New Geographies of Theory." *Regional Studies*, 43(6), 819–830.

Rutland, T. (2013). "Activists in the Making: Urban Movements, Political Processes and the Creation of Political Subjects." *International Journal of Urban and Regional Research*, 37(3), 989–1011.

Safransky, S. (2014). "Greening the Urban Frontier: Race, Property, and Resettlement in Detroit." *Geoforum*, 56, 237–248.

Safransky, S. (2018). "Land Justice as a Historical Diagnostic: Thinking with Detroit." *Annals of the American Association of Geographers*, 108(2), 499–512.

Saker, A. (2009, November 18). "Adult Bookstore Owners Sue Portland Commissioner, City for $1 Million over Alleged Harassment." *OregonLive*. https://www.oregonlive .com/portland/2009/11/adult_bookstore_owners_sue_por.html (last accessed August 7, 2020)

Saleeby, B. (1983). "Prehistoric Settlement Patterns in the Portland Basin of the Lower Columbia River: Ethnohistoric, Archaeological, Biogeographic Perspectives." PhD diss., University of Oregon.

Samayoa, M. (2020, August 6). "Portland Vacuums Tear Gas Residue from Storm Drains Downtown." Oregon Public Broadcasting. https://www.opb.org/article/2020/08/06 /portland-oregon-tear-gas-storm-drains-sewer-cleaning-protests/ (last accessed August 7, 2020)

Sandoval, C. (2009). "U.S. Third World Feminism: The Theory and Method of Oppositional Consciousness in the Postmodern World." In G. Henderson and M. Waterstone (eds.), *Geographic Thought: A Praxis Perspective*. London: Routledge, pp. 338–354.

Schlosberg, D. (2004). "Reconceiving Environmental Justice: Global Movements and Political Theories." *Environmental Politics*, 13(3), 517–540.

Schmid, T. (2018, May 23). "No Link between Homeless Villages and Crime Rates, Guardian Review Suggests." *The Guardian* (London). www.theguardian.com /us-news/2018/may/23/homeless-villages-crime-rate-seattle-portland (accessed August 7, 2020)

Schmidt, B. (2015, July 10). "Portland Explained: How Alleged Misspending Put City on Hook for Millions of Dollars." *OregonLive*. https://www.oregonlive.com/portland /index.ssf/2015/07/portland_explained_how_alleged.html (last accessed August 7, 2020)

Schrock, G., E. Bassett, and J. Green (2015). "Pursuing Equity and Justice in a Changing Climate: Assessing Equity in Local Climate and Sustainability Plans in U.S. Cities." *Journal of Planning Education and Research*, 35(3), 282–295.

Scott, A. (2012, February 17). "By the Grace of God." *Portland Monthly*. https://www .pdxmonthly.com/news-and-city-life/2012/02/african-american-churches-north -portland-march-2012 (last accessed August 7, 2020)

Serbulo, L., and K. Gibson (2013). "Black and Blue: Police-Community Relations in Portland's Albina District, 1964–1985." *Oregon Historical Quarterly*, 114(1), 6–37.

Sisters of the Road (2015). "Mission + Philosophies." https://www.sistersoftheroad.org/ mission-and-philosphy (last accessed 2015)

Slavin, M., and K. Snyder (2011). "Strategic Climate Action Planning in Portland." In M. Slavin (ed.), *Sustainability in America's Cities: Creating the Green Metropolis*. Washington, D.C.: Island Press, pp. 21–40.

Smith, A., and Q. Taylor (1980). "Racial Discrimination in the Workplace: A Study of Two West Coast Cities during the 1940s." *Journal of Ethnic Studies*, 8(1), 35–54.

Smith, N. (1992). "Contours of a Spatialized Politics: Homeless Vehicles and the Production of Geographical Scale." *Social Text*, 33, 55–81.

Smith, N. (1996). *The New Urban Frontier: Gentrification and the Revanchist City*. New York: Routledge.

Smith, N. (2002, February 16). "New Globalism, New Urbanism: Gentrification as Global Urban Strategy." *Antipode*, 34(3), 427–450.

Snow, D. (2001). "Framing Processes, Ideology, and Discursive Fields." In D. Snow, S. Soule, and H. Kriesi (eds.), *The Blackwell Companion to Social Movements*, Malden, Mass.: Blackwell, 380–412.

Sparks, T. (2010). "Broke Not Broken: Rights, Privacy, and Homelessness in Seattle." *Urban Geography*, 6, 842–862.

Sparks, T. (2017). "Neutralizing Homelessness, 2015: Tent Cities and Ten Year Plans." *Urban Geography*, 38(3), 348–356.

Speer, J. (2016). "The Right to Infrastructure: A Struggle for Sanitation in Fresno, California Homeless Encampments." *Urban Geography*, 7, 1049–1069.

Speer, J. (2017). "'It's Not like Your Home': Homeless Encampments, Housing Projects, and the Struggle over Domestic space." *Antipode*, 49(2), 517–535.

Speer, J. (2018). "The Rise of the Tent Ward: Homeless Camps in the Era of Mass Incarceration." *Political Geography*, 62, 160–169.

Speer, J., and E. Goldfischer (2019) "The City Is Not Innocent: Homelessness and the Value of Urban Parks." *Capitalism Nature Socialism*, 31(3), 24–41.

Spores, R. (1993). "Too Small a Place: The Removal of the Willamette Valley Indians, 1850–1856." *American Indian Quarterly*, 17(2), 171–191.

Starbird, E. (1972). "A River Restored: Oregon's Willamette." *National Geographic*, 141(6), 816–834.

Stephenson, R. B. (2021). *Portland's Good Life: Sustainability and Hope in an American City*. Lanham, Md.: Lexington Books.

Strom, S. (2003, August 18). "Oregon Steel Settles Pollution Lawsuit." *Portland Business Journal.* https://www.bizjournals.com/portland/stories/2003/08/18/daily10.html (last accessed August 7, 2020)

Stuart, F. (2016). *Down, Out, and under Arrest: Policing and Everyday Life in Skid Row.* Chicago: University of Chicago Press.

Sullivan, K. (2016). "Lonely Planet's Top Cities and Countries to Visit in 2017." *Newsday.* https://www.newsday.com/travel/lonely-planet-s-top-cities-and-countries-to-vis-it-in-2017-1.12633237 (last accessed August 10, 2019; not a working link)

Sundling, D., and S. Buck (2012). "Fish Consumption in the Portland Harbor." Brattle Group. https://www.brattle.com/wp-content/uploads/2017/10/6377_fish_consumption_in_portland_harbor_sunding_buck_oct_23_2012.pdf (last accessed August 7, 2020)

Swyngedouw, E. (2007). "Impossible 'Sustainability' and the Postpolitical Condition." In R. Krueger and D. Gibbs (eds.), *The Sustainable Development Paradox: Urban Political Economy in the United States and Europe.* New York: Guilford, pp. 41–65.

Swyngedouw, E. (2009). "The Antinomies of the Postpolitical City: In Search of a Democratic Politics of Environmental Production. *International Journal of Urban and Regional Research,* 33(3), 601–620.

Sze, J., and E. Yeampierre (2018). "Just Transition and Just Green Enough: Climate Justice, Economic Development and Community Resilience." In W. Curran and T. Hamilton (eds.), *Just Green Enough: Urban Development and Environmental Gentrification,* London: Routledge, 61–73.

Taylor, D. (2000). "The Rise of the Environmental Justice Paradigm: Injustice Framing and the Social Construction of Environmental Discourses." *American Behavioral Scientist,* 43(4), 508–580.

Taylor, Q. (1979). "The Emergence of Black Communities in the Pacific Northwest: 1865–1910." *Journal of Negro History,* 64(4), 342–354.

Temenos, C., and E. McCann (2012). "The Local Politics of Policy Mobility: Learning, Persuasion, and the Production of a Municipal Sustainability Fix." *Environment and Planning A,* 44(6), 1389–1406.

Theen, A. (2013a, November 15). "Michael Wright: Cocaine, Cracking Safes and Adult Book Sales in a Bygone Era of Portland's Chinatown." *OregonLive.* www.oregonlive.com/portland/2013/11/michael_wright_cocaine_crackin.html (last accessed August 7, 2020)

Theen, A. (2013b, November 15). "Michael Wright: Right 2 Dream Too Landlord and Portland Adult Bookstore Owner Awaits City Payout." *OregonLive.* www.oregonlive.com/portland/2013/11/michael_wright_right_2_dream_t.html (last accessed August 7, 2020)

Theen, A. (2014, April 29). "Portland Public Water District: Kent Craford Pushes for Reform as City Leaders Call Him a Corporate Shill." *OregonLive.* https://www.oregonlive.com/portland/index.ssf/2014/04/portland_public_water_district_6.html (last accessed August 7, 2020)

Tomlinson, S. (2013, November 7). The Big Pipe: Portland's Sewer and Stormwater Project Shows It Can Handle Big Rain. *OregonLive.* https://www.oregonlive.com/portland/2013/11/post_381.html (last accessed August 7, 2020)

Tuck, E., M. Smith, A. Guess, T. Benjamin, and B. Jones (2014). "Geotheorizing Black/

Land: Contestations and Contingent Collaborations." *Departures in Qualitative Research*, 3(1), 52–74.

Tveskov, M. (2017). "A 'Most Disastrous' Affair: The Battle of Hungry Hill, Historical Memory, and the Rogue River War." *Oregon Historical Quarterly*, 118(1), 42–73.

U.S. Department of Justice (n.d.). Title VI of the Civil Rights Act of 1964. https://www.justice.gov/crt/fcs/TitleVI-Overview (last accessed August 7, 2020)

VanderHart, D. (2016, April 13). "Portland's Finally Going to Talk to Disadvantaged Folks about Their Filthy River." *Portland Mercury*. https://www.portlandmercury.com/news/2016/04/13/17877389/portlands-finally-going-to-talk-to-disadvantaged-folks-about-their-filthy-river (last accessed August 7, 2020)

Vos, R. (2007). "Defining Sustainability: A Conceptual Orientation." *Journal of Chemical Technology and Biotechnology*, 82(4), 334–339.

Walker, G. (2012). *Environmental Justice: Concepts, Evidence and Politics*. New York: Routledge.

Walker, R. (1981). "A Theory of Suburbanization: Capitalism and the Construction of Urban Space in the United States." In M. Dear and A. Scott (eds.), *Urbanization and Urban Planning in Capitalist Society*. New York: Methuen.

Walker, S. (2009). "Beyond Distribution and Proximity: Exploring the Multiple Spatialities of Environmental Justice." *Antipode*, 41(4), 614–636.

Watson, V. (2006). "Deep Difference: Diversity, Planning and Ethics." *Planning Theory*, 5(31), 31–50.

Weissman, E. (2017). *Tranquility on the Razor's Edge: Changing Narratives of Inevitability*. Oakville, Ontario: Rock's Mills Press.

Weissman, E., and N. Dickson (2012). *Dignity in Exile: Stories of Struggle and Hope from a Modern American Shanty Town*. Toronto: Exile Editions.

Western Regional Advocacy Project (WRAP) (2010). *Without Housing: Decades of Federal Housing Cutbacks, Massive Homelessness, and Policy Failures*. https://wraphome.org//wp-content/uploads/2008/09/2010%20Update%20Without%20Housing.pdf (last accessed August 7, 2020)

Whaley, G. (2010). *Oregon and the Collapse of Illahee: U.S. Empire and the Transformation of an Indigenous World, 1792–1859*. Chapel Hill: University of North Carolina Press.

While, A., A. Jonas, and D. Gibbs (2004). "The Environment and the Entrepreneurial City: Searching for the Urban 'Sustainability Fix' in Manchester and Leeds." *International Journal of Urban and Regional Research*, 28(3), 549–569.

White, R. (1995). *The Organic Machine: The Remaking of the Columbia River*. Toronto: HarperCollins.

Wilkinson, C. (2010). *The People Are Dancing Again: The History of the Siletz Tribe of Western Oregon*. Seattle: University of Washington Press.

Wisdom of the Elders (2023). "Our Mission." https://wisdomoftheelders.org/ (accessed August 6, 2023)

Wolch, J., J. Byrne, and J. Newell (2014). "Urban Green Space, Public Health, and Environmental Justice: The Challenge of Making Cities 'Just Green Enough.'" *Landscape and Urban Planning*, 125, 234–244.

Wolfe, P. (2006). "Settler Colonialism and the Elimination of the Native." *Journal of Genocide Research*, 8(4), 387–409.

World Commission on Environment and Development (WCED—Brundtland Commission) (1987). *Our Common Future.* New York: Oxford University Press.

Yakama Nation (n.d.). "Honor. Protect. Restore" [online storymap]. https://geo.maps .arcgis.com/apps/Cascade/index.html?appid=41493a8d72d744abb16be70abcd137b6 (last accessed September 29, 2021)

Zapata M., J. Liu, L. Everett, P. Hulseman, T. Potiowsky, and E. Willingham (2019). "Governance, Costs, and Revenue Raising to Address and Prevent Homelessness in the Portland Tri-County Region." Portland: Portland State University.

Zenk, H., Y. Hajda, and R. Boyd (2016). "Chinookan Villages of the Lower Columbia." *Oregon Historical Quarterly,* 117(1), 6–37.

INDEX

GEOGRAPHIES OF JUSTICE AND SOCIAL TRANSFORMATION

Printed in the USA
CPSIA information can be obtained
at www.ICGtesting.com
CBHW051438020324
4901CB00004B/186